D1500843

*Gender in the Middle Ages*

*Volume 3*

# THE PASTORAL CARE OF WOMEN IN LATE MEDIEVAL ENGLAND

*Gender in the Middle Ages*

ISSN 1742-870X

*Series Editors*
Jacqueline Murray
Diane Watt

*Editorial Board*
Clare Lees
Katherine J. Lewis

This series investigates the representation and construction of masculinity and femininity in the Middle Ages from a variety of disciplinary and interdisciplinary perspectives. It aims in particular to explore the diversity of medieval genders, and such interrelated contexts and issues as sexuality, social class, race and ethnicity, and orthodoxy and heterodoxy.

Proposals or queries should be sent in the first instance to the editors or to the publisher, at the addresses given below; all submissions will receive prompt and informed consideration.

Professor Jacqueline Murray, Department of History, University of Guelph, Guelph, Ontario, N1G 2W1, Canada

Professor Diane Watt, School of Literature and Languages, University of Surrey, Guildford, Surrey GU2 7XH, UK

Boydell & Brewer Limited, PO Box 9, Woodbridge, Suffolk IP12 3DF, UK

*Previously published volumes in the series are listed at the end of this book.*

# THE PASTORAL CARE OF
# WOMEN IN
# LATE MEDIEVAL ENGLAND

*Beth Allison Barr*

THE BOYDELL PRESS

First published 2008
The Boydell Press
Paperback edition 2022


ISBN 978 1 84383 373 4 hardback
ISBN 978 1 83765 009 5 paperback


The Boydell Press is an imprint of Boydell & Brewer Ltd
PO Box 9, Woodbridge, Suffolk IP12 3DF, UK
and of Boydell & Brewer Inc.
668 Mt Hope Avenue, Rochester, NY 14620, USA
website: www.boydellandbrewer.com


A catalogue record for this book is available
from the British Library


This publication is printed on acid-free paper

# CONTENTS

For Jeb

# ACKNOWLEDGMENTS

I would like to express my gratitude to the many people who made this work possible.

First, I would like to thank the institutions who provided financial assistance, including the Graduate School at the University of North Carolina at Chapel Hill, the History Department at the University of North Carolina at Chapel Hill, the University Center for International Studies at the University of North Carolina at Chapel Hill, and the Richard III Society American Branch.

Second, I would like to thank the librarians and staff at the numerous archives in which I pursued research, especially the British Library, the Bodleian Library, Durham Cathedral Library, Southwell Minster Library, Leeds University Library, Cambridge University Library, St. John's College Cambridge Library, Gloucester Cathedral Library, Lincoln Cathedral Library, Dr. William's Library, Birmingham University Library, the Courtauld Institute, the Borthwick Institute, and the Chairman and Governing Body of Shrewsbury School.

Third, I would like to thank those who read, discussed, and commented on different aspects of this project, including Jennifer Ann Newton, Melissa Franklin-Harkrider, Roy Millhouse, Delayne Vaughn, David Bebbington (who helped me with a very last minute question), Jeffrey Hamilton, Barbara J. Harris, Cynthia B. Herrup, Stanley Chojnacki, and – most especially – Judith M. Bennett, whose invaluable guidance and insight significantly enriched this work.

Finally, I would like to thank my husband, Jeb, for his continuous patience and encouragement throughout the past ten years; my parents, Kathy and Crawford, for their encouragement and travel companionship; the Patel family in England, who hosted me in both London and Birmingham during my months of research; the History Department at Baylor University for their support and encouragement throughout this process; and, last but not least, Caroline Palmer and the staff of Boydell & Brewer.

# ABBREVIATIONS

BL      British Library

Bodl.    Bodleian Library

CUL     Cambridge University Library

EETS   Early English Text Society

*Festial*   *Mirk's Festial: A Collection of Homilies, by Johannes Mirku*s, ed. Theodore Erbe, EETS extra series 96 (London: Kegan Paul, Trench, Trubner & Co., 1905)

s.       shilling(s)

d.       penny/pence

# INTRODUCTION:
## "Be it husband, be it wife"

IN HIS *Festial*, the most popular vernacular sermon compilation in late medi-eval England, clerical author John Mirk included an exemplum about a Devon-shire vicar.

*In Devonshire beside Axe Bridge there dwelled a holy vicar who had one in his parish, a woman, that lay sick at the point of death half-a-mile from him in town. This woman at midnight sent after him [the priest] to do her her rites. Then this man with all the haste that he could muster, rose up, and went to the church, and took God's body in a box of ivory, and put it in his pocket … And he rode toward this woman, and went over a meadow that was nearby. Then as he hurried on his way and without his knowing, the box shook out of his bosom, and fell down on the earth; and in the falling the box opened, and the host rolled on the green. Then, when he had shriven [confessed] this woman, he asked her if she would be houseled [partake in Eucharist], and she said, "Yes." Then he put his hand in his bosom, and sought the box. When he found it not, he was very afraid, and said to the woman: "Dame, I shall fetch God's body with all possible haste." And so he came by a willow tree, and made from it a good stick, and made himself naked, and beat himself as fast as he might, until the blood ran down his sides, and said to himself thus: "You fool if you have lost your creator, you shall pay for it." And when he had beaten himself thus, he put on his clothes and ran forth. And then he became aware of a pillar of fire that went from the earth up to heaven. Then was he first aghast, but after he blessed him[self], he went near it. Then saw he all the beasts of the meadow gathered about that pillar. So when he came to this pillar, it shone as bright as any sun. Then was he aware of God's body lying on the grass, and the pillar of fire [leaping] from it up to Heaven. Then he fell down on his knees and asked mercy with all his heart, weeping sore for his negligence. But when he had made his prayer, he rose up, and looked about, and saw all the beasts kneeling on both their knees and worshipping God's body, save one black horse that kneeled but on his one knee. Then said this good man to him [the black horse] thus: "If you be any beast that may speak, I bid you in the virtue of this body that here lies, that you speak and tell me, why you kneel but on one knee, while all these other beasts kneel on both their knees." Then answered he [the horse] and said: "I am a fiend of hell and would not kneel on neither knee [of] my will, but I am made to do so against my will; for it is written that each man of Heaven, and earth, and hell shall bow to him." Then said he [the priest] to him [the horse]: "Why are you like a horse?" Then said he [the horse]: "I am like a horse, in order to make men forto steal me. And thus was a man of such a town hanged for me, and afterwards another, and at such a town the third." Then said this vicar: "I command you in the virtue of this body that is here that you go into the wilderness where no man comes, and be there till doomsday!" And so anon he [the horse] vanished away. And with all the reverence that he could, he [the vicar] took up the host, and put*

1

*it in the box, and so went again to the woman, and houseled her therewith. And so he went home, thanking God with all his heart for showing of his miracle.*[1]

This is an intriguing story, entertaining readers today with its supernatural miracles just as it probably entertained clerical readers and church audiences throughout the fifteenth century. But this tale is remarkable for more than its extraordinary events. It is also remarkable for its ordinary storyline. Hidden behind the kneeling animals, talking horse, and divine flames is a narrative about a priest fulfilling his pastoral obligations to a dying woman.[2]

In short, this story elucidates a critical problem – the challenge faced by late medieval English priests in caring for the spiritual needs of female parishioners. Women, like the men around them, needed someone to hear their confessions, administer penance, and advise in matters of daily life and religious instruction. Providing women with pastoral care was a clear duty for priests with cure of souls. Yet women, according to their portrayal in pastoral vernacular literature, were also different from men: women threatened clerical celibacy, undermined sacerdotal purity, and – many times – came to priests as dependants whose spiritual souls could not be cured without attention to the temporal authority of men. These factors created critical challenges for the very priests whose guidance women sought. Contradictory advice given by Mirk in his *Instructions for Parish Priests*, a late fourteenth-century manual of clerical instruction, illustrates this problem well. On the one hand, he ordered priests to care for all parishioners, "Be it husband, be it wife." On the other hand, he instructed priests to "forsake" at least some association with women "of evil fame lest they you make."[3]

So how did priests deal with these challenges? Were they able to overcome them and care for women in the same ways they cared for men? Or did these obstacles

---

[1]   John Mirk, *Mirk's Festial: A Collection of Homilies, by Johannes Mirkus*, ed. Theodore Erbe, EETS extra series 96 (London: Kegan Paul, Trench, Trubner & Co., 1905), 173–175. This edition is primarily based on Bodleian Library MS Gough Ecclesiastical Topography 4, in which this exemplum may be found on folios 100v–101r. Although I have examined the manuscripts of *Festial*, and other texts such as *Instructions for Parish Priests, Speculum Sacerdotal*, and *Middle English Sermons*, I found the printed editions to be accurate for the manuscripts they represent and thus, for the convenience of the reader, will cite the printed editions. In translating texts, I have (for the most part) simply modernized the language.

[2]   Exempla are sermon stories: short, colorful, didactic tales. Because their focus is not saints or biblical characters but contemporary characters and events, they serve as windows into the everyday life of medieval people. See Jacques Berlioz and Marie Anne Polo de Beaulieu, "*Exempla*: A Discussion and a Case Study," in *Medieval Women and the Sources of Medieval History*, ed. Joel T. Rosenthal (Athens: University of Georgia Press, 1990), 37–65, for further information about exempla as a source for women's history.

[3]   Most manuscripts read, "women's service you must forsake" while one manuscript reads "women's fellowship." *John Mirk's Instructions for Parish Priests: Edited from MS Cotton Claudius A II and Six Other Manuscripts with Introduction, Notes, and Glossary*, ed. Gillis Kristensson, Lund Series in English 49 (Lund: Gleerup, 1974), 70–71 (BL MS Cotton Claudius A II) and 178–179 (BL MS Royal 17 C XVII). I quote mostly from BL MS Cotton Claudius A II, as it is considered the "best" manuscript. It is also the main text used by Kristensson, although he includes variant readings from five of the other *Instructions* manuscripts. I also include quotes from BL MS Royal 17 C XVII, which – due to its significant differences from the other six manuscripts – Kristensson printed separately. For more information regarding the manuscripts, see: *John Mirk's Instructions for Parish Priests*, ed. Kristensson, 9–27, 57–62; 67–76 for BL MS Cotton Claudius A II; and 177–224 for BL MS Royal 17 C XVII. For a gendered analysis of *Instructions*, see Beth Allison Barr, "Gendering Pastoral Care: John Mirk and his *Instructions for Parish Priests*," in *Fourteenth Century England*, vol. IV, ed. J.S. Hamilton (Woodbridge, Suffolk: Boydell Press, 2006), 93–108.

hamper pastoral care, creating a rift between priests and the women they served? Through an analysis of Middle English pastoral literature (sermons, exempla, and pastoral handbooks), this study explores such questions in an attempt to understand how late medieval English priests perceived their spiritual obligations to female parishioners.

The picture that emerges is relatively bright. Popular sermon compilations regularly included women in sermon audiences and exempla; emphasized women's special pastoral needs; and gave advice about ways to handle those needs. Pastoral instruction manuals and other sermon compilations also reveal priests attuned to women's lifecycle stages, distinguishing not only between wives and singlewomen but also between singlewomen and prostitutes. Some pastoral writers even admonished men for mistreating their wives and for blaming women as the "cause" of sexual sin. Thus, Middle English pastoral literature reveals priests concerned about women: acknowledging women as distinct from men, recognizing the unique pastoral needs of women, and painting a more realistic picture of women than was often found in general Church ideology.[4]

But the picture still is cloudy in parts. For the many clerical writers who expressed concern for women and made room for women in the language of their writings, there were also those who ignored women. Moreover, because they portrayed women as prone to sexual sin, dubious about sacerdotal powers, fearful of confession, and complicating the assignation of penance, authors of vernacular pastoral literature presented women as problematic parishioners. This picture of tarnished female piety seems to have been inadvertent, created by clerics whose main aim was to provide women with proper counseling and spiritual care. Yet their advice perpetuated traditional cultural stereotypes that limited clerical perception of female parishioners. The dying female exemplum character from Devonshire received Eucharist one last time because of the tenacity of her vicar. As we shall see, some real women in late medieval England might not have been as lucky.

## PASTORAL CARE

In theory, pastoral care was a simple matter. Priests entrusted with the spiritual care of souls would teach their parishioners basic tenets of the Christian faith, including instruction on the seven deadly sins, the ten commandments, the seven articles of faith, the seven works of mercy, and scripture (both through preaching

---

4   Several historians have discussed the misogyny of the medieval Church, including: *Women Defamed and Woman Defended: An Anthology of Medieval Texts*, eds. Alcuin Blamires and Karen Pratt (Oxford: Clarendon, 1992); Jacques Dalarun, "The Clerical Gaze," in *A History of Women: Silences of the Middle Ages*, eds. Georges Duby, Michelle Perrot, and Christine Klapisch-Zuber (Cambridge: Belknap Press of Harvard University Press, 1992), 15–42; Dyan Elliott, *Fallen Bodies: Pollution, Sexuality, and Demonology in the Middle Ages* (Philadelphia: University of Pennsylvania Press, 1999); Eleanor McLaughlin, "Equality of Souls, Inequality of Sexes: Women in Medieval Theology," in *Religion and Sexism: Images of Women in the Jewish and Christian Traditions*, ed. Rosemary Radford Ruether (New York: Simon and Schuster, 1974), 213–266; and Jane Tibbetts Schulenburg, "Gender, Celibacy, and Proscriptions of Sacred Space: Symbol and Practice," in *Medieval Purity and Piety: Essays on Medieval Clerical Celibacy and Religious Reform*, ed. Michael Frassetto (New York: Garland, 1998), 353–376.

and personal interaction). They also would administer five of the seven sacraments whenever needed or requested – baptism, confession and penance, holy communion, matrimony, and extreme unction (confirmation and ordination could only be administered by bishops) – regularly remind their flocks of the importance of confession, and live godly lives worthy of emulation.[5] The compiler of Worcester Cathedral Library MS 172 summed up the "office of a Bishop or a priest" in "V manners." "The first is truly to preach Christ's gospel. The second is to pray [to] god continuously for the Church. The third is the sacraments freely to make and bear to whom it behooves. The fourth is only to study in holy scripture. The fifth is openly to prove and give example of perfection." Additionally, a priest should be a faithful example in conversation, chastity, charity, faith, and good works, as well as being poor, hungry, thrifty, sweet, merciful, quick to forgive, clean of heart, and willing to defend passionately his clerical office. Otherwise, the text warned, he should "understand himself to be no priest of his lord."[6]

Bringing such lofty commands closer to the ground, the fourteenth-century author of *Speculum Sacerdotal*, a vernacular sermon compilation contemporary and comparable to *Festial*, outlined precisely what priests were to do after performing mass. "The priests of them which are set to the governance of the parishioners after the reading of the gospel and of the offertory at mass turn them unto the people," he ordered, and they should then proclaim to the people all the feasts and holy days to honor during the next week. Priests should conclude this announcement with solemn prayers, praying for good crops, peace, their clerical brethren, all their parishioners including the sick, those traveling on pilgrimages and sailing on sea voyages, the living, and the dead. Although this was a routine assignment, *Speculum Sacerdotal* reminded priests that how devoutly people

---

5  For scholarship on pastoral care, issues related to pastoral care, and the pastoral care of women, see: Jacqueline Murray, "The Absent Penitent: The Cure of Women's Souls and Confessors' Manuals in Thirteenth-Century England," in *Women, the Book, and the Godly: Selected Proceedings from the St. Hilda's Conference 1993*, eds. Lesley Smith and Jane H.M. Taylor (Cambridge: D.S. Brewer, 1995), 13–26, and "Gendered Souls in Sexed Bodies: The Male Construction of Female Sexuality in Some Medieval Confessor's Manuals," in *Handling Sin: Confession in the Middle Ages*, eds. Peter Biller and A.J. Minnis (York: York Medieval Press, 1998), 79–94; Leonard E. Boyle, "The *Oculus Sacerdotis* and Some Other Works of William of Pagula," in his *Pastoral Care, Clerical Education, and Canon Law, 1200–1400* (London: Variorum Reprints, 1981), 81–110; Mary Flowers Braswell, *The Medieval Sinner: Characterization and Confession in the Literature of the English Middle Ages* (Rutherford, Madison, and Teaneck: Fairleigh Dickinson University Press, 1983); Leo Carruthers, "'No Woman of No Clerk is Preysed': Attitudes to Women in Medieval English Literature," in *A Wyf There Was*, eds. Paule Mertens-Fonck and Juliette Dor (Liège, Belgium: Dép. d'anglais, Université de Liège, 1992), 49–60; Sharon Farmer, "Persuasive Voices: Clerical Images of Medieval Wives," *Speculum* 61 (1986), 517–543, and "'It Is Not Good that [Wo]man Should Be Alone': Elite Responses to Singlewomen in High Medieval Paris," in *Singlewomen in The European Past, 1250–1800*, eds. Judith M. Bennett and Amy M. Froide (Philadelphia: University of Pennsylvania Press, 1999), 82–105; Michael Haren, *Sin and Society in Fourteenth-Century England: A Study of the Memoriale Presbiterorum* (Oxford: Clarendon, 2000); Ruth Mazo Karras, "Gendered Sin and Misogyny in John of Bromyard's Summa Predicantium," *Traditio: Studies in Ancient and Medieval History, Thought, and Religion* 47 (1992), 233–257; Ann Eljenholm Nichols, "The Etiquette of Pre-Reformation Confession in East Anglia," *Sixteenth Century Journal* 17:2 (1986), 145–163; Elizabeth A. Petroff, "Male Confessors and Female Penitents: Possibilities for Dialogue," in her *Body and Soul: Essays on Medieval Women and Mysticism* (New York and Oxford: Oxford University Press, 1994), 139–160.

6  Worcester Cathedral Library MS 172, f. 33r.

adhered to announcements of feast days and holy days rested on how devoutly a priest delivered the message.

> For the [more] honest and holy that they make their proclamation unto the people, the more they steer [guide] and should steer the people to that which they bid them. They should commend and praise the important holidays of God and of his saints excellently with all their might. And the cause wherefore they have been ordained openly to show, and to declare shortly some miracles that pertain unto the feasts that the people of God may be enlightened with unto the knowledge of truthfulness, and to the love thereof be inflamed and stirred.[7]

John Mirk also contributed to this conversation on clerical behavior, admonishing priests about pastoral care and dedicating one entire sermon to the matter. In *Denarracio de Morte Neronis Sermo*, Mirk described how the evil life of Nero met deservedly with an evil death.[8] But, before embarking on that tale, Mirk reminded his audience, "It is profitable and needful to the soul and to the life also to speak always that is good, and take that is honest, and namely to a priest; for his mouth is hallowed to speak God's words, and shall nothing speak, but that is profitable to the life and to the soul. For ribaldry and vice is poison to a priest's mouth, for it poisons his soul, and poisons others that hear him." A priest is responsible for remaining pure in both word and deed, Mirk continued, so "that none others be corrupt by example of him." The sermon concludes with a poignant exemplum of a hermit who prayed for the privilege to witness the soul of a holy man ascend into heaven. An angel appeared and guided him to the death of a supposedly holy man named Enklus. "Comforted in soul" for the opportunity to see his heart's desire, the hermit was cheered by the number of people also scurrying to attend the death. When he arrived, however, the hermit was horrified to see two horrible fiends sitting on the holy man's head, raking his soul from his throat. The angel explained that this man had done nothing for the love of God, but had been motivated by selfish ambitions. Consequently, he got what he deserved – eternal torment and separation from God. The angel then directed the hermit to another location. This time the hermit found a pilgrim lying dead in a chancel. Instead of surrounded by fiends, this body was surrounded by angels from heaven calling to the soul: "Come out, God's darling, come out, and go with us unto the bliss that ever shall last." Then King David danced into the room with his harp, followed by a musical host, and led the soul joyfully into heaven. Unlike the reputed holy man, the angel explained, this pilgrim had been a good man with no love for the world except to please God. Consequently, he also got what he deserved – eternal bliss. The exemplum concludes with a statement directed specifically to priests. "This is here written, to give priest's example, how they shall occupy holy feasts of the year ... For the higher that the feast is, the holier must a priest be; that is, more busily serve his God, not only outward with saying, but also inward with holy thinking." In other words, priests needed to walk the talk: outwardly act like holy men and inwardly keep their minds focused on the things of God.

Parishioners, in return for having such dedicated clerics, were expected to

---

[7] *Speculum Sacerdotal: Edited from British Museum MS. Additional 36791*, ed. Edward H. Weatherly, EETS original series 200 (London: Oxford University Press, 1936), 2.
[8] *Festial*, 191–196.

attend mass and confession regularly (at least once a year), perform penance dutifully, pay tithes promptly, and behave respectfully toward both priests and sacred property. Pastoral manuals made these duties clear, ordering parishioners to "church come, and be confessed all and some, and to receive Eucharist without disruption on Easter day"; "believe on that sacrament"; "leave their many words, their idle speech, and nice jokes, and put away all vanity" and not to stand in the church nor "lean to pillar nor to wall, but fair on knees they shall sit" when attending church services; "ball and bares and such play, out of church yard put away;" and to "tithe well and true."[9] The laity should also memorize the basic tenets of Christianity, as taught by their priests. The *Lay Folk's Catechism* ordered that "parsons and vicars and all parish priests" diligently ask their parishioners if they knew the fourteen points of truth, the ten commandments, the seven sacraments, the seven deeds of mercy, the seven virtues, and the seven deadly sins; if they rehearsed these regularly; and if they taught them to their children. "And if it be found that they know them not, then enjoin them upon their behalf, and of pain of penance" to learn them.[10]

Gender was part of this dyadic relationship between priest and parishioners. Priests were not to discriminate in administering the sacraments; nor were male and female parishioners to use gender as an excuse in shirking their spiritual responsibilities. *Omnis utriusque sexus*, from the Fourth Lateran Council in 1215, is perhaps the most famous statement dictating gender inclusivity for confession and penance. "All the faithful of either sex, after they have reached the age of discernment, should individually confess all their sins in a faithful manner to their own priest at least once a year, and let them take care to do what they can to perform the penance imposed on them."[11] This decree echoed in pastoral literature throughout the late Middle Ages, from Archbishop Thoresby's, "each man and woman, that of age is, ought for to receive [communion] once in the year, that is to say, at Easter, as holy church uses, when they are cleansed of sin through penance," to John Mirk's, "Thus you most also often preach, and your parishioners carefully teach: When one has done a sin, Look he lie not long therein, But soon that he him shrive [confess], Be it husband, be it wife," to the advice in the *Book of Vices and Virtues* that, "the sinful man or woman should shrive them wholly, that is of all things, for they should say all their sins, great and small." Clerical authors thus reminded clerical colleagues of their duty to make pastoral care available for all parishioners, regardless of sex.[12]

In some ways, then, a symbiotic relationship existed between priests and parishioners in late medieval England. Priests, in exchange for fulfilling their spiritual and physical obligations to parishioners, expected parishioners to fulfill their spiritual and physical obligations to priests. Neither priests nor parishioners of appropriate age could shirk these responsibilities, and, if they did, they faced

---

9   *Instructions for Parish Priests*, 81–87 and 185–186.

10  *The Lay Folk's Catechism*, eds. Thomas Frederick Simmons and Henry Edward Nolloth, EETS original series 118 (London: Kegan Paul, Trench, Trubner & Co., 1901), 20–22.

11  As printed in *Pastors and the Care of Souls in Medieval England*, eds. John Shinners and William J. Dohar (Notre Dame: University of Notre Dame Press, 1998), 169–170.

12  *Lay Folk's Catechism*, 66; *Instructions for Parish Priests*, 71 and 179; *The Book of Vices and Virtues: A Fourteenth Century English Translation of the Somme le Roi of Lorens d'Orleans*, ed. W. Nelson Francis, EETS original series 217 (London: Oxford University Press, 1942), 176–177.

consequences. The compiler of *Middle English Sermons* warned priests to confess and cleanse themselves of deadly sin before performing mass and administering the sacrament.[13] Those who lazily thought to avoid these duties might have changed after hearing some sermon stories. *Alphabet of Tales*, for example, relays an exemplum about a lecherous priest who conducted mass without repenting of his sin. A white dove prevented him from completing the service, to his great embarrassment, by flying down from heaven and consuming the consecrated bread and wine. This occurred three times before the priest finally confessed.[14] Other stories admonished priests to exemplify holiness because of the example they set for parishioners. *Festial* contains the tale of a priest who, instead of presenting a good example, "was lusty to speak of ribaldry and jests that turned men to lechery." One night demons came and dragged him from his sleep. When they returned him to his bed three nights later, he was beaten and burned full of wounds that never would heal. It was only after suffering this torture and punishment that the priest became the example that he always should have been. "And all his life after when he heard any man speak of ribaldry, he would say, 'Sir, beware of me.'"[15] Another exemplum shared the story of a priest who cared more about eating, drinking, and sex than meeting the needs of his parishioners. When he died, the souls of those he had neglected accused him into damnation: "We were committed unto you and you have forgotten us; for when we sinned; you neither reproved us with good word nor example, and therefore you are the cause of our damnation." The story concludes with the priest falling into the pit of hell from which he was never heard again.[16]

Priests who refused to heed such supernatural warnings also risked worldly consequences. They could be deprived of a benefice; censured by church overseers; or, if they upset their parishioners enough, lose financial support and even find themselves victims of physical violence. The early fifteenth-century vicar of Remmesbury and chaplain of Netheravene illustrate these consequences well. The first was suspended from performing his spiritual duties by an official of the dean of Salisbury and publicly denounced for adultery in 1409. The second had his life threatened in 1406 by parishioner Ralph Hobbes, over a matter of sacrament administration and perhaps also rape accusations.[17]

Laity likewise faced consequences for spiritual misbehavior. Those who failed to attend confession or take communion might die with unconfessed sins and without sufficient grace, thereby condemning believers to an extended stay in purgatory or hell. Mirk told the frightening story of the evil merchant who refused to repent, even after Jesus visited him on his deathbed. "My son, why will you not shrive yourself and put you into my mercy, as I am ready always to give mercy to all those who will meekly ask," pleaded Jesus. The stubborn man replied, "For I know well I am unworthy to have mercy; wherefore you will give me no

---

13 *Middle English Sermons edited from British Museum MS. Royal 18 B. xxiii*, ed. Woodburn O. Ross, EETS original series 209 (London: Oxford University Press, 1940), 287–288.

14 *An Alphabet of Tales: An English 15th Century Translation of the Alphabetum narrationum of Etienne de Besancon. From Additional Ms. 25, 719 of the British Museum*, ed. Mary MaCleod Banks, EETS original series 127 (London: Kegan Paul, Trench, Trubner & Co., 1905), 462–463.

15 *Festial*, 192.

16 *Alphabet of Tales*, EETS original series 127, 463–464.

17 *The Register of John Chandler, Dean of Salisbury, 1404–17*, ed. T.C.B. Timmins, Wiltshire Record Society 39 (Devizes: Wiltshire Record Society, 1984), 101, 30, xviii.

mercy." Jesus responded by flinging blood in the dying man's face, yelling, "You fiend-child, this shall be ready token between me and you in the day of doom, that I would have done you mercy, and you would not [receive it]." "Alas! Alas!" cried the man, "I am damned forever!" He then promptly died – his face red as blood, his body black as pitch.[18] If such fictional tales were not enough to frighten parishioners into good behavior, priests could also refuse them burial in sacred ground or, if the parishioners were still alive, censure and recommend them for excommunication. The parish priest of Ousby, for example, was ordered in 1306 to impose a penalty of forty shillings on parishioners for misdeeds discovered during a recent visitation. If they failed to comply, the priest would "suspend twelve of the better men of the said parish from entering church and strike them down with the sentence of major excommunication if their rebellion so demands." The Great Sentence, which appeared frequently in pastoral manuals, reminded priests and parishioners that excommunication could be the spiritual consequence of disobedient living.[19]

Theoretically, priests and parishioners had incentive enough to keep the system of pastoral care working smoothly and efficiently. In practice, matters were more complicated. First, the behavior of many priests indicated that either they did not understand their duties as listed in manuscripts like Worcester Cathedral MS 172 or did not fear the consequences of malfeasance. The compiler of *Middle English Sermons* quoted St. Bernard lamenting the proliferation of sinful priests in the second Sunday of Advent sermon. "Lord Jesus it is not now to say such is the priest as the people is, but how even as the worst of the people is, so is the priest now-a-days."[20] The lives of some priests reveal that this lament was rooted in reality. The burgesses of Saltash complained in 1406 that their vicar had spent most of his six-year tenure violating pastoral responsibilities instead of fulfilling them. He got drunk and revealed confessions, sold the sacramental items, refused to minister last rites, failed to teach either the Gospel or God's law, "nor set any other good example to his parishioners by which they could amend their lives, because he carries on like a mere layman." Visitation and various parish records from Kent, Salisbury, Shropshire, and Oxford indicate that this vicar was only one of many misbehaving clerics. Priests in Sturry, Thanington, Hoath, Sandwich, Charlton, Buckland, Dover, and Wooton failed to sing mass regularly and some failed to administer the sacraments when needed so that parishioners died without receiving confession or communion.[21] A rector in Stockton received multiple citations for his nonresidence until he finally was "absolved and deprived … from any cure and rule of the said church and of the parishioners."[22] The Bishop of Hereford received word from the Bishop of London in 1350 that many priests were

---

18 *Festial*, 91–92.

19 *The Bishop's Register: A Translation of Documents from Medieval Episcopal Registers Designed to Illustrate their Contents as well as Various Phases of Medieval Episcopal Activity*, trans. and ed. Clifford J. Offer (London: Society for Promoting Christian Knowledge, 1929), 222. The Great Sentence can be found in multiple pastoral manuals, such as *Instructions for Parish Priests*, 104–107, and *Quattuor Sermones: Printed by William Caxton*, ed. N.F. Blake, Middle English Texts 2 (Heidelberg: Winter, 1975), 81–85.

20 *Middle English Sermons*, 118.

21 *Catholic England: Faith, Religion and Observance before the Reformation*, trans. and annotator R.N. Swanson (New York: Manchester University Press, 1993), 261 and 262–265.

22 Offer, *The Bishop's Register*, 126–128.

endangering the cure of souls by charging for ordinary services. And the chaplain Thomas Dyer, appointed by Merton College, Oxford, was declared in 1484 not "good and virtuously disposed in his living as a priest should be who has such a cure." His parishioners accused him of stealing candles and votive offerings from the church, revealing confessions, and denying the sacraments unless paid extra.[23] Hence some priests in late medieval England failed to provide their parishioners with critical components of pastoral care, including confession, penance, holy communion, and extreme unction.

Second, parishioners often complicated pastoral care by misbehaving as badly as some priests. The fifteenth-century chancery case of Rev. William Pierson of London reveals John Coll and his wife Agnes attempting to frame their priest (Pierson) for sexual misconduct and then blackmailing him, saying "that if he did not give them a great reward they would send him to prison and utterly shame him." Sir John Hickson, a vicar in Sussex, knelt at the altar during mass one Sunday to offer intercessions and prayers and found himself instead assaulted by several disgruntled parishioners. They attacked him, restrained him, threw him in the stocks, and finally imprisoned him on false charges.[24] Other parishioners in Kent withheld or cheated on tithes, refused to attend services, talked evil of their priests, intimidated clerical assistants, and refused to partake in confession and communion. Some parishioners even extended this disrespect toward priests to the teachings of holy church. Sermons, for example, were filled with tales of faithless parishioners not believing in the efficacy of the host (spitting it out, hiding it at home, or selling it) and penitents lying during confession.[25] One exemplum portrayed a woman as combining these sins of sacrilege, lying about forgiving a fellow parishioner, and then partaking of Eucharist immediately afterward to avoid sanction by her priest.[26] Such attitudes manifest difficulties in the pastoral care process, for how could parishioners receive the sacraments from their priests if they neither trusted nor respected them, and how could they respect the sacraments if they did not believe in them? Likewise, how could priests be expected to provide pastoral care for parishioners who defamed them, abused them, and refused to believe in the teachings of holy church? The alleged words of one rector reflect this tension between priests and parishioners, as he shouted from pulpit at his congregation in 1405, "You are excommunicated rustics."[27]

Finally, even if both priests and parishioners had good intentions, such individual factors as social status and life-stage complicated the pastoral relationship. Instruction manuals warned priests to be mindful of what "degree [rank]" each parishioner was and to deal with them accordingly. *Instructions for Parish Priests* ordered:

---

[23] Shinners and Dohar, *Pastors and the Care of Souls*, 253–255 and 268. *The Register of John Chandler* similarly indicates that parishioners frequently accused priests of failing to administer pastoral care. A rector in the deanery of Salisbury was accused in 1408 of being too drunk to visit the sick; the vicar of Holnest and Bourton was accused in 1408 of refusing to visit the sick, even when repeatedly asked, 85 and 86; and the vicar of Sutton in 1405 was accused of not instructing parishioners nor preaching and of allowing Walter Ky to die without the sacraments, 11.

[24] Shinners and Dohar, *Pastors and the Care of Souls*, 272–273 and 276–278.

[25] Swanson, *Catholic England*, 265–267.

[26] Shrewsbury School MS 3, ff. 55v–56r.

[27] The rector denied having said this. *Register of John Chandler*, 21–22.

First you must this remember,
What he is that does the sin,
Whether it be she or he,
Young or old, serf or free,
Poor or rich, or in office,
Or man of dignitary if he is,
Single or wedded or cloistered,
Clerk or lewd or secular,
Bishop or priest or man of high rank,
You must know this by all means.[28]

On the one hand, this sensitivity was purely practical, helping priests assess the severity of sin and assign penance correctly. For example, fornication between a single lay man and single lay woman was considered a lesser sin than fornication between a religious man and religious woman. Thus penance in the first case was less than penance in the second. On the other hand, this sensitivity to personal degree was also protective, helping shield priests from giving inappropriate counsel and parishioners from receiving bad pastoral advice. Once a cleric realized his penitent was married, he would know to disallow certain vows without spousal approval. Mirk addressed this in *Instructions for Parish Priests*.

To preach them also you must not hesitate,
Both to wife and also husband,
That neither of them no penance take,
Nor no vow to chastity make,
Nor no pilgrimage take to do,
But if both assent thereto.[29]

Moreover, knowledge of economic, familial, or even physical status would help clerics refrain from imposing too difficult penance – such as assigning a long pilgrimage for a poor peasant or decreeing fasting for those doing strenuous manual labor. The author of *Speculum Sacerdotal* articulated this in his chapter on penance. "It is fitting for the priest to consider the feebleness of man and to temper their penance to be lighter or shorter so that they might bear it … And they that may not fast for labor of harvest or of going, let each man of them give a penny to feeding and clothing of poor men … and poor men that may not fast nor pay, let them say for each day that they fast not 40 Pater Nosters, or 50, or at least 30."[30]

But while clerical sensitivity to parishioner degree was beneficial to priests and parishioners, it could also be detrimental. Simply knowing the name of the penitent, what position the penitent held in the parish, how much money the penitent made, and whether the penitent was male or female erected barriers that hindered the process of pastoral care. For example, if the penitent was a member of a politically powerful or wealthy family, the priest might be less inclined to ask the probing questions required for confession and more inclined to assign lighter penance. *The Book of Margery Kempe* provides two stories showing this

---

[28] *Instructions for Parish Priests*, 147–148 and 211.
[29] Ibid., 88–89 and 186–187.
[30] *Speculum Sacerdotal*, 75–76.

worldly pressure that some parishioners exerted on clerics to try and sway spiritual matters. Some pressure was direct and active. Before leaving on pilgrimage to Jerusalem, Margery told a respectable lady that her husband was in purgatory and that the lady too would be a long time coming to heaven. Offended by the obvious inference about the sinfulness of her (and her husband's) life, the woman commanded that the confessor disagree with Margery's prediction and abandon Margery. If he did not, the priest would lose the respectable woman's friendship, which possibly encompassed her financial and political support as well. Other pressure was more indirect and passive. Once the Bishop of Worcester attempted to soothe Margery's wrath after he asked her to a meeting which she did not want to attend. "Margery," he said, "I have not summoned you, for I know well enough you are John of Brunham's daughter from Lynn. I beg you not to be angry, but be pleasant with me, and I shall be pleasant with you, for you shall eat with me today." In other words, he seems to have remembered that Margery's father was a powerful burgess, frequent Mayor of Lynn, alderman of the Trinity Guild, Member of Parliament, and holder of various other influential offices, and thus thought it better to appease Margery than to provoke. It is quite probable that Margery Kempe owed at least some of the assistance and tolerance she received from local clerics to the political and social position of her father. Otherwise, she might have suffered the fate often threatened her – burning as a Lollard.[31]

Hence pastoral care was a fragile process. Priests walked a delicate line between providing for spiritual needs indiscriminately and yet still acting with an awareness of differences among parishioners. Perhaps it was for this reason that clerical authors regarded clerical behavior as a critical component of pastoral care. Mirk, in his *Instructions for Parish Priests*, placed strict rules for how clerics should govern themselves *before* embarking on how clerics should provide for their parishioners. He reminded priests to be "chaste," to perform their services without "haste," and to practice what they preached if "you wish that god you hear." The text continues, specifying exactly how priests should and should not live:

> In word and deed you must be mild,
> Both to man and to child.
> Drunkenness and gluttony,
> Pride and sloth and envy,
> All you must put away,
> If you will serve god to satisfaction.
> That you need, eat and drink,
> But slay your lust at any cost.
> Taverns also you must forsake,
> And merchandise you shall not make.
> Wrestling and shooting and such manner [of] sport,
> You must not use without blame.
> Hawking, hunting and dancing,
> You must forgo at any cost,

[31] *The Book of Margery Kempe: The Text from the Unique MS Owned by Colonel W. Butler-Bowdon*, ed. Sanford Brown Meech with prefatory note by Hope Emily Allen and notes and appendices by Sanford Brown Meech and Hope Emily Allen, EETS original series 212 (London: Kegan Paul, Trench, Trubner & Co., 1940), 46, 47, 109–110, 28–29.

Cutted clothes and piked shoes,
Your good fame they will ruin.
Markets and fairs I you forbid,
But it be for great need.
In honest clothes you must go;
Dagger nor girdle wear you none.
Beard and crown you must shave,
If you will your rank save.
Of food and drink you most be free,
To poor and rich by their rank.
Eagerly you must your psalter read,
And of the day of doom have dread;
And ever do good against evil,
Or else you cannot live well.[32]

Despite the difficulties (not to mention improbabilities) involved in attaining such a high ideal, contemporary clerical literature encouraged priests to live as perfectly as possible. "For little is worth your preaching, if you be of evil living," explained Mirk.[33] British Library MS Royal 17 XXVI uses the word *angel* in describing priests, suggesting that all who had taken the high order of priesthood should be so clean from sin and fleshly deeds that they would appear as heavenly beings to their earth-bound flock.[34] Perhaps clerical authors hoped that if they could convince priests to act like angels, their pastoral care would be angelic as well.

To conclude, the day-to-day practice of pastoral care spun a complex web of religious obligations, spiritual needs, social constraints, cultural perceptions, and tenuous relationships. One careless move or wrong turn, and priests and parishioners alike could find themselves face to face with a poisonous spider. Even worse, they could tear the web entirely.

## THE PASTORAL CARE OF WOMEN

One potentially venomous spider was gender. Although priests *should* have cared for women as carefully as they cared for men, the association of women with sexual sin and the social and legal status of women as dependent on men complicated how priests *could* have provided this care.[35] To begin with, as medieval

---

[32] *Instructions for Parish Priests*, 68–70.
[33] Ibid., 68.
[34] BL MS Royal 17 A XXVI, f. 23.
[35] Although basing his comments on Latin and Continental sources, Peter Biller has discussed the difficulties of gender in the confessional. "The dangers of confession becoming the occasion of sexual entanglement is reflected in warnings which are commonplace in the instructional literature: the priest was to avoid looking at the woman and to hear confession in a place where both can be seen. Even with modest and chaste confessors and penitents, the difference of gender could still make things awkward. It might induce considerable shame and embarrassment which went beyond, and were different from, the shame which the penitent appropriately felt about the sins she had committed." Peter Biller, "Confession in the Middle Ages: Introduction," in *Handling Sin: Confession in the Middle Ages*, eds. Peter Biller and A.J. Minnis (York: York Medieval Press, 1998), 13.

culture commonly associated women with sexual temptation, priests – vowed to celibacy – were expected to be especially cautious when counseling women.[36] Mirk suggested in his *Instructions for Parish Priests* that priests not gaze on female penitents, as if merely looking at women would entice clerics to sin.[37] Some Latin penitentials suggested that priests place women at their sides so that they could not accidentally see a female penitent's face, "especially if she is young." Women were required to cover their hair for confession, and priests were not to place their hands on the heads of female penitents as they sometimes did with men. Furthermore, as "female penitents presented a particular challenge" not only in their bodies but also in the subject matter of their confessions, priests were warned about listening to women confessing sexual sins. Priests were still to help these female penitents, but they were forbidden to write down the women's confessions, lest the written word later inspire sinful thoughts and desires. The author of one manual even ordered women confessing sins of an erotic nature to go to priests who did not know them personally – even if this meant bypassing their usual parish priests.[38] Although clerics created these rules with the laudable aim of protecting themselves (and perhaps also the women they served) from immorality, they reflect a cautious approach to women that would have hindered their ability to counsel female parishioners.[39]

In addition to threatening priests personally (their celibacy), the sexual hazard posed by women threatened priests professionally (their sacerdotal purity). The Fourth Lateran Council stated in 1215 that a priest found guilty of "incontinence" who continued to practice "the divine mysteries" should be "deprived of his ecclesiastical benefices" and "forever deposed." Incontinent priests or even priests suspected of incontinence could be considered unworthy of performing the sacraments.[40] As R.N. Swanson has written, this "quasi-donatism" stemmed from the papacy's struggle to impose celibacy on unwilling clerics in the eleventh century, "urging lay boycotts of the ministrations of married or concubinary priests. It

---

[36] Alcuin Blamires has summed this up well. "Associated, perhaps, with the clerical suspicion of the female body's power to provoke sexual arousal was a deep-seated male apprehension about, or inferiority complex about, the female capacity for extended sexual activity. Not only did women excite men to sinful thoughts; women were actually held to be more lustful creatures by nature. From here it was a short step to the equation, woman equals lust." Blamires, *Woman Defamed and Woman Defended*, 5.

[37] *Instructions for Parish Priests*, 113.

[38] Thomas N. Tentler, *Sin and Confession on the Eve of the Reformation* (Princeton: Princeton University Press, 1977), 82–83 and 86–87; Elliott, *Fallen Bodies*, 24. But John Mirk explicitly stated that parishioners were always to confess to their own parish priest with only a few exceptions. *Instructions for Parish Priests*, 108–112.

[39] Of course, some late medieval clerics might have been more tempted sexually by male parishioners than female parishioners. Ordinances from the early medieval *Penitential of Theodore*, describing penance for "a male who commits fornication with a male" and calling the "effeminate" partner an "adulteress," make it clear that homosexual relations did exist in the Middle Ages and that clerical authorities were aware of it. *Medieval Handbooks of Penance: A Translation of the Principal Libri Poenitentiales and Selections from Related Documents*, trans. and eds. John T. McNeill and Helena M. Gamer (New York: Columbia University Press, 1990), 185. But, because of medieval cultural assumptions, even a priest who preferred men to women would have needed to behave cautiously around female parishioners to avoid accusations of sexual misconduct.

[40] *Christianity through the Thirteenth Century*, ed. Marshall W. Baldwin, et al. (New York: Harper and Row, 1970), 306. Not quite as specific, the seventh-century *Penitential of Theodore* declared, "a bishop, presbyter or deacon guilty of fornication ought to be degraded and to do penance at the decision of a bishop." McNeill, *Medieval Handbooks of Penance*, 192.

was a short step to deny the validity of the sacraments they performed – even though this was formal heresy."[41] For clerics who derived much of their social and religious status from their ability to celebrate mass, perform baptisms, and grant forgiveness, having this sacerdotal power questioned posed a critical problem. To help priests avoid such challenges to their authority, Robert Mannyng of Brunne suggested that priests not stare at women, not touch women, not be alone with women, not stand next to women during church services, not kiss women, and not think about women at all.[42]

Yet proper observance of clerical duties made this impossible. Priests *had* to spend time with women – especially since evidence suggests that women were often more active in parish life than their male counterparts.[43] Katherine French has shown that some women participated more vigorously than some men in parish activities.[44] Churchwarden accounts reveal that women frequently labored in cleaning the nave, washing church linens, sweeping the floors, decorating for holidays, baking the holy loaf for mass, and embroidering altar cloths for the celebration of the Eucharist.[45] Men participated less frequently in these activities. Also, female groups often raised more money than their male counterparts for parish churches. Accounts from Croscombe (Somerset) reveal that a "maiden's guild" raised thirty percent of the total parochial income in 1493; accounts from

---

[41] R.N. Swanson, "Angels Incarnate: Clergy and Masculinity from Gregorian Reform to Reformation," in *Masculinity in Medieval Europe*, ed. D.M. Hadley (New York: Longman, 1999), 160–177, at 172.

[42] Robert Mannyng, *Robert of Brunne's Handlyng Synne, A.D. 1303, with Those Parts of the Anglo-French Treatise on which it was Founded, William of Wadington's 'Manuel des pechiez'*, ed. Frederick J. Furnivall, EETS original series 119 and 123 (London: Kegan Paul, Trench, Trubner & Co., 1901 and 1903), 280, 245, 240, 277, and 57. Similar commands can be found in the *Penitential of Theodore*. It stated that "if a priest is polluted in touching or in kissing a woman he shall do penance for forty days" and "if a presbyter kisses a woman from desire, he shall do penance for forty days." It also stated that women should not "stand among ordained men in the church, nor sit at a feast among priests." McNeill, *Medieval Handbooks of Penance*, 191 and 205.

[43] Peter Heath has written that "contact with women could not be avoided; some incumbents doubtless enjoyed without abusing the friendship of women in the parish; and many, no doubt, had occasion to give confidential advice to women in their cure. For these reasons, when some girl, or even some wife, of the parish was suspiciously with child, the culprit would find it easy to promote accusation of the incumbent or his assistant; the parishioners would find it easy to believe, if only because it was sometimes true." Peter Heath, *The English Parish Clergy on the Eve of the Reformation* (Toronto: University of Toronto Press, 1969), 106–107.

[44] Katherine French, "Parochial Fund-raising in Late Medieval Somerset," in *The Parish in English Life 1400–1600*, eds. Katherine French, Gary G. Gibbs, and Beat A. Kumin (New York: St. Martins Press, 1997), 115–132; "'To Free Them From Binding': Women in the Late Medieval English Parish," *Journal of Interdisciplinary History* 27:3 (1997), 387–412; "Maidens' Lights and Wives' Stores: Women's Parish Guilds in Late Medieval England," *Sixteenth Century Journal* 29:2 (1998), 399–425. As French has put it, "[w]hen both a men's and women's Hocktide collection took place, the women's half consistently earned more money than the men's." French, "'To Free Them from Binding,'" 401. Andrew Brown has also recorded that women often raised more money for parish churches than did men. Andrew Brown, *Popular Piety in Late Medieval England: The Diocese of Salisbury, 1250–1550* (Oxford: Clarendon, 1995), 257.

[45] French, "'To Free Them from Binding,'" 394. French has also discussed women purchasing church seats, participating in preparing the church for parish celebrations, and even serving as churchwardens. French, *The People of the Parish: Community Life in a Late Medieval English Diocese* (Philadelphia: University of Pennsylvania Press, 2001), 162–173, 188–190, 87–88. Nick Alldridge has found women participating in similar circumstances in his, "Loyalty and Identity in Chester Parishes," in *Parish, Church, and People: Local Studies in Lay Religion 1350–1750*, ed. S.J. Wright (London: Hutchinson, 1988), 85–124, at 91.

Salisbury reveal the "wives of the parish" earning almost enough money to buy new windows for the nave during a 1497 Hocktide festival; and accounts from Ashburton (Somerset) in 1491 show – in French's estimation – the wives "to be more enthusiastic about their work" in the church than men and contributing "more money than the men."[46]

Other historians have emphasized the special devotion of female parishioners. Peter Biller has cited a mid-thirteenth-century preacher accusing women of going "more readily to church than men," attending "sermons more readily than men," and praying more than men.[47] Sharon Farmer has noted that priests considered women especially devoted parishioners, relying on them to convince their husbands to participate in religious activities, and Patricia Crawford and Susan Groag Bell have described women engaging in such acts of private devotion as reading religious literature and teaching it to their children.[48] Moreover, historical accounts record that some medieval women asked for communion frequently, sometimes even once a day, and paid regular visits to their confessors. Margery Kempe claimed that she actively pursued the company of priests – engaging them in theological debates, employing some as confessors, and frequently asking for advice. Although she was exceptional in the number of times she met with priests, Kempe's need for clerical attention has been judged by Elizabeth A. Petroff as similar "to what most medieval women sought."[49] One woman from the diocese of Canterbury even turned the tables on the proper administration of mass, and instead of being on the receiving end, ministered Eucharist to her chaplain on three different occasions.[50] Women's abundant participation within church life has led Swanson to suggest that men's "questionable" commitment to parish churches might have stemmed from their perception of women as "overly familiar" with priests. Women were so active in parishes that their husbands, fathers, and sons might have grown resentful towards priests and, in rebellion, refused to attend religious services and even attacked clerics.[51]

Thus priests were faced with a difficult challenge: how to provide effective

---

46  French, "Parochial fund-raising," 125–126. Brown, *Popular Piety*, 120. French, "Maidens' Lights and Wives' Stores," 409. Gervase Rosser also has noted that the maidens' guild was "particularly successful in raising such contributions" to the Croscombe parish. Gervase Rosser, "Communities of Parish and Guild in the Late Middle Ages," in *Parish, Church, and People*, ed. S.J. Wright, 29–55, at 41.

47  Peter Biller, "The Common Woman in the Western Church in the Thirteenth and Early Fourteenth Centuries," in *Women in the Church: Papers Read at the 1989 Summer Meeting and the 1990 Winter Meeting of the Ecclesiastical History Society*, eds. W.J. Sheils and Diana Wood, Studies in Church History 27 (Oxford: Basil Blackwell, 1990), 127–157, at 140. G.R. Owst remarked that "men were in the minority, and the churches were attended mainly by womenfolk." G.R. Owst, *Preaching in Medieval England: An Introduction to Sermon Manuscripts of the Period, c. 1350–1450* (Cambridge: Cambridge University Press, 1926), 173 (footnote).

48  Sharon Farmer, "Persuasive Voices: Clerical Images of Medieval Wives"; Patricia Crawford, *Women and Religion in England, 1500–1720* (New York: Routledge, 1993), 73–97; Susan Groag Bell, "Medieval Women Book Owners: Arbiters of Lay Piety and Ambassadors of Culture," in *Sisters and Workers in the Middle Ages*, ed. Judith M. Bennett, et al. (Chicago: University of Chicago Press, 1989), 135–161.

49  Petroff, "Male Confessors and Female Penitents: Possibilities for Dialogue," 153.

50  *English Historical Documents III, 1189–1327*, ed. Harry Rothwell (New York and Oxford: Oxford University Press, 1975), 716.

51  R.N. Swanson, *Religion and Devotion in Europe, c.1215–c.1515* (Cambridge: Cambridge University Press, 1995), 305–308.

pastoral care for female parishioners who needed their guidance and supported their churches but who also potentially threatened their clerical celibacy and sacerdotal purity. But did this challenge affect how priests cared for women? Evidence presented by some historians suggests that it did. Jacqueline Murray has argued that an androcentric construction of sin in Latin pastoral manuals and a misogynist portrayal of women in medieval theology could have alienated priests from the women they served. Consequently women would have received relatively poor pastoral guidance. For example, Margery Kempe gave an account of a priest who came to "shrive" her immediately after she gave birth. "When she came to the point to say that thing which she had so long concealed, her confessor was a little too hasty and began sharply to reprove her before she had fully said what she intended." Superficially, this story told of a routine duty that faced most priests: acting as confessors for pregnant or post-partum women. But this ordinary priestly visit had an extraordinary outcome: Margery Kempe went mad. She sank into a state of deep depression that lasted several months, a depression partly caused by a priest who had refused to listen to her and reproved her too harshly. The priest had failed to understand and address her needs. Although this terrible scenario might have been an isolated event, Jacqueline Murray has suggested otherwise. After comparing Margery's account to instructions for the treatment of women in another clerical manual, Murray writes that "Margery's problem with an unsympathetic confessor might reflect a harsh and critical attitude towards female penitents which was more systemic and misogynistic."[52]

Dyan Elliott and Ruth Mazo Karras have lent further support to this idea that misogynist ideas in texts written and read by clerics could have translated into shoddy pastoral care for female parishioners. Elliott has claimed that because high standards of clerical purity drove priests to repress their libidinal desires, clerical imaginations conflated women and demons, eventually fusing them into the image of the early modern witch. Thus women, shut out of sacred spaces by clerical obsession with sexual purity, returned as demonic figures – haunting sleeping clerics, polluting holy places, and darkening the lives of real women with their omnipresent shadows. In a similar but less provocative fashion, Karras has explored how the association of female characters in exempla with particular sins negatively shaped medieval people's conception of women. For example, John of Bromyard depicted women as particularly prone to commit sins of lust. This, Karras has argued, perpetuated a misogynist belief that women were more dangerous sexually than men – a concept which, "as transmitted by preachers, helped construct the mental world of Chaucer, of Margery Kempe, and of the people who underwent the demographic and social changes of the post-plague century."[53]

In more recent work, Karras has taken this idea one step further to argue that misogynist ideas about female sexuality narrowed clerical vision about real women. Because they believed that women's dangerous sexuality could only be safely contained within marriage, clerics did not allow conceptual space to exist

---

[52] Jacqueline Murray, "The Absent Penitent: The Cure of Women's Souls and Confessors' Manuals in Thirteenth-Century England," 25–26. The encounter between Margery and her priest can be found in *The Book of Margery Kempe*, 7–9.

[53] Elliott, *Fallen Bodies*: this comment is a general assessment; Karras, "Gendered Sin and Misogyny," 257.

in their writings for sexually active women who were neither married nor prostitutes. Using several examples from Latin pastoral manuals, Karras argued that medieval English clerics conflated singlewomen and prostitutes. "Where the texts went into more detail about fornication, listing the possible partners with whom the sin might be committed, it becomes clear that the sexually active singlewoman was viewed in quite narrow terms – indeed, defined as a prostitute." Sharon Farmer makes a similar argument about thirteenth- and fourteenth-century clerics in Paris, arguing that because these religious men viewed women through a marriage prism, they often denied (or at least ignored) the existence of women who violated their ideology that all women should live under the control of men. "Because they defined women – especially lower-status women – through their sexuality and because they assumed that all women should be subordinated to men, Parisian clerics tended to ignore the existence of a large number of working singlewomen in the cities: singlewomen who were neither household servants nor prostitutes."[54]

Thus, by presenting the pastoral care of women through a lens of clerical misogyny, many historians have produced a dire picture of how priests might have cared for their female parishioners. Because priests viewed women through an androcentric construction of sin, misogynist ideas about feminine sexuality, and a marriage prism, they saw women not as real people living, working, and dying in the parish, but as fabricated manifestations of "womanhood" that reflected more mythology than reality. Singlewomen and working women slipped through the cracks; married women were defined by their husbands; and difficult women, such as Margery Kempe, were left with impatient and disinterested confessors. By limiting the ways that priests saw women, clerical misogyny could have limited the ways in which priests provided spiritual care to women.

Other historians have glossed over the difficulties posed by female parishioners, seeming to indicate that the pastoral care of women was either similar to the pastoral care of men, or just not an important concern. Michael Haren, in his examination of a fourteenth-century confessor's manual, has done exactly this. Although writing that "women penitents are dealt with under a number of headings in the treatise," he discusses the pastoral care of women very superficially, primarily in a short paragraph at the end of his section on "Miscellaneous Penitents." His study reveals more about how priests dealt with bureaucrats, manorial officers, knights, merchants, and pardoners than it does about medieval England's female population.[55]

Nor is Haren alone with this insufficient attention to the pastoral care of women. Thomas Tentler, in his comprehensive examination of pre-Reformation Latin pastoral manuals, mostly ignored gender distinctions despite dealing specifically with auricular confession. G.R. Owst and J.W. Blench, although finding interesting information about the pastoral care of women in their surveys of

---

[54] Ruth Mazo Karras, "Sex and the Singlewoman," in *Singlewomen in the European Past*, eds. Judith M. Bennett and Amy M. Froide (Philadelphia: University Pennsylvania Press, 1999), 127–145, at 129; Sharon Farmer, "'It Is Not Good That [Wo]man Should Be Alone,'" 91. I emulate Judith M. Bennett and Amy M. Froide in their use of the compound form of the words "singlewoman" or "singlewomen." Bennett and Froide, "A Singular Past," in their *Singlewomen in the European Past*, 1–37.

[55] Michael Haren, *Sin and Society in Fourteenth-Century England*, 184.

Middle English sermon literature, mentioned women only in reference to other subjects, not as subjects in of themselves. Owst, for example, discussed women in regards to lay preaching, clerical condemnation of sins from the pulpit, and lay interruption of sermons. But he did not use this information to discuss how medieval sermon literature portrayed women in general. Again, despite examining many pastoral manuals containing references to the pastoral care of women and despite focusing on religious life in fifteenth-century parishes, Eamon Duffy has continued this trend of treating gender as an irrelevant factor.[56]

Limited by their vision and by their sources, most historians have understood the pastoral care of women within the bleak context of clerical misogyny, subsumed it under the pastoral care of men, or ignored it altogether. Consequently they have created a limited picture of how late medieval English priests cared for women.

## GENDERED LESSONS

In his article, "'No Woman of No Clerk is Preysed': Attitudes to women in Medieval English Religious Literature," Leo Carruthers did things differently. Instead of studying pastoral care through Latin manuals and sermon compilations, he turned to vernacular sources. Instead of classifying clerical discussions of women as anti-feminist, he argued that some clerical authors wrote of women in tolerant, even kind, ways. "Many Middle English treatises on Confession would indicate that good confessors had a humane and understanding attitude to women, even praising them at times," he wrote.[57] Similarly, in her study of late medieval sermons in France, Larissa Taylor has argued that "a surprising number of late medieval preachers stressed the dignity of woman and her equal role in Christian life." Preachers in France recognized that women were more reliable in church attendance than men, spoke out against the mistreatment of wives by husbands, and regularly "expressed views that were quite the opposite of the antifeminism of which they are so often accused."[58] Consequently, both Carruthers and Taylor have presented a more neutral view of clerical attitudes toward women.

Pressing such ideas further, this study argues for a more realistic understanding of how priests viewed and cared for female parishioners. The first chapter, *Pastoral Vernacular Literature*, establishes the critical role vernacular sermon compendiums and pastoral care handbooks played in the education and training of clerics with *cura animarum* – suggesting that this literature helped shape clerical attitudes towards pastoral care. The second chapter, *Pastoral Language*, traces the use of gender inclusive language in vernacular sermon literature and pastoral care handbooks to argue that clerical writers recognized their responsibilities to teach,

---

[56] These comments are general assessments. Tentler, *Sin and Confession on the Eve of the Reformation*; Owst, *Preaching in Medieval England*; J.W. Blench, *Preaching in England in the Late Fifteenth and Sixteenth Centuries* (Oxford: Basil Blackwell, 1964); Eamon Duffy, *The Stripping of the Altars: Traditional Religion in England, c.1400–c.1580* (New Haven and London: Yale University Press, 1992).

[57] Leo Carruthers, "'No Woman of No Clerk is Preysed'," 60.

[58] Larissa Taylor, *Soldiers of Christ: Preaching in Late Medieval and Reformation France* (New York and Oxford: Oxford University Press, 1992), 157, 172, 167–169, and 166

preach, and care for women.[59] Using John Mirk's *Festial* as a case study, it asserts that, despite varying in their use of gender inclusive language, clerical writers persistently and explicitly included women when addressing pastoral matters. Through their particular use of gender inclusive language, clerics acknowledged the important role female parishioners played in pastoral matters and seemed to accept clerical obligations to provide women with proper pastoral care. *Pastoral Perceptions*, the third chapter, details the attention that John Mirk and other clerical authors paid to female parishioners, recognizing women's lifecycle stages and their special pastoral needs. Yet this realistic concern was tempered by the limited ability of clerics to perceive women outside of their dependence on men and by their continued portrayal of women as sexually dangerous. Although both male and female parishioners presented gendered challenges to priests, the final chapter *Pastoral Care* suggests that the unique problems associated with women hampered the pastoral care process. Whether they liked it or not, priests had to exercise special caution when caring for women, and that caution – if implemented as suggested by pastoral literature – would have constrained the quality of care received by female parishioners.

In short, this study contends that clerical authors of Middle English pastoral literature taught their audiences to think differently about women. Sometimes such gendered lessons were helpful. Priests reading John Mirk's pastoral literature would have learned that women were important parishioners who needed to be addressed specifically in their sermons and not overlooked when they administered sacraments. They also would have learned that married women had pastoral needs different from singlewomen; that pregnant women had pastoral needs different from widows; and that, at least in some instances, female parishioners needed to be dealt with differently than their male counterparts. By their own writings, then, many late medieval English priests acknowledged the important role that female parishioners played in their ministry and professed concern about the quality of care they received.

Sometimes, however, such gendered lessons were also harmful. By focusing so much on the distinctiveness of women, clerical authors of Middle English pastoral literature seem to have branded female parishioners as particularly problematic. They assumed that female parishioners were especially ashamed about revealing sensitive confessions, therefore making the confessor's job more difficult as he attempted to unearth concealed sins. They claimed that assigning penance to married women was complicated by their dependent status. They even portrayed female parishioners as cynical about sacerdotal powers. Most damning, however, clerical authors continued to uphold the long tradition of obsessing about female sexuality – perhaps encouraging priests to consider female parishioners as more guilty than their male counterparts when it came to sexual sin. In these respects,

---

[59] By clerical writer/author I am referring to the cleric who compiled each individual manuscript. As most clerics borrowed sections from other manuals, such as taking a few sermons from *Festial* and a passage on the seven deadly sins from Richard of Lavynham's famous treatises, they are not authors in the sense of being the original creators (even John Mirk borrowed extensively from *Legenda Aurea* and other texts). But they are authors in the sense of being compilers and editing each collection of sermons or instructional book to their own individual specifications. I have found that when copying sections from other texts, many clerics changed language and added their own explanations or examples, thus creating new text from the existing version.

the literature designed to help priests serve women better only widened the gap between them.

In the end it seems that medieval priests faced a complex challenge. Caught between the difficulties of trying to provide appropriate care for women yet being hindered by cultural and religious restraints, as well as their own preconceptions, priests had to overcome critical challenges when caring for the pastoral needs of female parishioners. Clerics with *cura animarum* had to care for women – and most seemed to want to care for women – yet they simultaneously had to be more careful when providing that care. Simply by reminding priests of their duties toward female parishioners and giving advice on how to handle problems associated with women, clerical authors of vernacular instruction manuals and sermon collections attempted to solve this conundrum. Did they ever succeed? The answer is difficult to know. But what we do know is that at least some tried.

# Chapter 1

# PASTORAL VERNACULAR LITERATURE

God says himself, as written we find,
That when the blind leads the blind,
Into the ditch they fall both,
For they see not whereby to go.
So act priests now-a-days;
They be so blind in god's law,
That when they should the people read [teach]
Into sin they do them lead.
Thus they have now done for a long time,
And all is for lack of knowledge.
Wherefore you parish priest,
If you [wish to] please your savior,
If you be not great [learned] clergyman,
Look [study] you must on this work;
For here you might find and read
That which behooves you to know;
How you shall [to] your parish preach,
And what you need them to teach,
And which you must yourself be,
Here also you might it see;
For little is worth your preaching,
If you be of evil living.[1]

WITH THESE opening words, John Mirk made the intent of his *Instructions for Parish Priests* clear: to better educate priests – in their pastoral duties as well as their daily conduct – so that they could better educate parishioners. The author of *Speculum Sacerdotal* similarly stated that he had composed his work at the request of priests to help them preach and teach to their parishioners:

Therefore, you certain priests who are dear and familiar unto me before all others …
that for the instance and prayers which that you have made unto me for this present
work I have here disposed and written after my simpleness of the observance of all

---

[1] *John Mirk's Instructions for Parish Priests: Edited from MS Cotton Claudius A II and Six Other Manuscripts with Introduction, Notes, and Glossary*, ed. Gillis Kristensson, Lund Series in English 49 (Lund: Gleerup, 1974), 67–68.

saints the which should worshipfully each Sunday be showed unto your people that God may be glorified in your churches by the matters written after, and devotion and knowledge of the people may be the more informed to worshipping and glorifying of him that is almighty ... God.[2]

In short, clerical education served as a primary motive for the creation of pastoral vernacular literature, as it was believed that a better-educated clergy would produce a better-educated laity. Because of this particular design function, as well as the ubiquity of vernacular sermon compendiums and pastoral guides throughout the late medieval period, pastoral vernacular literature represented one of the most accessible ways for clerics to learn their craft. Thus it could have significantly influenced how late medieval priests conceptualized and conducted pastoral care.

CLERICAL EDUCATION

Two exempla from *Festial* help illuminate clerical education in the fourteenth and fifteenth centuries. In the first, a bishop, after discovering a priest in his diocese knew only enough Latin to sing requiem mass, forbade the priest to continue his pastoral duties. Soon thereafter, the bishop rode toward the church to matins, and when he came to the churchyard, a great number of dead bodies rose all around him, saying: "You say no mass for us and now you have taken our priest from us. Do that this be amended, other for sooth you shall be dead." Not surprisingly, the terrified bishop acquiesced, returning the clerical license to the semi-literate priest and allowing him to continue singing mass. In the second exemplum, a small child confronted a "master of divinity who studied busily." Sitting on a beach, the child was pouring water into a sand hole. When the cleric asked him why, the boy responded he was trying to fit all the water of the ocean into the hole. The cleric declared the impossibility of the task, to which the child answered, "I shall as soon do this, as you shall do that which you are about." Realizing that this was a divine messenger, the cleric abandoned his academic pursuits and "thanked God who so fairly warned him."[3]

Superficially, these exempla illustrate sermon points, such as the importance of providing mass and prayers for souls in purgatory, believing in the Trinity, and of

2  *Speculum Sacerdotal: Edited from British Museum MS. Additional 36791*, ed. Edward H. Weatherly, EETS original series 200 (London: Oxford University Press, 1936), 2–3.
3  *Festial*, 271, 167–168. It is tempting to link the second exemplum with late medieval complaints of priests who took advantage of Boniface VIII's *cum ex eo*, which afforded some clerics a seven-year leave of absence from their parishes to attend university. Much to the chagrin of their parishioners, they would often appoint a poorly trained lower cleric to perform their pastoral duties. Moreover, many of these priests who took advantage of *cum ex eo* found they could only pay for their academic training through pluralism (retaining of more than one benefice), thereby leaving more than one parish without its designated priest. If this story represents one of those priests seeking a university education and leaving either a single parish or multiple parishes, then it would seem that God ordered him not only to leave his studies, but also to return to his parishioners. For more about absenteeism and pluralism, see A.K. McHardy, "Careers and Disappointments in the Late-Medieval Church: Some English Evidence," in *The Ministry: Clerical and Lay: Papers Read at the 1989 Summer Meeting and the 1989 Winter Meeting of the Ecclesiastical History Society*, ed. W.J. Sheils, Studies in Church History 26 (Oxford: Basil Blackwell, 1989), 111–130.

caring for souls more than study. But these exempla also illustrate an intriguing view of clerical education: that academic training was not essential for all clerics. The first exemplum emphasized the importance of meeting parishioners' needs over the importance of knowing Latin; the second emphasized God's disapproval of excessive education. Consequently, both stories downplayed the importance of academic pursuits, suggesting that (at least for some late medieval English clerics) institutionalized education did not always provide the key to success.

This does not mean that clerics were to forsake education. Literacy was a necessary skill for church vocation. Clerics with *cura animarum* needed to read sermons intelligibly, understand and implement confessor manuals, and teach their parishioners prayers and creeds. Literacy was also critical for the practical administration of a benefice. Both beneficed and unbeneficed clerics needed to keep records of payments received (tithes and oblations), expenses paid (such as chancel repairs and the purchasing of sacramental items), and services rendered (such as marriages and funerals) – or at least have the capacity to understand records kept by a hired clerk. Late fifteenth-century ministerial accounts from the parish of Hornsea illustrate this well, as three different people using different methods of record-keeping authored the accounts from 1481–1485. The parochial chaplain John Wilson – the one most interested in composing check lists for payments, tithes, and oblations – filled his part of the accounts with the names of parishioners who paid, descriptions of what they paid, and explanations for why they paid. Wilson sometimes recorded payments that William Hubbylday (warden of the abbey's fishpond) and John Proktour (the vicar) seem to have overlooked. Hubbylday, more interested in the general income and expenses of the parish, merely inserted corrected amounts into Wilson and Proktour's accounts, while Proktour recorded total amounts received from oblations, tithes, and the glebe.[4] Thus for both the vicar and chaplain in Hornsea, literacy was essential for the daily upkeep of the benefice – for Proktour with his interest in the bottom line and for Wilson with his interest in proceeds and expenditure.

What is not quite so clear, however, is *how much* literacy was necessary. Must all clerics have been fluent in both Latin and English, as was John Mirk? Must all have been able to write as well as read, like Proktour and Wilson? Or could some clerics have thrived on English reading skills alone?

No seminaries or divinity schools existed in the medieval world. Pastoral training was a haphazard affair with would-be-priests gleaning information and skills from a variety of sources. Yet, as the priesthood only boasted a few requirements for free men (twenty-four years of age at time of ordination, progression

---

4    Peter Heath has written that "such accounts must have been common. A check list of tithe-payers was surely a necessity in a parish of any size or population, even if the habit of counting expenditure was less urgent." But, despite their probable proliferation, only a small number of clerical accounts seem to have survived. *Medieval Clerical Accounts*, ed. Peter Heath, Borthwick Papers 26 (York: St. Anthony's, 1964), 3. A historian from the University of Hull, Heath is one of the only scholars to have researched extensively clerical accounts. He organized and published the 1481–1493 accounts of two Hornsea vicars, John Proktour and William Ottway, and explored many of the challenges posited by the text. Heath has tentatively concluded that Wilson, Proktour, and Hubbylday were the most likely candidates to have written the accounts, 7–8. Moreover, by using the accounts to illuminate the financial problems and the declining living standards of the late medieval English parish clergy, he clearly demonstrated how valuable clerical accounts are to the study of parish priests, 135–174.

through the previous orders, and ordination by a bishop), persistent candidates could gain admittance. Advancement through the four minor orders (porter, lector, exorcist, acolyte) required minimal effort: tonsure, some reading ability, and a willingness to perform menial tasks and assist other clerics. Progression through the major orders (subdeacon, deacon, priest, and bishop) required more commitment: at least a vow of celibacy and enough literacy skills to pass ordination exams.[5] But, because many incontinent priests received only minor reproofs for their transgressions and many ordination exams tested only rudimentary skills, this level of commitment still might not have been arduous.[6] For example, thirteenth-century ordination exams queried candidates about basic Bible skills (such as explaining the gospel) and knowledge of missal and psalter chants recited during services, information that most candidates could have gleaned from attending mass and sermons as well as from the tutelage of other clerics. The mid-thirteenth-century Bishop of Durham merely required that:

> every shepherd of souls and every parish priest know the Decalogue [the Ten Commandments]: let him also know the seven mortal sins, the seven sacraments, and their effects; the requisites of a true confession; the form of baptism; and let him have a least a simple understanding of the faith as it is contained in the three creeds.[7]

Demanding even less formal training, a late fourteenth-century exam scrutinized candidates about their age, lifestyle (recommending a "temperate" one), and physical appearance (whether the candidates were marred, deformed, or diseased), asking little about their education.[8]

---

5    *Pastors and the Care of Souls in Medieval England*, eds. John Shinners and William Dohar (Notre Dame: University of Notre Dame Press, 1998), 49–55; Geoffrey F. Bryant and Vivien M. Hunter, *'How Thow Schalt Thy Paresche Preche': John Myrc's Instructions for Parish Priests, Part One Introduction and Text* (Barton-on-Humber: Workers' Educational Association Barton-on-Humber Branch, 1999), 30–41.

6    On the one hand, many historians have discussed the incontinence (failure to remain celibate) of priests. While assuredly many priests took celibacy seriously and remained chaste throughout their ecclesiastical careers, many other priests seemed to consider this vow a suggestion rather than an order. For example, the fifteenth-century parson of Orsett repeatedly shared a rented room with a married woman; the rector of St. Mary Axe visited prostitutes; a fourteenth-century London transvestite claimed that he preferred priests as customers; and even Margery Kempe related stories of clerical infidelity. The first three examples were paraphrased from Peter Heath, *The English Parish Clergy on the Eve of the Reformation* (Toronto: University of Toronto Press, 1969), 104–105. Ruth Mazo Karras has discussed brothels for clerics in Southwark, York, London, and Westminster, as well as the case of the transvestite. Ruth Mazo Karras, *Common Women: Prostitution and Sexuality in Medieval England* (New York and Oxford: Oxford University Press, 1996), 45 and 77. As for Margery Kempe, one particular cleric whom she accused of fornication confessed readily. *The Book of Margery Kempe: The Text from the Unique MS Owned by Colonel W. Butler-Bowdon*, ed. Sanford Brown Meech with prefatory note by Hope Emily Allen and notes and appendices by Sanford Brown Meech and Hope Emily Allen, EETS original series 212 (London: Oxford University Press, 1940), 61–62. On the other hand, many historians also have discouraged discussions of clerical immorality. Christopher Harper-Bill has claimed that few clergy were actually convicted of immorality during the late medieval period and that many accusations were probably nothing more than rumor. "The easiest way for any disgruntled parishioner to cause trouble for his priest was to initiate a rumour," especially of sexual indiscretion. Christopher Harper-Bill, *The Pre-Reformation Church in England 1400–1530* (New York: Longman, 1996), 49.

7    Bryant and Hunter, *'How Thow Schalt Thy Paresche Preche,'* 36.

8    Shinners and Dohar, *Pastors and the Care of Souls in Medieval England*, 57–71.

Yet because ordination exams consistently required reading skills (English and at least rudimentary Latin) and because admittance to higher church positions (such as bishoprics) required advanced academic training, many clerical candidates attended schools. Although often little more than a local priest teaching four or five boys their *Pater Noster*, clerical schools became a staple of English society – evolving into the sprawling halls of Oxford and Cambridge. According to Helen Jewell, "The English educational system had developed for training clergy. The song and grammar schools and the universities came into existence to provide boy choristers, Latinate ordinands, and qualified holders of degrees ... with higher office in the church."[9] David Cressy similarly has written that most formal schooling in late medieval and early modern England was "geared as much to the preparation of priests as to the education of the laity."[10] Elementary (or song) schools provided young clerical candidates with basic reading and writing skills in English, some skills in Latin, and knowledge about simple prayers, catechisms, and creeds. Secondary (or grammar) schools provided students with advanced Latin skills. Universities provided training in rhetoric, logic, and Latin grammar for bachelor degrees, and training in philosophy, astronomy, geometry, arithmetic, and music for advanced degrees.[11]

Medieval schools played an important role in clerical education, but they did not monopolize it. To begin with, most priests never attended advanced grammar schools or universities. Examining 15,000 wills and references to more than 200 primary and grammar schools, J.A.H. Moran found that fifteenth-century clerics in Yorkshire mostly attended elementary schools – if they attended school at all. Only a few progressed to grammar schools, and even fewer attended university.[12] R.N. Swanson explored the formative obstacles (both financial and ecclesiastical) that blocked clerical access to university education, concluding that only a few were able to afford the costs. Moreover, students who succeeded in attending Oxford or Cambridge and gaining a degree rarely returned to pastoral duties. Most used their credentials to become canons, bishops, and members of the ever-growing civil service or royal court.[13]

In sum, the priests who worked in parishes were not the priests who attended advanced schools. They, instead, were the "mean clerics" who came from middling families, lacked regular salaries, often subsided on the generosity of local parishioners, rarely obtained benefices, and yet shouldered the bulk of pastoral responsibilities.[14] A.K. McHardy has found that unlettered and unbeneficed priests who

9   Helen Jewell, *Education in Early Modern England* (New York: St. Martin's, 1998), 60–61.

10  David Cressy, *Education in Tudor and Stuart England* (New York: St. Martin's, 1975), 3.

11  Alan Cobban, *English University Life in the Middle Ages* (Columbus: Ohio State University Press, 1999), 149–156.

12  J.A.H. Moran, *The Growth of English Schooling, 1340–1548: Learning, Literacy, and Laicization in Pre-Reformation York Diocese* (Princeton: Princeton University Press, 1985).

13  R.N. Swanson, "Universities, Graduates, and Benefices in Later Medieval England," *Past and Present* 106 (1985), 28–61. Peter Heath also has written: "A major deterrent, of course, was the cost of living and the fees, which could together amount to fifty shillings a year even in the early fifteenth century. This not only prevented some aspirants from entering altogether, but also compelled a very significant proportion of those who did to depart before they had completed the seven years necessary for a master's degree, let alone the fourteen required to incept in theology or to take a doctorate in law." Heath, *The English Parish Clergy*, 79. Dorothy Owen, *The Medieval Canon Law: Teaching and Transmission* (Cambridge: Cambridge University Press, 1990), 3–9.

14  BL MS Cotton Claudius A II, f. 3v.

provided *cura animarum* outnumbered their educated and beneficed counterparts in late medieval England. Aside from the rare figure of Robert Grosseteste who benefited from influential patrons and extraordinary circumstances, most priests with *cura animarum* never would have advanced beyond elementary schools and never would have learned academic skills beyond the basics.[15]

Because educational standards began to decline in the late fourteenth century, few would-be priests needed skills beyond the basics to gain ordination. Arguing that the Black Death significantly altered pastoral functions in the diocese of Hereford, William Dohar has concluded that the plague cut into both clerical numbers and clerical profits – forcing a reduced number of priests to perform pastoral duties for a reduced amount of money.[16] Expanding Dohar's argument, J.A.H. Moran has argued that these conditions created a "man-power" shortage for the church.[17] Fewer boys viewed the church as a lucrative profession and, with more options available to them in the post-plague economy, fewer chose to become clerics. Hard pressed for more parish, chantry, and household priests, the church responded pragmatically by lowering educational standards in an attempt to bolster clerical recruitment. Consequently post-1350 clerics faced less academic hurdles than their pre-1350 counterparts.

Many historians have interpreted this decline in academic qualifications as detrimental to the clerical profession. William J. Courtenay has argued that the lowering of educational standards contributed to more clerics accepting unbeneficed positions and fewer university graduates taking priestly vows.[18] This created a "crisis of patronage" for English universities, as G.F. Lytle and R.N. Swanson have argued. No longer gaining as many recruits from universities, fewer ecclesiastical patrons supported Oxford and Cambridge, causing them to suffer from a shortage in both funds and students. Thus, according to this argument, a decline in educational standards translated into a decline in status for the clerical profession. As poorly trained candidates gained access to sacerdotal orders, highly trained candidates chose more prestigious lines of work.[19] On a more severe note, other historians have linked this lowering of academic qualifications to the sixteenth-century caricature of a pre-Reformation priest as "barely literate, barely celibate, barely sober bumpkin, more at home in a tavern or *in flagrante delicto* than at an altar or a *prie-dieu*."[20]

Yet it is possible that this decline in educational standards was also a shift in

---

15  McHardy, "Careers and Disappointments in the Late Medieval Church," 111–130.

16  William J. Dohar, *The Black Death and Pastoral Leadership: The Diocese of Hereford in the Fourteenth Century* (Philadelphia: University of Pennsylvania Press, 1995).

17  J.A.H. Moran, "Clerical Recruitment in the Diocese of York, 1340–1530: Data and Commentary," *Journal of Ecclesiastical History* 34:1 (1983), 19–54.

18  William J. Courtenay, "The Effect of the Black Death on English Higher Education," *Speculum* 55:4 (1980), 696–714.

19  G.F. Lytle, "Patronage Patterns and Oxford Colleges, c. 1300–1500," in *The University in Society*, vol. 1, ed. Lawrence Stone (Princeton: Princeton University Press, 1974), 111–149; and R.N. Swanson, "Universities, Graduates, and Benefices in Later Medieval England," *Past and Present* 106 (1985), 28–61.

20  Shinners and Dohar, *Pastors and the Care of Souls in Medieval England*, xiii. In short, it seems as if many historians would agree with John Colet's contemporary assessment.that "the broad gate of holy orders opened, every man that offers himself is all where admitted without pulling back." John Colet was the sixteenth-century dean of St. Paul's Cathedral. He berated clerics for ignorance, negligence, and incontinence, proclaiming, "Physician, Heal Thyself!" J.H. Lupton, *A Life of John*

educational models. The wane in formal educational standards coincided with a waxing of vernacular pastoral literature.[21] Instead of needing Latin to read the Vulgate, the *Sarum Manual*, or John of Bromyard's *Summa Predicantium*, priests could read Mirk's *Festial* to learn stories about saints and stories from the Bible, the *Lay Folk's Mass Book* to learn prayers and creeds, and *Instructions for Parish Priests* to learn about penance and confession. Consequently priests equipped with vernacular sermons, exempla collections, prayers, catechisms, and penitentials needed less formal training to conduct their pastoral duties.[22]

Moreover, these vernacular compilations provided priests with something that formal education did not offer: practical advice on how to care for parishioners. Serving as the primary spiritual intercessors and counselors for ordinary people, parish priests (along with their various clerical assistants) exercised considerable control over the quality of parishioners' religious experiences. As such, teaching clerics how to provide pastoral care properly should have been a critical issue for all involved. Yet, from what we know of formal education, neither song schools, nor grammar schools, nor basic university courses would have taught priests how to handle parishioners like Margery Kempe. Nor did they teach the fundamentals of pastoral care, such as how to conduct confession, impose penance, console the sick and dying, perform churching ceremonies, instruct midwives in birthing procedures, arbitrate among feuding parishioners, and even handle domestic difficulties between husbands and wives. These were skills (and knowledge) that priests would have learned informally: from personal experience, from observation of other clerics, and from reading pastoral literature.[23]

---

*Colet, D.D., Dean of St. Paul's, and Founder of St. Paul's School. With an Appendix of Some of his English Writings* (London: G. Bell and Sons, 1909), 300 and 299.

[21] For more information about the proliferation of vernacular pastoral manuals in late medieval England, see: Vincent Gillespie, "Vernacular Books of Religion," in *Book Production and Publishing in Britain 1375–1475*, eds. Jeremy Griffiths and Derek Pearsall (Cambridge: Cambridge University Press, 1989), 317–341; and W.A. Pantin, *The English Church in the Fourteenth Century*, Medieval Academy of America Reprints for Teaching 5 (Toronto: University of Toronto Press in association with the Mediaeval Academy of America, 1980), 189–243. Katherine French also has commented on this trend (drawing from Pantin and Heath), writing, "The fifteenth-century growth in vernacular manuals for priests suggests that, although knowledge of Latin might have been declining, the desire for knowledgeable and literate clergy was not." Katherine French, *The People of the Parish: Community Life in a Late Medieval English Diocese* (Philadelphia: University of Pennsylvania Press, 2001), 180. She also has discussed how vernacular literature such as *Festial* helped educate both clergy and laity. Ibid., 176–186.

[22] R.L. Storey found that in London, the largest number of recruits came from the lesser-educated immigrant population, not from the London graduates of grammar schools and universities. R.L. Storey, "Ordination of Secular Priests in Early Tudor London, Part One," *Nottingham Medieval Studies* 33:1 (1989), 122–131.

[23] "As for the liturgical aspect of his training, that would have been nurtured by youthful and life-long attendance at church, before he began his apprenticeship as an ordained assistant first in the services and then in the cure of souls. Much he would learn by imitation and by conversation with other clergy." And, after learning basic reading skills, "he could complete his education from books, such as had been written in the vernacular as well as Latin from the early fourteenth century for the guidance of just such a priest." Heath, *The English Parish Clergy on the Eve of the Reformation*, 85–86. John Lawson and Harold Silver also emphasized this in their discussion of clerical education, *A Social History of Education in England* (London: Methuen, 1973), 42–90. Also see Cobban, *English University Life in the Middle Ages*, 149–156.

## PASTORAL VERNACULAR LITERATURE

Representing one of the most accessible ways for priests to acquire practical advice about their craft, pastoral vernacular literature played a critical role in educating late medieval clerics. The Fourth Lateran Council provided the original impetus for didactic religious literature in 1215. The decree *Omnis utriusque sexus* required all Christians of proper age to give confession and take communion at least once a year (usually Easter); thereby making instruction about the proper conduction of communion and confession necessary for both priests and parishioners.[24] Following suit, the English Church promulgated their own decrees, encouraging such literature as Archbishop Pecham's *Ignorantia Sacerdotum*, Robert Grosseteste's *Templum Domini*, Thomas of Chobham's *Summa de penitentia*, and William of Pagula's *Oculus Sacerdotis*. The Bishop of Lichfield, Alexander of Stavensby, even demanded in the mid 1230s that all priests retain copies of his detailed instructions for how parish priests should conduct the sacraments.[25]

While most of the thirteenth-century authors concentrated on such tenets as the Ten Commandments, Articles of Faith, Works of Mercy, Seven Vices and Virtues, and the Seven Sacraments, later fourteenth- and fifteenth-century clerics prescribed sweeping advice on pastoral care. Leonard Boyle first noticed this difference in his study of William of Pagula's *Oculus Sacerdotis*. He argued that although manuals like *Oculus Sacerdotis* extended from thirteenth-century concerns about clerical education (as exemplified by the Fourth Lateran Council in 1215, the Council of Oxford in 1222, and the Council of Lambeth in 1281), it represented a different genre from thirteenth-century homiletic, moralistic, and penitential treatises because it reflected a comprehensive approach to pastoral care and included contemporary theology.[26]

In other words, comprehensive pastoral care literature included the basic elements of past texts as well as providing clerics with practical knowledge about their craft – enumerating for priests exactly what they needed to teach their parishioners, how to administer the sacraments, and how to preach and perform the divine office. For example, John Mirk's *Instructions for Parish Priests* elucidated the exact word order *not* to be used while baptizing a child.

---

[24] Leonard E. Boyle posited the argument that the Fourth Lateran Council and the constitution *Omnis utriusque sexus* generated a revolution in pastoral care that clearly defined the pastoral responsibility of priests and encouraged a type of literature that taught priests how to care for penitents. Leonard E. Boyle, "The Fourth Lateran Council and Manuals of Popular Theology," in *The Popular Literature of Medieval England*, ed. Thomas J. Heffernan, Tennessee Studies in Literature 28 (Knoxville: University of Tennessee Press, 1985), 30–43.

[25] Although a plethora of scholars have discussed this, here is a statement from a pioneer in the study of vernacular pastoral literature: W.A. Pantin. "The starting point of the manuals of instruction is the legislation of the Lateran Council of 1215 and particularly the decree *Omnis utriusque sexus*, making annual confession to the parish priest and annual communion at Easter obligatory on all Christians. If this legislation was going to be carried out seriously, it meant that both priest and laity must be educated up to it, priests must be instructed in the elements of moral theology, particularly in the technique of hearing confessions, and the laity too must receive a minimum of necessary instruction." Pantin, *The English Church in the Fourteenth Century*, 191–192.

[26] Leonard Boyle, "The *Oculus Sacerdotis* and Some Other Works of William of Pagula," in his *Pastoral Care, Clerical Education, and Canon Law, 1200–1400* (London: Variorum Reprints, 1981), 81–110.

> But if chance occurs thus,
> That he the words said amiss,
> Or thus, In nominee Filij and Patris and Spiritus Sancti. Amen.
> Or any other way [except in the right order]
> As the Father and the Son and the Holy Ghost,
> In nomine Patris and Filij and Spiritus Sancti. Amen.
> If it be other ways altered …
> Say the service all once more.[27]

Such detail was unnecessary for clerics well schooled in Latin. But for the average cleric who narrowly passed his ordination exams, it would have been a boon. The Premonstratensian monk who compiled British Library MS Sloane 1584 included a recipe for making Eucharist bread, instructions for sub-deacons and deacons on how to conduct mass, and a detailed list of penitential questions carefully arranged to assist different types of penitents.[28] *Instructions for Parish Priests* even explained what priests were to do if they spilled consecrated wine on the altar, "Suck it up at once."[29] Similarly, sermon compilations provided enough preaching material to guide clerics through the potentially bewildering morass of holy days. Often divided into the *sanctorale* (sermon cycle based on commemoration of the saints) and *temporale* (sermon cycle based on religious holidays, Easter, Christmas, etc.), these compilations became increasingly important in the fourteenth and fifteenth centuries as parochial clerics undertook regular preaching in order to stay competitive with mendicant friars.[30] The sermon collection *Festial* even included a sermon detailing how priests should answer the diverse questions of "lewd men" who challenged their authority.[31]

This new genre of pastoral literature targeted a growing audience of needy readers: ordinary clergymen. Pantin described these men as a "very large clerical proletariat of priests working for a salary, 'parish priests' or 'chaplains' (*capellani curati*), who acted as assistants to or deputies for the beneficed parish priests," while Christopher Harper-Bill has described them as the "only effective representatives of the universal church" for the "vast majority of the English people, living in isolated rural communities."[32] Intending his work for just such men, John Mirk pleaded at the end of *Instructions for Parish Priests* for clerics to:

> Read this often, and so let others;
> Hide it not in concealment,
> Let other [people] more read this book …
> It is made to show [instruct] them
> Who have no books of their own,

---

27  *Instructions for Parish Priests*, 99–100. The context of these instructions was to help priests distinguish if a baptism had been performed properly (especially if it had been performed by a lay person).

28  BL MS Sloane 1584, ff. 7r–10v.

29  *Instructions for Parish Priests*, 169.

30  For more on the controversy between secular clergy and friars, see Pantin, *The English Church in the Fourteenth Centuries*, 124–6; and A.G. Little, *Studies in English Franciscan History* (Manchester, UK: The University Press, 1917), 116–22.

31  *Festial*, 124–129.

32  Pantin, *The English Church in the Fourteenth Century*, 28; Harper-Bill, *The Pre-Reformation Church in England*, 44.

And others that be of mean knowledge,
Who would gladly know more.[33]

Even the author of *Speculum Sacerdotal* acknowledged that he created his collection at the request of priests "dear and familiar" so that those in their charge might be "more informed to worshipping and glorifying ... God."[34] Evidence thus suggests that clerical authors wrote pastoral vernacular literature for the education and edification of their clerical brethren, sometimes at the specific request of friends and acquaintances.

Hence, prolific and practical, pastoral vernacular literature was designed to play a critical role in clerical education. "For the many parish priests of England [who] would have found [Latin] treatises quite beyond the range of their linguistic and theological knowledge, vernacular pastoral guides would have proven essential," argued G.H. Russell.[35] Such clerics *should* have welcomed utilitarian manuals that provided immediate answers to pastoral care problems and homily compilations that provided ready-to-preach sermons. The sheer number of surviving texts suggests that many did.

## SOURCES: SERMONS, EXEMPLA, AND JOHN MIRK

Among the many men who produced comprehensive pastoral care literature, John Mirk stands out as the most popular and most influential in late medieval England.[36] An Augustinian prior from Lilleshall Abbey in Shropshire, Mirk was

---

[33] *Instructions for Parish Priests*, 175.

[34] *Speculum Sacerdotal*, 2–3.

[35] G.H. Russell, "Vernacular Instruction of the Laity in the Later Middle Ages in England: Some Texts and Notes," *The Journal of Religious History* 2:2 (1962–1963), 98–119, at 102.

[36] See Appendix I for a more indepth discussion of the *Festial* manuscripts. I am particularly fortunate that many scholars have conducted codiological and technical studies of Mirk's manuscripts, including tracing the dissemination of the manuscripts. Fewer, however, have examined the content (and when so, these few usually have focused on its orthodoxy and how Mirk was probably combating Lollardy); while none have investigated the gendered nature of the texts. Aside from Fletcher, Powell, and Elsasser, to whom references have been made, these scholars have worked on Mirk: Judy Ann Ford, *John Mirk's Festial: Orthodoxy, Lollardy, and the Common People in Fourteenth-Century England* (Cambridge: D.S. Brewer, 2006); Geoffrey F. Bryant and Vivien M. Hunter, *'How Thow Schalt Thy Paresche Preche'*; William Alpheus Edwards, "John Myrc's Conception of the Function of Medieval Parish Priests," B.D. thesis, Duke University, 1943; Herbert W. Stroup, "John Mirk: Tutor to England's Medieval Preachers," *Lutheran Theological Seminary Bulletin* 47:3 (Summer 1967), 26–38; D.S. Brewer, "Observations on a Fifteenth-Century Manuscript," *Anglia* 72 (1954), 390–399; Margaret J. Bunn, "John Mirk's *Festial*: A Study of the Medieval English Sermon," M.A. thesis, University of Leeds, 1954; D.B. Foss, "John Mirk's *Instructions for Parish Priests*," in *The Ministry: Clerical and Lay: Papers Read at the 1989 Summer Meeting and the 1989 Winter Meeting of the Ecclesiastical History Society*, ed. W.J. Sheils, Studies in Church History 26 (Oxford: Basil Blackwell, 1989), 131–140; James M. Girsch, "An Elizabethan Manuscript of Mirk's *Festial* Sermon on St. Winifred and Observations on the 'Shrewsbury Manuscript'," *Neuphilologische Mitteilungen* 96:3 (1995), 265–269; Carl Horstmann, *Altenglische Legenden, Neue Folge* (Heilbronn, Germany: Gebr. Henniger, 1881); Charles Lee, "'Tales Olde': The *Festial* of John Mirk and its Historical Context," Ph.D. diss., University of Missouri-Columbia, 1992; Veronica M. O'Mara, "A Middle English Sermon Preached by a Sixteenth Century 'Atheist': A Preliminary Account," *Notes and Queries* n.s. 34:2 (1987), 183–185; Urania Contos Petalas, "The Sermons of John Mirk," Ph.D. diss., University of California at Los Angeles, 1970; Lillian L. Steckman, "A Late Fifteenth-Century Revision of Mirk's *Festial*," *Studies in Philology* 34 (1937), 36–48; Martyn F. Wakelin, "An Edition

literate, educated, and concerned about helping less fortunate priests.[37] Living in the aftermath of the Great Plague, he seems to have worried that many priests with cure of souls lacked basic pastoral skills – a legitimate concern, considering the *ad hoc* nature of pastoral training in late medieval England. Thus, to help priests who suffered from poor education (or poor learning skills), Mirk wrote *Festial*. "In help of such mean clerics, as I am myself," he claimed in the prologue, "I have drawn this treaty from the *Legenda Aurea* with more adding to it. So he that desires to study therein, shall find ready for all the principal feasts of the year a short sermon needful for him to teach and others to learn."[38] Completed in the late fourteenth century, *Festial* was organized by Mirk to be a valuable asset for parish priests: containing seventy-four sermons written in English, arranged in chronological order, and created for immediate delivery. Because of its practicality and usefulness (as well as its ubiquity), Alan Fletcher concluded that *Festial* would have been "central to preaching in English in the fifteenth century" and that "probably most *Festial* MSS were owned by parish priests and the lower clergy."[39] As such, *Festial* plays a central role in this study of how clerics with *cura animarum* were trained to view (and perhaps treat) their parishioners.[40]

Numerous manuscripts and printed copies survive of Mirk's *Festial*, including twenty-two extant "major" manuscripts that contain substantial copies of *Festial*, an ever-growing group of "minor" manuscripts that contain various sermons and sermon fragments, and at least twenty-four printed copies from the late fifteenth and early sixteenth centuries.[41] For the purposes of this project, I am mostly concerned with the major manuscript compilations which contain the majority of *Festial*'s sermons, as found in the oldest manuscript, BL MS Cotton Claudius A II. Scholars have divided the major manuscripts into two primary recensions. Group A, descended from Mirk's original composition, contains sermons arranged in chronological order (as they would be preached through the year). Group B manuscripts stem from a later redaction that contains significant

---

of John Mirk's *Festial* as it is contained in the Brotherton Collection Manuscript," M.A. thesis, University of Leeds, 1960; ibid., "The Manuscripts of John Mirk's *Festial*," *Leeds Studies in English* n.s.1 (1967), 93–118.

[37] Mirk probably began his clerical career as a vicar for the church of St. Alkmund in Shropshire – thus his interest in pastoral care. Alan Fletcher has written that the *Festial* prologue "could well imply that Mirk had had cure of souls." Alan Fletcher, "John Mirk and the Lollards," *Medium Aevum* 56:2 (1987), 217–224, at 223 and footnote 24.

[38] BL MS Cotton Claudius A II, f. 3v. Mirk also wrote two instructional manuals for priests, one in English (*Instructions for Parish Priests*) and one in Latin (*Manuale Sacerdotis*).

[39] Alan Fletcher, "Unnoticed Sermons from John Mirk's *Festial*," *Speculum* 55:3 (1980), 514–515. M.F. Wakelin provided the basic information for the county origins of each manuscript. Wakelin, "The Manuscripts of John Mirk's *Festial*," 93–118.

[40] Judy Ann Ford, in her very recent study of *Festial*, has commented on its contemporary popularity and current value for historians. "[T]he *Festial* offers an unrivaled opportunity to study late-fourteenth-century Christianity as it was expounded to the ordinary, rural men and women who comprised the majority of the English population. John Mirk's position as a rural canon, rather than a university or court preacher, gave him the chance to work with ordinary country people and become closely aware of their point of view. The success of his sermon collection provides evidence that the *Festial* was found attractive, at the least, by relatively uneducated priests, and at the most, by a broad spectrum of their parishioners." Ford, *John Mirk's Festial*, 13–14.

[41] I include Trinity College Dublin MS 201 in this account, although it contains only thirty-six of the original seventy-four *Festial* sermons. Unfortunately I was unable to view the original manuscript (I only studied a microfilm copy) and thus do not include a description of it within Appendix I.

textual variations and an altered sermon order.[42] Group B manuscripts divide the sermons into *Temporale*, homilies devoted to time-specific celebrations such as Sundays and religious holidays like Easter (these are *moveable* dates), and *Sanctorale*, sermons devoted to various saints and the veneration of relics (these are *fixed* dates). Textual variations, inclusion/omission of sermons, inclusion/omission of the prayer and prologue, and dialect have helped further parcel the manuscripts into tentative family groups.

Although surviving in significantly fewer manuscripts than *Festial*, John Mirk's pastoral care handbook, *Instructions for Parish Priests*, has been christened as "the best-known 15th-century manual of religious instruction in English."[43] Directed toward humble clerics, this poem of approximately 1934 lines outlined the basics for pastoral care: instructions for baptism, marriage, confession; copies of the Lord's Prayer, the Creed, the doctrine of the Trinity, and the Seven Sacraments; questions for confession; and guides for prescribing penance. Like *Festial*, *Instructions* was probably written in the late fourteenth century, with most manuscripts dating from the fifteenth century (one perhaps from the sixteenth century). Unlike *Festial*, only one *Instructions* manuscript stands alone; the remaining manuscripts are incorporated into larger pastoral care manuals.

Both the manuscripts of Mirk's *Festial* and *Instructions for Parish Priests* give testimony to how everyday clerics collected, filtered, and used the pastoral vernacular literature at their disposal. The texts that they copied, lifted, and modified were chosen to meet certain needs and often were combined with other literature, such as Richard of Lavynham's treatise on the Seven Deadly Sins. Surely the scribe who compiled the "Bedfordshire cycle" – the minor *Festial* manuscripts of Gloucester Cathedral MS 22, Durham Cathedral Cosin MS V IV 3, Lincoln Cathedral MSS 50 and 51, and Bodleian Library MS E Museo 180 – thought he had created a useful package worth the effort of copying four times over. The careful late sixteenth-century hand that recorded Southwell Minster MS 7 seems to have valued his acquisition equally high, as he took great pains to copy his *Festial* neatly and accurately. Since these were the sermons and literature that clerics would

---

[42]  Susan Powell has noted that the Group B manuscripts are "marked by consistent textual variations." Her evidence is in agreement with earlier evidence produced by Wakelin. "My own comparison with this collation of these MSS not at the time known to Wakelin has in the main confirmed the grouping inferred by the arrangement of the sermons." She also has enumerated specific differences between Group A and Group B manuscripts. "Apart from differences in sermon arrangement and text, other diversions can be noted in the two recensions. Of the Group B MSS only one, MS Durham University Library Cosin V. III. 5, contains the Introductory Prayer and Prologue which are found in several of the Group A MSS. In the Group A MSS the sermon for Good Friday precedes the details of church ritual for Maundy Thursday and Holy Saturday, while in the Group B MSS this order is reversed, presumably in accordance with the chronological precedence of Maundy Thursday over Good Friday. The Group A MSS provide one sermon for Ss. Philip and James, while the Group B MSS divide that sermon into two. The Group A MSS contain two sermons on the Assumption of Mary, but of the Group B MSS only [BL MS Harley 2247 and BL MS Royal 18 B XXV] contain the first of these. Moreover, several sermons are never found in any of the Group B MSS – the second sermon for the first Sunday in Lent, the sermons for the saints local to Mirk's home at Lilleshall, the sermon for St. Barnabas, that on the death of Nero, and those appended in some Group A MSS only, which deal with marriage, burial and the salutation and miracles of Mary." Susan Powell, "A Critical Edition of the *Temporale* Sermons of MSS Harley 2247 and Royal 18 B. xxv," Ph.D. diss., University of London King's College, 1986, Part II, 8 and 12–13.

[43]  *Instructions for Parish Priests*, 9.

use on a weekly basis for preaching and teaching, one would surmise that when choosing texts, most chose wisely.

In addition to *Festial* and *Instructions for Parish Priests*, I have examined other contemporary sermon compilations and pastoral handbooks to shed light on the ordinary and extraordinary nature of John Mirk's texts (especially in regards to the pastoral care of women). Non-*Festial* sources bound with Mirk's homilies comprise the first set of non-Mirk sermon compilations studied, such as BL MS Royal 18 B XXIII (otherwise known as *Middle English Sermons*). This eclectic sermon compilation was a contemporary of the *Festial* manuscripts and contains three *Festial* homilies embedded within a much larger tract of vernacular sermons drawn from a variety of sources (including the borderline heretical Sidney Sussex sermon cycle).[44] Also comparable with *Festial* and circulating throughout much of the same area (the Midlands), the Sidney Sussex cycle stems from Cambridge University Library MS Sidney Sussex 74, a manuscript written by a cleric with Lollard leanings. Nevertheless, the sermons attracted the attention of orthodox priests who lifted and modified bits and pieces of it to fit into their own collections (such as by the compiler of *Middle English Sermons*). Surviving in the Bedfordshire cycle, Shrewsbury School MS 3, Bodleian Library MS Bodley 95, and Bodleian Library MS Bodley 110, the Sidney Sussex cycle moved in the same circles as *Festial* and dealt with many of the same issues. I also have drawn much evidence from the single compilation of BL MS Additional 36791, otherwise known as *Speculum Sacerdotal*. Written at the same time as *Festial* by a cleric who lived in the same region as Mirk and who seems to have shared Mirk's purpose, *Speculum Sacerdotal* provides an ideal model for comparison with *Festial*. Both state their concern to help other priests; both were compiled in the late fourteenth and early fifteenth centuries in neighboring counties (Shropshire and Warwickshire); both relied largely on the same two sources, *Legenda Aurea* of Jacobus de Voragine and *Rationale Divinorum Officorum* of Joannes Belethus; and both include a similar number of sermons (74 vs. 70).[45] Finally, this study draws from several pastoral care manuals contemporary with *Instructions for Parish Priests* and similar in content to Mirk's work. Some of these are multiply-occurring texts, such as the late fifteenth-century pastoral care handbook *Quattuor Sermones* which Wynkyn de Worde bound with printed copies of *Festial*, and some are singly occurring manuscripts compiled by individual clerics for personal use, such as Durham Cathedral MS V IV II, CUL St. John's College MS S 35, BL MS Vespasian A XXV, and BL MS Sloane 1584.[46]

In general, comprehensive pastoral care manuals and sermon compilations are of foremost importance to the study of medieval women as the sermons, exempla, and pastoral advice they contain speak directly about the "Common Woman."[47] Indeed, women parade throughout these texts. We can see them in their life-

---

[44] See Helen Spencer for a detailed analysis of the Sidney Sussex cycle. H. Leith Spencer, *English Preaching in the Late Middle Ages* (Oxford: Clarendon, 1993).

[45] Weatherly noted these similarities in the introduction to his edition of *Speculum Sacerdotal*, xxxviii–xliv.

[46] The few that I have examined, however, scarcely represent the possible hundreds that lurk on library shelves, often masked by catalogue references to the better-known literature that they also preserve.

[47] Peter Biller, "The Common Woman in the Western Church in the Thirteenth and Early Fourteenth Centuries," *Women in the Church: Papers Read at the 1989 Summer Meeting and the 1990 Winter*

cycle stages, as daughters, singlewomen, wives, mothers, and widows; we can see them interacting in everyday life, as gossips and neighbors, loving mothers and angry wives, pious daughters and crafty nuns; we can see them praying for their families, weeping for their sins, and even partaking in the sacraments. Sketching vignettes about the diurnal lives of medieval women, however, encompasses only part of the usefulness of pastoral vernacular literature. Sermons and exempla also are "worth studying" – as Ruth Mazo Karras has commented – "for the ideas to which medieval men and women were regularly exposed." She readily admits that exempla, because they are repeated "century after century" by religious texts, do not reflect "the teller's experience." "Yet the tales would not have been retold nor criticisms repeated if they were not consistent with their tellers' view of the world, and the ideas were not less meaningful to those who read and heard them because they were conventional," she has argued. "To be appreciated, exempla had to be adjusted to fit the social relations of their day; they thus represent the adaptation of theological ideas to popular mentalities."[48] In other words, because they convey contemporary ideas and relay messages designed to shape the actions and beliefs of those who read and listened to them, sermons, exempla, and pastoral care handbooks shed light on the mental world of late medieval priests and the parishioners they served.

Despite the richness of pastoral vernacular literature, however, it has limitations. Religious literature used and created by clerics in the practice of their trade was designed for specific purposes: to aid priests in the pastoral care process and to help them communicate orthodox belief and practice to their parishioners. Because of this didactic function, sermons and exempla can only reveal how priests were taught to care for their parishioners and how parishioners were taught to behave and believe. It cannot reveal what priests and parishioners actually did. Moreover, pastoral literature was written by clergy. As such, it was a dialogue by men, often for men, that discussed the world from a distinctly clerical perspective. Thus, even though it reveals much about how clerics perceived women, depicted women's behavior, and attempted to care for the souls of women, it cannot reveal what women actually did in the late medieval parish. Neither can it reveal how female parishioners interpreted the pastoral care they received.

As a final point, modern readers must be aware that medieval pastoral literature is rarely original. Clerical authors gleaned bits and pieces of sermons and stories from a variety of sources, many times assimilating entire homily collections, devotional treatises, and instruction books, and then mixing them up to produce unique blends. Yet, even though pastoral literature was personalized by clerical authors to fit their individual needs, it stemmed mostly from a composite body. Clerical authors drew from a corpus of traditional texts, such as the *Golden Legend*, *Gesta Romanorum*, treatises on the seven deadly sins, writings of the church fathers, various exempla collections, and stock sermon compilations (like *Festial*), in order to create their "original" compositions. Hence, when studying pastoral vernacular literature, we must consider the roots and the trunk of the tree as well as the individual branches.

*Meeting of the Ecclesiastical History Society*, eds. W.J. Sheils and Diana Wood, Studies in Church History 27 (Oxford: Basil Blackwell, 1990), 127–157, at 132.
48  Karras, *Common Women*, 105.

*

Because it was prolific, practical, and didactic by design, pastoral vernacular literature represented one of the most accessible ways for ordinary clerics in late medieval England to learn their craft. As such, it was in a unique position to influence clerical attitudes toward pastoral care. Concentrating on the works of John Mirk, this book utilizes vernacular sermon compilations and comprehensive pastoral care manuals to illuminate the shadowy world of pastoral care. It is not an exhaustive study. Much pastoral vernacular literature remains unexamined. Nor does this study reveal how parishioners perceived pastoral care, as it is limited only to sources from the clerical perspective. But it is a window revealing how a few influential sermon compilations and pastoral guides could have shaped the perceptions, attitudes, and – perhaps – actions of fourteenth- and fifteenth-century priests.

*Chapter 2*

# PASTORAL LANGUAGE:
## "CHRIST'S PEOPLE, BOTH MEN AND WOMEN"

JOHN MIRK concluded his *Festial* sermon on the Lord's Prayer with an exemplum about a woman who had lived in sexual immorality for many years. One day when she was in church, she listened to a sermon about the "horrible pains of hell ordained" for those who lived in lechery and "would not leave it." The words of this sermon so convicted her that "she was contrite and stirred by the Holy Ghost, that she went, and shrove her, and took her penance, and was in full purpose forto have left her sin for always after." Yet on her way home she met her lover who seduced her with calming words. "If all things were such that is preached, there should no man nor woman be saved; and therefore leave it not, for it is not such. But be we hereafter of one assent, as we have been before, and I will plight you my troth that I will never leave, but hold you always." Then "turned the woman her heart, and did the sin as they did before." Shortly thereafter they both suddenly died. A concerned priest prayed that God would show him the state of their souls, and as he walked past a body of water one day, he saw a dark mist hovering above the surface and heard the voices of this man and woman emanating from the darkness. "Then said the woman to the man, 'Cursed be you of all men, and cursed be the time that you were born, for by you I am damned into everlasting pains.' Then answered the man: 'Cursed be you and the time that you was born, for you have made me damned forever! For had I once been contrite for my sins as you were, I would never have turned as you did; and if you had held good covenant with him that made you, you might have saved us both. But I promised that I would never leave you. Wherefore go we now both into the pain of hell that is ordained for us both!'" The sermon then abruptly concludes, "From the which pain God keep you and me, if it be his will. Amen."[1]

This story illuminates several provocative points about men and women in the late medieval parish, including at least two about male and female spirituality. First, the story portrays the fictional female parishioner as an ordinary member of sermon audiences who listened and attempted to implement the spiritual lessons she learned. Second, the story portrays the fictional male character as not in church with his lover, and – as implied by his shout, "you might have saved us both" – perhaps even dependent on her for (some) spiritual assistance. In short,

---

[1]  *Festial*, 287–288.

this story suggests that women were active in the pastoral world of late medieval England: listening to sermons (perhaps more than their male counterparts), attempting to implement the spiritual lessons they learned, and – for better or for worse – influencing the spirituality of men around them.

From this perspective, it is not surprising that the sermon in which the story is embedded uses language targeting female, as well as male, parishioners. For example, it opens with the salutation: "*Good men and women*, you shall know well that each curate is held by all the law in holy church, to expound the 'Pater Noster' to his parishioners once or twice in the year; and if he do not so, he shall be hard accused of God for his negligence." The sermon text then explains: that the "'Pater Noster' be vii prayers the which *each man and woman* have great need to pray God for; for that puts away the vii deadly sins, and gets grace of God … both to the life and to the soul"; that parishioners who acknowledged God as their father, as the Pater Noster demanded, were "*brother and sister* in God"; and that parishioners should employ the Pater Noster to defend themselves against the "enticing fiends" who slyly "bring a *man or a woman* into sin." Hence, through the use of explicit gender-inclusive language, this sermon makes its purpose clear: to convince all parishioners – both men and women – of their need for understanding and using spiritual teachings in their everyday lives.[2]

Nor is the explicitly gendered language of this sermon anomalous. The compiler of Lincoln Cathedral MS 133 echoed the pattern found in the Lord's Prayer sermon, generously incorporating both implicit gender-inclusive language (gender neutral nouns, such as *people* and *friends*, and pronouns, such as *they*) and explicit gender inclusive language (specifically stating *men and women*) within the nine sermons he copied from *Festial* – sometimes even going beyond the gender sensitivity of other *Festial* manuscripts. The Septuagesima sermon from Bodleian Library MS Gough Ecclesiastical Topography 4, for example, records:

Thus, *good men*, know that Adam and Eve were both holy.[3]

Lincoln Cathedral MS 133 records instead:

Thus *good man and woman* may know that Adam and Eve were both good and holy.[4]

Similarly, in the Quadragesima Sermon, the Gough manuscript records the fasting of Jesus in the desert as:

showing to us and all *christian men and people* the virtue and the reward that comes of fasting.[5]

The copyist of the Lincoln Cathedral manuscript does not include the male generic phrase, recording simply "*all christian people*."[6] Thus we see the language variation – first in the Septuagesima sermon from male generic, "*good men*," to the explicit

---

[2]  *Festial*, 282, 285–286.
[3]  *Festial*, 68.
[4]  Lincoln Cathedral MS 133, f. 106r.
[5]  *Festial*, 82.
[6]  Lincoln Cathedral MS 133, ff. 111v–112r.

gender-inclusive phrase, "*good man and woman*"; and second in the Quadragesima sermon from male generic and implicit gender-inclusive, "*christian men
and people*," to completely implicit gender-inclusive, "*christian people*."

In sum, Lincoln Cathedral MS 133 reveals the choices a clerical scribe made
about language within his text – what words to include, what words to exclude,
and what phrases to alter. These choices were certainly influenced by the base
text used, but they were also influenced by the copyist himself. Helen Spencer has
noted that, "Because a compiler selects and rearranges his materials, he is making
something new out of what was old ... A compiler may reveal much about
himself by his selection of extracts, even though he expresses himself through
the words of others."[7] As this chapter demonstrates, the choices made in sermon
manuscripts such as *Middle English Sermons* and John Mirk's *Festial* reveal clerics
intentionally providing room for women within the language of their texts. Like
Mirk's sermon on the Lord's Prayer and Lincoln Cathedral MS 133, clerical attentiveness to women within sermon language occurred often and in ways suggesting
both individual attentiveness on the part of clerics as well as a general pattern of
attentiveness at moments of pastoral care. Thus, when Margery Kempe declared
that she "would give every day a noble to have every day a sermon," perhaps some
of her attraction to hearing sermons stemmed from the female-friendliness of
pastoral language.[8]

Yet scholars of Middle English pastoral literature often have overlooked the
significance of gendered language in sermons. W. Nelson Francis, in his examination of the extant manuscripts of *The Book of Vices and Virtues*, reduced the
omission of explicit gender-inclusive language in BL MS Additional 22283 to a
"simplification." "[M]any minor alterations, almost all involving single words
or at most short phrases, have been made with varying frequency throughout
... such as 'a man and a woman' ... The commonest form of simplification in
[the manuscript] is merely to omit 'and a womman' and its variations."[9] In other
words, Francis realized that one copier of *The Book of Vices and Virtues* chose to
exclude explicit gender-inclusive language from the text; but he saw this exclusion
as a matter of editing, not as a matter of substance. Fifty years later, Helen Spencer
made a similar decision about the use of explicit gender-inclusive phrasing in her
comprehensive study of Late Middle English sermon literature, remarking that
"we need not dwell" on the point that medieval clerical writers regularly included
references to both sexes in their sermons.[10] Even Susan Powell, who stands as a
leading authority on the manuscripts of John Mirk, has remarked little on the
addition and subtraction of implicit and explicit gender-inclusive language in
*Festial*. One of the few times she addressed it was in reference to the significantly

---

7   H. Leith Spencer, *English Preaching in the Late Middle Ages* (Oxford: Clarendon, 1993), 270.

8   Margery Kempe, *The Book of Margery Kempe: The Text from the Unique MS Owned by Colonel W.
    Butler-Bowdon*, ed. Sanford Brown Meech with prefatory note by Hope Emily Allen and notes and
    appendices by Sanford Brown Meech and Hope Emily Allen, EETS original series 212 (London:
    Oxford University Press, 1940), 142.

9   *The Book of Vices and Virtues: A Fourteenth Century English Translation of the Somme le Roi of
    Lorens d'Orléans*, ed. W. Nelson Francis, EETS original series 217 (London: Oxford University
    Press, 1942), lxxv. Dominican friar Lorens d'Orleans composed the *Somme le Roi* in the thirteenth
    century and it soon became very popular, with numerous versions both in French and translated
    into English.

10  Spencer, *English Preaching*, 65.

altered *Festial* sermons contained in BL MS Harley 2247 and BL MS Royal 18 B XXV. "Evidence that the revision [contained in the above two manuscripts] was aimed at a socially more significant audience than Mirk's is afforded at the beginning of each sermon, where Mirk addresses his congregation as 'Good men and woymen' or perhaps 'Goddys blessyd pepull' or 'Goddy's worschypfull servantys', or some such phrase. In the revision the mode of address consistently affords much greater dignity to the audience, who are termed 'Worshipfull frendis', with the occasional variation of 'right worshipfull frendis'," she has written.[11] But this statement overlooks rather than addresses the use of gendered language, focusing on the "dignity" of the audience members instead of their gender.

Leo Carruthers has been an exception to this trend. In his examination of didactic treatises belonging to the *Somme le Roi* textual tradition, such as *Jacob's Well*, he has paid careful attention to the language used by Middle English writers. Like his peers, he has noted that "the preacher of Jacob's Well is plainly addressing a mixed audience of both men and women, married and single, as is clear from his frequent use of direct address and his references to their status." Unlike his peers, however, he has noted that the specific and continued recognition of male and female parishioners could indicate something more significant than church attendance. "Nevertheless, some medieval English clerics," wrote Carruthers, "seem capable of rising above the general wave of anti-feminism, of being at least neutral and occasionally positive in their attitude towards the female sex and marriage."[12] This chapter extends Carruther's insight to argue that through their use of gender inclusive language, some medieval English clerics rose "above the general wave of anti-feminism": recognizing the critical role female parishioners played in pastoral matters and accepting clerical obligations to provide women with proper pastoral care. Thus when clerical authors repeated the tale found in Mirk's Lord's Prayer homily of the fictional female parishioner who listened to the sermon and attempted to implement its lessons, they should not have been surprised by either her attention or her initial response. Because, according to the implicit and explicit gender inclusive language of their texts, this would have been exactly what sermon authors had intended.

## WORDS THAT MATTER:
## THE SIGNIFICANCE OF "GOOD MEN AND WOMEN"

Words and their meanings – this is the subject I have chosen. Some of you, no doubt, will wonder at my choice; for the subject will strike you as odd and unimportant, even rather silly … This is a most unfortunate attitude. For the fact is that words play an enormous part in our lives and are therefore deserving of the closest study … They are matters of the profoundest ethical significance to every human being. *Aldous Huxley*[13]

11  Susan Powell, "A Critical Edition of the *Temporale* Sermons of MSS Harley 2247 and Royal 18 B XXV," Ph.D. diss., University of London King's College (1980), Part II, 37.
12  Leo Carruthers, "'No Woman of No Clerk is Preysed': Attitudes to Women in Medieval English Religious Literature," in *A Wyf There Was*, eds. Paule Mertens-Fonck and Juliette Dor. Liège (Liège, Belgium: Dép. d'anglais, Université de Liège, 1992), 49–60, at 55 and 60.
13  Aldous Huxley, *Words and their Meanings* (Los Angeles: Ward Ritchie, 1940), as quoted in Wendy

Before discussing the evidence from pastoral sermon literature, the immediate question to resolve is: why might it be significant that some clerical writers included women in the language of their texts? The answer is straightforward: because including women in didactic clerical literature was unnecessary. Priests could have composed, read, and copied their texts without explicitly evoking female parishioners.

Feminist critics in recent decades have revealed multiple problems with excluding women from language. In 1959, G. Milton discovered that female students performed less satisfactorily on math problems containing male-related situations than those problems containing female-related situations.[14] Researchers Sandra and Darl Bem found in 1973 that job-advertisements using masculine pronouns and the generic "man" discouraged women from applying.[15] Wendy Martyna published her findings in 1980 that females, when asked to complete one hundred sentence fragments with pronouns, used the generic *he* fewer times than their male counterparts, suggesting that women relate less well to the "generic" pronoun than do men.[16] Confirming Martyna's work, Jeannette Silveria (in 1987) summarized fourteen studies examining men and women's understanding and interpretation of words like *he* and *man*. Overall, women are "more likely to interpret the masculine 'generic' generically than are males, and less likely to use the form themselves in producing language ... both women and men report that they usually image males when they read or hear the masculine 'generic.'"[17]

Thus, according to these studies, word choice matters in modern female and male responses to language. Women seem to have difficulty comprehending, processing, and applying language directed toward men; but they seem able to use language directed toward themselves. As the Association for Women in Psychology has written, "We do not know, but we can guess at the psychological costs of being a nonperson in one's own language ... to say that subtleties of language are trivial and thus can't affect us is to fall into the trap of psychological ignorance."[18] Dale Spender, in *Man Made Language*, made an even more direct assessment of linguistic androcentrism. "When there are a sexist language and sexist theories culturally available, the observation of reality is also likely to be sexist. It is by this means that sexism can be perpetuated and reinforced as new objects and events, new data, have sexist interpretations projected upon them."[19]

Martyna, "The Psychology of the Generic Masculine," in *Women and Language in Literature and Society*, eds. Sally McConnell-Ginet, Ruth Borker, Nelly Furman (New York: Praeger, 1980), 69–78, at 69.

[14] G.A. Milton, "Sex Differences in Problem Solving as a Function of Role Appropriateness of Problem Context," *Psychological Reports* 5 (1959), 705–708.

[15] Sandra Bem and Daryl Bem, "Does Sex-Biased Job Advertising 'Aid and Abet' Sex Discrimination?" *Journal of Applied Social Psychology* 3:1 (1973), 6–18, as discussed by Martyna, "The Psychology of the Generic Masculine," 69–78.

[16] Martyna, "The Psychology of the Generic Masculine," 70–73.

[17] Jeannette Silveria, "Generic Masculine Words and Thinking," in *The Voices and Words of Women and Men*, ed. Cheris Kramarae (Oxford: Pergamon, 1980), 165–178; as discussed by Barrie Thorne, Cheris Kramarae, and Nancy Henley, "Language, Gender and Society: Opening a Second Decade of Research," in their *Language, Gender and Society* (Rowley, Mass.: Newbury House, 1983), 7–24, at 10.

[18] As quoted by Martyna, "The Psychology of the Generic Masculine," 76.

[19] Spender's argument can be summarized in a single comment: "Males, as the dominant group, have produced language, thought, and reality. Historically it has been the structures, the categories, and

This secular concern about gender-inclusive language also has permeated the religious arena, convincing modern clergy and laity to examine the effects of male generic language in present-day liturgy.[20] "The communal nature of liturgy demands that all participants be included in the experience of worship," Ronald D. Witherup, a Catholic priest and seminary professor, has argued. "The Church's liturgy is never *my* liturgy (this goes for the priests who preside at Eucharist as well), it is *ours* as a faith community. This means, of course, that the rights and responsibilities of the entire believing community take precedence over those of individuals." His book, *A Liturgist's Guide to Inclusive Language*, outlines strategies celebrants can employ to make Catholic services truly universal, such as using the words "friends" and "dearly beloved" in admonitions and invitations.[21] Keith Watkins made a similar argument in *Faithful and Fair: Transcending Sexist Language in Worship*, noting that the use of male generic language "contributes to the impression that the church belongs to men rather than to women and that God holds men in higher esteem than women."[22] He, like Witherup, has used his book to provide ministers with useful methods for overcoming gender biased language.

Concern for gender sensitivity within ministerial language has grown to such an extent that even theologians from conservative seminary traditions have begun to argue for gender inclusivity within biblical texts as well as liturgy. They are supporting gender-sensitive translations, such as *Today's New International Version*, because they replace "man" with "humanity," "he" with "they," and "mankind" with "people." "This is not political correctness (though gender sensitivity in our culture may have made us more sensitive to the issue)," argues Darrell L. Bock, a New Testament Studies professor at Dallas Theological Seminary. "It is an attempt to render more clearly and faithfully Scripture and its intended scope in terms of who is addressed in many texts … when gender sensitive rendering is done carefully, it actually helps us appreciate the meaning of the biblical text in a less potentially ambiguous way than not rendering the text with such sensitivity."[23]

Clerical writers in late medieval England did not have access to such modern research and theories. Little evidence exists to suggest that clerics thought about the psychological impact their word choice had on parishioners. Standards of the time allowed the Middle English word "man" to function as a generic for "people." The Middle English Dictionary defines "man" in several ways, including "A person, a man or woman," "An adult male of the human species … with emphasis on maleness," "A husband," "A male child," and an indefinite pronoun. Thus the word "man" (and its derivatives) functioned as both a male-generic

---

the meanings which have been invented by males – though not of course by all males – and they have been validated by reference to other males. In this process women have played little or no part." Dale Spender, as extracted by Deborah Cameron, "Extracts from *Man Made Language*," in her *The Feminist Critique of Language: A Reader* (New York: Routledge, 1990), 102–110, at 105.

[20] It is important to note that this project uses "gender-inclusive language" to refer only to men and women; not to the gender of God.

[21] Ronald D. Witherup, *A Liturgist's Guide to Inclusive Language* (Collegeville, Minnesota: Liturgical Press, 1996), 69 and 53.

[22] Keith Watkins, *Faithful and Fair: Transcending Sexist Language in Worship* (Nashville: Abingdon Press, 1981), 17.

[23] Darrell L. Bock, "Do Gender Sensitive Translations Distort Scripture? Not Necessarily," *Journal of the Evangelical Theological Society* 45:4 (December 2002), 651–669, at 667–668.

and androcentric term. Similarly, *A Book of Middle English*, by J.A. Burrow and Thorlac Turville-Petre, defines "man" specifically as an indefinite pronoun for which modern English has no "exact equivalent." "We select from a range of indefinite pronouns to suit the occasion – one, anyone, they, people, we, you – or a passive construction is used instead. All these possibilities must be considered when translating Middle English." Although the authors do not include a definition of "man" as masculine (neither do they include a definition of "woman" as feminine), they seem to take this at face value, incorporating texts such as Chaucer's *Canterbury Tales* which clearly use the word "man" to describe the masculine sex – such as using an example from *The Prioress's Tale* which describes an abbot as a "holy man."[24]

Hence the Middle English word "man" has two meanings: the indefinite pronoun encompassing "one" to people and the masculine sex. These meanings coexist in the fluid nature of Middle English literature, flowing from one meaning to the other usually without clarification. *Speculum Sacerdotal* illustrates this well. The sermon for Easter day states that on this day

> each *true Christian man* receives the body and the blood of his savior.[25]

Similar statements throughout the sermon employing the words "friends" and "people" indicate that, in this instance, "man" means "people." Shortly thereafter the sermon records the story of a bishop who could see the sins of his parishioners. The text specifies that when "*each man*" came to receive the sacrament, the bishop could see if he was worthy to kneel at God's board. In the context of the previous use of "man," one might assume that "*each man*" encompasses both male and female parishioners. But then the text specifies that after dealing with the men, the bishop turned and:

> began to deal to *women* and to behold what manner souls they had.[26]

In this instance, then, the "man" kneeling for the sacrament literally means a male person. Similarly, Cambridge University Library MS Gg VI 16 shows the dual meaning of "man." First, it employs it as "people," such as when the text describes the woman of Canaan as representing "*sinful man's soul*." Second, it employs the word "man" as masculine, such as when the text clarifies:

> Therefore must *every man and woman* do when he has misspent his time through sinful living.[27]

24 *Middle English Dictionary*, eds. Sherman M. Khun and John Reidy (Ann Arbor: University of Michigan Press, 1975), vol. M, part 1, 107–117; J.A. Burrow and Thorlac Turville-Petre, *A Book of Middle English: Second Edition* (Oxford: Blackwell Publishers, 1996), 43 and 313.

25 *Speculum Sacerdotal: edited from British Museum MS. Additional 36791*, ed. Edward H. Weatherly, EETS original series 200 (London: Oxford University Press, 1936), 117.

26 Ibid., 123–124.

27 CUL MS Gg. VI. 16, ff. 56v–57r and 35v. For more information about the meanings of "man" in Middle English, see: A.C. Baugh and T. Cable, *A History of the English Language* (Englewood Cliffs, NJ: Prentice Hall, 1978); Norman Blake, *The English Language in Medieval Literature* (London: J.M. Dent, 1977); J.D. Burnley, *The Language of Chaucer* (London: Macmillan Education, 1989); Ralph W.V. Elliot, *Chaucer's English* (London: A. Deutsch, 1974); J.A. Sheard, *The Words We Use* (London: A. Deutsch, 1954); and Barbara M.H. Strang, *A History of English* (London: Methuen, 1974).

Pastoral literature, a discourse by men and for men, functioned foremost as a guide to help clerics with their spiritual duties. Authors expected that their words would be modified in practice to adapt to specific circumstances; their goal was to create a simple, easy-to-copy text that could be passed from cleric to cleric and thus help improve the overall quality of pastoral care.[28] Consequently, phrases such as "man and woman," "he or she" might have often been reduced to "man" and "he" to expedite the replication process. Finally, even if women did read sermon collections or witness sermons preached with male generic language, little evidence remains to suggest that medieval women would have heard these texts in the same ways as modern women. Male generic language simply might not have affected female parishioners in fifteenth-century England the way that it seems to affect many modern women today.

Despite these considerations, however, many late medieval clerical authors chose to direct their language specifically to male and female parishioners. The compiler of Bodleian MS Gough Ecclesiastical Topography 4 clearly specified:

*Christ's people, both men and women.*[29]

Did this make these authors feminist or anti-misogynist? Not necessarily. But their use of explicit and implicit gender-inclusive language at a time when masculine terms could be unquestionably understood to include both sexes does seem to indicate a particular concern for female parishioners to experience spiritual care on a more personal and individual level.


## GENDERED LANGUAGE

Because the word "man" could function in Middle English as "one" or "people," clerical writers regularly employed the male generic within their sermon compendiums. The author of *Speculum Sacerdotal*, for example, seemed most comfortable using male generic and androcentric phrases when referring to humanity and his sermon audience. In his sermon for the Nativity of Our Lord, he wrote that Adam's sin had caused "great discord between God and *man*, between *man* and angels, between *man and man*," and that through Eve "all *mankind*" was lost. Despite this male-generic tendency, however, the language of *Speculum Sacerdotal* still specifically recognized women as ordinary parishioners who needed pastoral care. The sermons remind priests that both men and women owe confession and need penance; that Christian people should attend church regularly, especially on holy days such as Candlemas; and that both male and female parishioners needed reminders about their obligations before participating in holy festivals such as Easter day.[30]

In a similar fashion, *Middle English Sermons* also illustrates how clerical authors

---

[28] Both John Mirk and the author of *Speculum Sacerdotal* make this goal clear in the introductions to their sermon compilations. BL MS Cotton Claudius A II, f. 3v; *Speculum Sacerdotal*, 1–3.

[29] *Festial*, 129.

[30] *Speculum Sacerdotal*, 75–86, 26–29, and 125–129.

of pastoral vernacular sermons regularly employed implicit and explicit gender-inclusive language when emphasizing the teaching and preaching of *pastoralia*. *Middle English Sermons* contains three *Festial* sermons bound within a larger tract of 51 sermons and was written specifically to prepare ordinary clerics for preaching and teaching parishioners. Woodburn O. Ross, editor of the collection, stated "that the sermons are designed to be preached, not simply to be read. One sermon, for instance, contains a brief quotation from St. Bernard concerning the Last Judgment, which is followed by what must be a recommendation to preachers for a possible expansion of the discussions: 'And that this is dreadful, narrate these 15 signs.'" Further internal evidence confirms that these sermons were intended to instruct clerics as well as designed for immediate delivery to "lay audiences."[31] Sermon thirteen, for example, speaks directly to priests, demonstrating that the sermon was indeed intended for clerical instruction:

> *Reverent friends*: Iii things there be that make the preacher of God's word to be heard and dread: one is temporal lordship, the second is holiness of living, and the third is high craft of knowledge.[32]

Likewise, the first sermon speaks directly to a lay audience, explaining to the faithful listeners, "*Good men and women*," that the compiler employed English "to your understanding."[33] *Middle English Sermons* was created to assist clerics in practicing their spiritual duties and in preaching to their parishioners in a useful manner.[34]

Despite the practical bent of *Middle English Sermons*, the language of the homilies is not explicitly female-friendly. Sermon ten, for example, overflows with the male generic, as the following phrases demonstrate:

> For all the service that a *man* may do to his lord here in earth, love should be most acceptable, for iii reasons: one for love makes a *man* kindly; and love makes a *man* full of dread; and love makes a *man* diligent in service.

> Many *men* would lose their property and their good for their friends, and be sore wounded.

> Thus also love makes a *man* full of dread and afraid to misplease God either in thought, word, or deed.

> *Good men*, nature steers a *man* to love that *man* that loves him.

> Christ, God's Son of heaven, in this gospel says to *every Christian man* in this manner.[35]

The sermon never specifically addresses women. Sermon 35 continues this trend of (mostly) overlooking women. Although it opens with the implicit gender-

---

[31] *Middle English Sermons edited from British Museum MS. Royal 18 B. xxiii*, ed. Woodburn O. Ross, EETS original series 209 (London: Oxford University Press, 1940), xviii–xix.

[32] Ibid., 69–70.

[33] Ibid., 3.

[34] Unlike *Festial*, however, the sermons in *Middle English Sermons* were not written as a cohesive unit. Rather they were combined from a variety of sources. See Spencer, *English Preaching*, 308–311.

[35] *Middle English Sermons*, 59–61.

inclusive phrase "*Friends*," additionally states, "Dear *friends*, these words the which that I have said," and even incorporates two explicit gender-inclusive addresses to the sermon audience, "*men and women*," it still mostly relies on male generic and androcentric phrasing – substituting "*man*," "*mens*," or "*mankind*" for people at least fifty times and even using the unambiguous term "*Sirs*."[36] This preference for male generic phrasing proliferates throughout *Middle English Sermons*, abounding in homilies like sermon 16 (b) for the Third Sunday in Lent which uses the male generic "*men*" approximately twenty times and never contains female-friendly phrasing.[37]

Nevertheless, the sermons within *Middle English Sermons* do specify "*men and women*" on several occasions. Ross tentatively argued that the sermons fell into several groups written by at least six different clerics. The first group of sermons, one through eight as numbered by Ross, contain the most gender-inclusive language. Six of these open with "*Good men and women*," along with frequent references to male and female parishioners. The third sermon addresses two paragraphs to "*Sir*" and "*Sirs*."[38] This androcentric usage is understandable as the sermon is reiterating a (probably staged) conversation between a priest and male parishioner.

'*Sir*,' you say perchance, 'it is forbidden by *[y]ou priests and prelates* of holy church any *lewd man* to study of holy writ.' *Sir*, I say nay: but it is forbidden any *lewd man* to misuse holy writ, For God himself bids his people to understand it.[39]

Shortly thereafter, the sermon returns its focus to parishioners in general, warning priests that:

God bids *every man Christian and woman* to understand his law, and all more not come to the perfect understanding thereof … I pray *every man and woman* know and believe, and I charge you (the priests) in pain [of everlasting death].[40]

Thus this sermon displays its goal: to help priests in their spiritual duties toward both male and female parishioners.

Nor is it alone. Sermons 11 and 14 also use gender-specific language when discussing the spiritual responsibilities of parishioners (such as the seven sacraments, or learning church law and creeds). Sermon 11 begins "*Worshipful sirs*," but quickly thereafter states that:

*every man and woman* that they presume not himself to receive that worthy Lord but they be worthy.[41]

The author of this sermon chose to specifically state "*men and women*" when

---

36  Ibid., 187–198.

37  Ibid., 93–99.

38  When the terms "Sir" and "Sirs" are used in pastoral literature, they often seem to refer to the clerics who (presumably) will be using the sermons. As such, they are androcentric terms used to refer to men. They never seem to imply both men and women, such as the implicit gender inclusive term "men."

39  *Middle English Sermons*, 13.

40  Ibid., 14.

41  Ibid., 61–62.

reminding penitents to make sure they had cleansed themselves of sin before partaking in Eucharist. Sermon 14 incorporates much male generic language, but its author relied on the word "*man*" when referring to no one in particular, and on the words "*man and woman*" when discussing the specific responsibilities of Christians. For example, he wrote:

> For right as a *man* that is in a strong flood of water there *he* may not began set *his* feet, but if *he* turn soon again to the land *he* is like to fall to the ground and so to be drowned in the water.[42]

This clearly is a generic example, understood to mean "people". Later, however, the text states:

> I understand *every Christian man and woman* that ought to have one love to God.[43]

Unlike the generic reference, this time the author is discussing how every Christian is to live: as the one footed beast described by Hilarius in "De Ymagine Mundi" that relies on its foot (God) for everything – shelter, rest, and protection. Christians were to do this, and *Middle English Sermons* makes it explicit by stating "*every Christian man and woman*."[44]

It is significant that *Middle English Sermons* explicitly includes women when referring to the spiritual duties of parishioners because it suggests that clerical authors thought of their spiritual charges as both male and female. Several additional sermons in *Middle English Sermons* provide testimony to this. Sermon 20, for example, falls in the midst of several gender-insensitive sermons (12 through 22) that rely almost exclusively on male generic phrasing. Sermon 20 fares little better, until one sentence discussing the importance of open confession states:

> the which is needful to each *sinful man and woman*.[45]

Sermon 23 similarly records:

> *Good men and women*, now is passed the holy time of Easter, and *each man and woman* is shriven and houseled.[46]

Sermon 38:

> So by this example you may well see that Christ will not have *no man nor woman* lost and they will ask mercy and be shriven of their sins.[47]

Sermon 47:

> the which pain should stir *every man and woman* to draw to confession and contrition, to virtue and cleanness.[48]

42  Ibid., 76.
43  Ibid., 77.
44  Ibid., 77.
45  Ibid., 116.
46  Ibid., 133.
47  Ibid., 217.
48  Ibid., 312.

Finally the third sermon states:

> I pray every *man and woman* know and believe.[49]

When gender-inclusive language appears in *Middle English Sermons*, it appears in sermons emphasizing the spiritual responsibilities of Christians. Thus the very use of explicit gender-inclusive language reveals clerical authors acknowledging their spiritual debt to care for women as well as men. In fact, as we will see, clerical writers of manuscripts contemporary with *Middle English Sermons* also commonly included gender-inclusive language when writing about pastoral care issues – such as confession, contrition, penance, church attendance, Eucharist, belief in the tenets of holy church, and the responsibilities of both priests and parishioners.

## JOHN MIRK'S *FESTIAL*: A CASE STUDY

The manuscripts of John Mirk's *Festial* provide an excellent case study of how clerical copiers of medieval sermon literature persistently included women within the language of their texts. By tracing language changes within the major manuscripts of *Festial*, this section finds that the use of gender-inclusive language varied dramatically within manuscripts stemming from the same sermon collection.[50] The earlier manuscripts (*sanctorale* and *temporale* sermons combined), dubbed "Group A" by M.F. Wakelin, Alan Fletcher, and Susan Powell, display the most concern for specifically including women while the later "Group B" manuscripts (*sanctorale* and *temporale* sermons separated) display the least concern. Nevertheless, each *Festial* manuscript employed gender-inclusive language when discussing pastoral matters.

### a. Group A manuscripts

Organized with *sanctorale* and *temporale* sermons combined, dating from the mid-fifteenth century or earlier (excepting the early sixteenth-century manuscript Southwell Minister 7), and stemming from the region in which John Mirk lived, this first recension of *Festial* manuscripts includes BL MS Cotton Claudius A II, Bodl. MS Douce 108, Bodl. MS Douce 60, Gonville and Caius College Cambridge MS 168/89, Bodl. MS Gough Ecclesiastical Topography 4, and Southwell Minster MS 7. Although BL MS Cotton Claudius A II is the oldest and most complete version of *Festial*, it does not set the pattern for the incorporation of gender inclusive language within these first recension texts. Out of its seventy-four sermons, thirty-six open with no gendered language (beginning with phrases such as, "This day is called" and "Such a day you shall have"), eighteen open with male generic salutations ("*Good men*"), five open with implicit gender-inclusive salutations (such as "*Blessed people of god's mouth*" or "*Good christian children*"), and fifteen

---

[49] Ibid., 14.
[50] For further description about each major *Festial* manuscript and an introduction to the minor manuscripts, see Appendix I.

open with the explicit gender-inclusive phrase, "*Good men and women*."[51] Thus, within its sermon salutations, the Cotton Claudius manuscript includes specific references to both sexes – but it is the exception, not the rule.

In contrast, the remaining first recension manuscripts evoke female parishioners much more frequently. Sixty-two of the sixty-nine homilies in Bodl. Library MS Gough Ecc. Top. 4 begin with a variation of "*Good men and women*," instead of the androcentric and gender neutral salutations of the Cotton Claudius manuscript. For example, the sermon for St. Andrew's day in BL MS Cotton Claudius A II begins with:

> *Good men* you shall have.[52]

Bodl. Library MS Gough Ecclesiastical Topography 4 opens, instead, with:

> *Good men and women*, such a day you shall have.[53]

Again, the sermon for the conception of the Virgin Mary begins in BL MS Cotton Claudius A II with:

> Such a day you shall have the conception of our lady the which day holy church makes mention of the conception of her.[54]

Bodl. Library MS Gough Ecc. Top. 4 states instead:

> Also, *good men and women*, such a day you shall have our Lady day that is called the Conception. Of the which day holy church makes mention of the conception of her.[55]

The compiler of the Gough manuscript also traded explicit gender inclusive introductions for the implicit gender inclusive introductions found in the Cotton Claudius manuscript. Folio 73v opens the sermon for the vigil before Pentecost in BL MS Cotton Claudius A II with:

> *Good christian creatures.*[56]

Gough Ecc. Top. 4 opens instead with:

> *Christian men and women.*[57]

Perhaps the clerical copyist of the Gough manuscript simply preferred the phrase

---

51 Counting sermons in manuscripts is not always straightforward, as sometimes the manuscripts contain only sermon fragments or split a single sermon (such as the sermon for the feast of St. Philip and St. Jacob) into two sermons. As such, scholars sometimes vary in their sermon counts. In general, I have attempted to count according to the presumed intent of the clerical author – if a separate sermon was intended, I counted it as a separate sermon (for example, I included sermon fragments).

52 BL MS Cotton Claudius A II, f. 6r.

53 *Festial*, 6.

54 BL MS Cotton Claudius A II, f. 11v.

55 *Festial*, 15.

56 BL MS Cotton Claudius A II, f. 73v.

57 *Festial*, 155.

"*Good men and women*"; perhaps he merely copied the phrase from another, hitherto unknown manuscript; or perhaps he intentionally incorporated the gender-sensitive phrasing because he believed that by specifically addressing both men and women, he could better gain the ear of the sermon audience. Whatever the reasons, the textual changes in Bodl. Library MS Gough Ecc. Top. 4 produced a very gender attentive sermon compilation.

Such gender sensitivity continues throughout the first recension manuscripts, becoming even more accentuated in some. Gonville and Caius College MS 168/89 opens sixty-six of its seventy sermons with variations of "*Good men and women*"; Southwell Minster MS 7 (the latest *Festial* manuscript) likewise opens sixty-four of its seventy-one homilies with explicit gender-inclusive salutations; and Bodl. Library MSS Douce 60 and Douce 108 open eighty-five of their collective eighty-eight sermons with "*Good men and women.*" A further examination of language within sermon bodies, such as the Epiphany sermon, reveals the Douce manuscripts to be more gender attentive than their counterparts. For example, the Epiphany sermon in Bodl. Library MS Gough Ecc. Top. 4 records:

> Now, *good men*, you have heard how our Lord Jesus Christ was this day showed by these kings offering.[58]

The Epiphany sermon in Bodl. Library MS Douce 60 (as well as similarly in 108) records instead:

> Now *good men and women* you have heard how our lord Jesus Christ was this day showed by the three kings offerings.[59]

The same sermon in Bodl. Library MS Gough Ecc. Top. 4 records:

> All this was done, for to teach *each christian man* his belief. For each *christian man or woman* is held forto believe.[60]

Bodl. MS Douce 60 (also similarly in 108) records instead:

> All this was done to teach *every christian man and woman* his belief. For every *christian man and woman* is bound to believe this.[61]

In a final example from the Epiphany sermon, Bodl. Library MS Gough Ecc. Top. 4 records:

> Now, *good men*, you have heard, how our Lord Jesus Christ this day was showed by king's offering ...[62]

Bodl. Ms Douce 60 (again similarly in 108) records instead:

> Now *good men and women* you have heard how Lord Jesus Christ this day was showed by three king's offering.[63]

---

[58] *Festial*, 50.
[59] Bodl. MS Douce 60, f. 63v. Also see Bodl. MS Douce 108, 98 (each page is numbered separately, instead of by folio).
[60] *Festial*, 51.
[61] Bodl. MS Douce 60, f. 64v. Also see Bodl. MS Douce 108, 101.
[62] *Festial*, 52.
[63] Bodl. MS Douce 60, f. 66r. Also see Bodl. MS Douce 108, 102–103.

In sum, BL MS Cotton Claudius A II contains the oldest and most complete version of *Festial*. Within the same time frame that it was produced, editors compiled four similar copies of Mirk's compendium. More than a century later, a sixth extant copy was made. These manuscripts rescind from the same family, yet Bodl. Library MS Gough Ecc. Top. 4, Gonville and Caius College MS 168/89, Southwell Minster MS 7, and Bodl. Library MSS Douce 60 and 108 reflect a much greater concern for explicit and implicit gender-inclusive language than BL MS Cotton Claudius A II.

What does this indicate? First it suggests the possibility that the Cotton Claudius manuscript may not be the best representative of John Mirk's original text. Five manuscripts in this recension, excepting Southwell Minster MS 7, were written at approximately the same time and in approximately the same area, thus making it difficult to pinpoint which came first and from where. As Cotton Claudius MS A II still seems to have been written in the area closest to Mirk's home and contains the most complete set of *Festial* sermons, it retains an authoritative status. Yet the fact that it contains language strikingly different from the other five manuscripts might be significant. Second, as none of the six manuscripts are verbatim copies of any of the others, the language differences emphasize the choices that individual copiers made about how they wanted their manuscripts to read. It is especially crucial to note that five of the six compilers chose to include (some more extensively than others) language specifically addressed to women.

The alterations to *Festial* had only begun. At least seven more Group A manuscripts spiraled from the Cotton Claudius family, each displaying concern for explicit and implicit gender-inclusive language. On the Warwick/Staffordshire border sometime before 1450, a clerical copyist produced BL MS Lansdowne 392. Every one of its fifty-one sermons opens with a variation of "*Good men and women*." Lansdowne 392 also incorporates explicit gender-inclusive phrases within its sermon bodies, rather than relying on the male generic as used in many of the other manuscripts. For example, in Mirk's Epiphany sermon, Lansdowne 392 records:

> Now *good men and women* you have heard how our lord Jesus christ was this day showed by iii kings offering.[64]

Gough Ecc. Top. 4 records only:

> Now, *good men*, you have heard, how our Lord Jesus Christ this day was showed by king's offering.[65]

Two more Group A manuscripts seem directly related to Lansdowne 392: Harley 2403 and CUL Dd. X. 50. Yet, despite the textual kinship, the compilers of each manuscript made individual choices about gender inclusive language. The compiler of Harley 2403 echoed the concern of the Lansdowne compiler for incorporating women into sermon audiences, opening sixty-seven of its seventy homilies with, "*Good men and women*," as well as including at least some explicit gender-inclusive language within sermon bodies. Although the compiler of CUL

[64] BL MS Lansdowne 392, f. 25v.
[65] *Festial*, 52.

Dd. X. 50 reflected only moderate concern about specifically incorporating women into his sermon salutations (only thirty-four of the fifty-nine sermons open with explicit gender inclusive phrasing), he reflected significant concern about specifically including women within the language of sermon bodies.[66] For example, in the Epiphany sermon, CUL Dd. X. 50 both echoes the gender-specific language and includes even more female-friendly phrases than Lansdowne 392 and Harley 2403.

Lansdowne 392 records:

> Now *sirs* you have heard how our lord Jesus christ was this day showed both god and man by these iii kings offering.

> Now *good men and women* you have heard how our lord Jesus christ was this day showed by iii kings offering.[67]

Likewise, Harley 2403 records:

> Now *good men* you have heard how our lord Jesus Christ was this day showed both god and man by these iii kings offerings.

> Now *good men* you have heard how our lord Jesus Christ this day was showed by kings offerings.[68]

CUL Dd. X. 50, however, records:

> Now *good men and women* you have heard that our lord jesus christ was this day both god and man by the offering of three kings.

> Now *good men and women* you have heard how our lord jesus christ was showed this day by offering of the kings[69]

The final four Group A manuscripts, Dr. William's Library MS Ancient 11, Bodl. Library MS Hatton 96, BL MS Harley 2420, and BL MS Harley 2417, display considerable variety within organization and language choices. Yet each also incorporates women within the words of its text. The compiler of Dr. William's Library MS Ancient 11 opened twenty-five of his fifty-six sermons that have sermon salutations with a variation of, "*Good men and women*", thirty-one with implicit gender-inclusive salutations, such as: "*Christian people*," "*Dear friends*" or "*Worshipful friends*," and none with male generic or androcentric phrases.[70] The compiler also explicitly addressed women within sermon bodies. For example, the now familiar Epiphany sermon includes the phrases:

> Now *good men and women* you have heard how our lord jesus christ was this day showed.

---

66 The author also mostly used "Dear Friends" or "Christian people" as his sermon salutations when he did not use "Good men and women."

67 BL MS Lansdowne 392, ff. 24v and 25v.

68 BL MS Harley 2403, ff. 34r and 35v.

69 CUL MS Dd. X. 50, ff. 31r and 32v.

70 For example, see 13, 17, 36, 45, and 101, in Dr. William's Library MS Ancient 11. Two sermons are incomplete at the beginning.

Now *good men and women* you have heard how our lord jesus christ this day was showed very god and man.[71]

Dr. William's Library MS Ancient 11 augments this attentiveness to gender sensitivity by adding one more phrase with the word woman to the Epiphany text. BL MS Gough Ecc. Top. 4 states:

All this was done, forto teach *each christian man* his belief. For *each christian man or woman* is held forto believe in the Father, and in the Son, and in the Holy Ghost, that be three persons and one God.[72]

Dr. William's Ancient 11 states instead:

that was done to teach *every christian man and woman* ... for each *Christian man and woman* should believe in the father and in the son and in the holy ghost.[73]

The mid-fifteenth-century Staffordshire composer of Bodl. MS Hatton 96 jumbled his sermons haphazardly. Although he directed salutations of fifty-three sermons within the *Festial* section explicitly to men and women, the compiler of Hatton 96 incorporated female-friendly language inconsistently within his sermon text – sometimes including it and sometimes not.[74] The Epiphany sermon, again, illustrates this well. Like most other Group A manuscripts, the compiler of Hatton 96 introduced the sermon to, "*Good men and women*," and incorporated women explicitly within the sermon bodies on several occasions.

Bodl. MS Gough Ecc. Top. 4, again for example, records:

Now, *good men*, you have heard how our Lord Jesus Christ was this day showed by these king's offering.[75]

Bodl. MS Hatton 96 records instead:

Now *good men and women* you have heard how our lord jesus christ was this day showed by these kings offering.[76]

As the sermon progressed, however, the compiler of MS Hatton 96 became less gender-aware – tacking "or of woman" on awkwardly to the end of a phrase in which the word "woman" was smoothly incorporated by other manuscripts. Bodl. Library MS Gough Ecc. Top. 4 records:

For there is no gold in this world so precious to God, as is a meek heart and a love of a *man or of a woman*.[77]

In Bodl. MS Hatton 96, however, the word "woman" appears more as an afterthought:

---

71  Dr. William's Library MS Ancient 11, 53, 54.
72  *Festial*, 51.
73  Ibid., 56.
74  For example, see ff. 141v, 145v, 149v, 152v, and 154v.
75  *Festial*, 50.
76  Bodl. MS Hatton 96, f. 249v.
77  *Festial*, 50.

For there is no gold in the world so precious to gods sight as is the meek heart *of a man* and a devout or *of woman.*[78]

By the end of the sermon, the compiler of Bodl. MS Hatton 96 neglected specific inclusion of women, concluding with a male generic phrase:

Now *good men* you have heard how our lord jesus Christ this day was showed by the kings offering.[79]

In contrast, the last two Group A manuscripts, BL MSS Harley 2420 and Harley 2417, demonstrate great concern for gender inclusive language. Originally written as a single unit, they open 64 of 67 sermons that have salutations with "*Good men and women*" and incorporate much explicit gender-inclusive language within sermon bodies. On one occasion, the compiler reversed the usual order and, instead of dropping "*women*" in favor of "*Good men*" (as clerical writers did presumably for the sake of brevity), he – at least temporarily – dropped "*men,*" opening the sermon only with, "*Good women.*"[80] Thus the compilers of each Group A manuscript made similar yet seemingly individual choices about incorporating women into the language of *Festial* – suggesting that at least some late medieval clerics considered the specific inclusion of women within the language of their texts as important.

## b. Group B manuscripts

Although containing the same *Festial* sermons, the nine Group B manuscripts appear quite different from the Group A manuscripts for two reasons: their sermons are divided into *sanctorale* and *temporale*, and they display less concern for explicit gender-inclusive language.

Bodl. Library MS Rawlinson A 381 and Bodl. Library MS University College 201 resemble the Group A manuscripts more than any other of the Group B manuscripts – except in concern for explicit gender inclusive language.[81] Rawlinson A 381 opens a mere three of its sixty-three *Festial* sermons with the explicit gender-inclusive phrase, "Good men and women." University College 201 fares little better, as only three of its sixty-two Festial homilies open with "*Good men and women.*" This lack of concern for explicit gender-inclusive language continues throughout the remaining Group B manuscripts. Of the thirty-six *Festial* sermons in Trinity College Dublin MS 201, a mere five open with "*Good men and women.*" Of the sixty-two *Festial* sermons in Durham Cathedral MS Cosin V III 5, only four open with "*Good men and women.*" Of the fifty-seven *Festial* sermons with salutations in Harley 2391, six open with "*Good men and women.*" Of the fifty-six *Festial* sermons in Brotherton 502, only four open with "*Good men and women.*"

---

[78] Bodl. MS Hatton 96, f. 249v.

[79] Ibid., f. 251r.

[80] BL MS Harley 2417, f. 67.

[81] Susan Powell has suggested further "groupings" for the Group B manuscripts. See: Powell, "A Critical Edition of the *Temporale* Sermons," 13–21; Powell, "The Advent and Nativity Sermon from a Fifteenth-Century Revision of John Mirk's *Festial,*" Middle English Texts 13 (Heidelberg, 1981), 22–27.

Finally, of the sixty sermons that have salutations in Harley 2371, only four open with "*Good men and women.*"

The final two Group B texts tell a similar story. BL MSS Harley 2247 and Royal 18 B XXV represent the most altered of the *Festial* manuscripts. Abandoning John Mirk's mission to provide sermon literature for less-educated clerics, these compilers revised *Festial* to make it more attractive for the literate and educated – removing many of Mirk's fanciful exempla, buttressing biblical points with quotes from the *Vulgate*, and combining fifty-seven of the original homilies with thirty homilies from a Dominican sermon cycle.[82] These modifications did indeed result in a more erudite edition of *Festial*. Yet these same "improvements" also created a much less explicit gender-inclusive compilation. First, all of the Harley 2247 and Royal 18 B XXV sermons begin with either implicit gender-inclusive phrases ("*Worshipful friends*") or non-gendered ones ("This day"). Second, much of the explicit gender-inclusive phrasing of *Festial* has disappeared from the sermon bodies of Harley 2247 and Royal 18 B XXV. For example, in the Rogation Days sermon, in which all but two of the Group A and B manuscripts that include the sermon reiterate the gender specific phrasing "husband, wife and servant," Harley 2247 and Royal 18 B XXV delete the phrase. Bodl. MS Gough Ecc. Top. 4 records:

> *Good men and women*, these three days following Monday, Tuesday, and Wednesday you shall fast and come to church: *husband, wife, and servant*; for all we be sinners, and need the mercy of God.[83]

BL MS Harley 2247 records instead:

> These iii days, Monday, Tuesday and Wednesday by command by constitution to be fasted of them that be of lawful age, and full necessary it is to *every Christian creature* to come to Holy Church and go in procession, for all we be sinners and greatly need of God's mercy.[84]

Likewise, in the sermon for Epiphany, Harley 2247 and Royal 18 B XXV often omit the gender sensitivity of the Group A manuscripts. Bodl. MS Gough Ecc. Top. 4 records:

> For each *Christian man or woman* is held to believe in the Father, and in the Son, and in the Holy Ghost, that be three persons and one God.[85]

BL MS Harley 2247 records simply:

> *every man* must believe that there be iii persons and but one God in Trinity.[86]

82  See Powell, "A Critical Edition of the *Temporale* Sermons"; Alan Fletcher and Susan Powell, "The Origins of a Fifteenth-Century Sermon Collection: MSS Harley 2247 and Royal 18 B XXV," *Leeds Studies in English* 10 (1978), 74–96; and Lillian L. Steckman, "A Late Fifteenth-Century Revision of Mirk's *Festial*," *Studies in Philology* 34 (1937), 224–231, for further discussion of the compilers and intended audience for Harley 2247 and Royal 18 B XXV.

83  *Festial*, 149.

84  BL MS Harley 2247, f. 105r.

85  *Festial*, 51.

86  BL MS Harley 2247, f. 30r.

Third, the scribes of Harley 2247 and Royal 18 B XXV changed the dying-woman-from-Devonshire exemplum character, in the Corpus Christi day sermon, to a man. Bodl. MS Gough Ecc. Top. 4 begins the story:

> In Devonshire beside Axe Bridge there dwelled a holy vicar and had one of his parish, a *woman*, that lay sick at the point of death half a mile from him in town. The which at midnight sent after him to do her her rights.[87]

BL MS Harley 2247 records instead:

> I read that in Devonshire, beside a town called Axe Bridge, dwelled a holy priest and well-disposed curate of that town that had a *sick man* in his parish. And about midnight the sick creature sent after the curate in great haste to minister his rights unto him.[88]

Harley 2247 and Royal 18 B XXV provide the only time in *Festial* manuscripts in which this exemplum character is not female. Although perhaps not a substantial alteration in of itself, this change in gender of the sick parishioner seems indicative of the overall pattern of gender sensitivity within BL MS Harley 2247, BL MS Royal 18 B XXV, and the remaining Group B manuscripts: they reflect less concern for explicit gender-inclusive language than the Group A manucripts.

## c. Gender inclusivity and pastoral care

Regardless of the overall quantity of explicit gender-inclusive language contained within the sermons and the nature of the salutations (explicit gender-inclusive, implicit gender-inclusive, male generic, or not-gendered), however, the clerical compilers of the Group A and Group B manuscripts persistently incorporated women into passages discussing pastoral care. Thus each major manuscript of *Festial* reminds readers that women were just as important as their male counterparts when it came to spiritual matters.

For example, most of the Group A and Group B manuscripts record an almost identical explicit gender-inclusive phrase for the Rogation Days sermon, inviting parishioners to participate in the upcoming pieties.[89]

**Group A manuscripts**

| | |
|---|---|
| Cotton Claudius A II: | *Good men* these three days following Monday Tuesday and Wednesday you shall fast and come to church *husband wife and servant* for all we be sinners and need to have mercy of god.[90] |
| Gough Ecc. Top. 4: | *Good men and women*, these three days following Monday, Tuesday, and Wednesday you shall fast and come to |

---

[87]  *Festial*, 173.
[88]  BL MS Harley 2247, ff. 129r–v.
[89]  Bodl. MS Douce 60 and BL MS Harley 2371 do not include the Rogation Days sermon, and the variation of BL MSS Harley 2247 and Royal 18 B XXV has already been discussed.
[90]  BL MS Cotton Claudius A II, f. 71v.

church: *husband, wife, and servant*; for all we be sinners, and need the mercy of God.[91]

Douce 108:  *Good men and women* these three days following, Monday, Tuesday, and Wednesday you shall fast and come to church, *husband, wife, and servant,* for all we be sinners and need to have the mercy of god.[92]

Gonville and Caius 168/89:  *Good men and women* these iii days following Monday Tuesday and Wednesday you shall fast and come to church *husband wife and servant* for all be we sinners and need for to have mercy of god.[93]

Southwell Minster 7:  *Good men and women* these iii day following Monday Tuesday and Wednesday you shall fast and come to church *husband wife and servant* for all be sinners and need to have mercy of god.[94]

Lansdowne 392:  *Good men and women* these iii days following that is Monday Tuesday and Wednesday you shall fast and come to church *husband wife and servant* for all we be sinners and need to have the mercy of god.[95]

Harley 2403:  *Good men and women* these iii days following that is Monday Tuesday and Wednesday you shall fast and come to church *husband wife and servant* for all we be sinners and need to have the mercy of god.[96]

Harley 2420:  *Good men and wome*n these three days following that is Monday Tuesday and Wednesday you shall fast and come to church *husband wife and servant* namely Monday and Wednesday you must needly fast for all we be sinners and need to have the mercy of god.[97]

Hatton 96:  *Good men and women* these iii days following Monday Tuesday and Wednesday you shall fast and come to church *husband wife and servant* for all we be sinners and need to have the mercy of god.[98]

Dr. William's Ancient 11:  *Good men and women* you shall come to church these iii days following that is Monday Tuesday and Wednesday and you shall fast *husband wife and servant* and for all we be sinners and have need of mercy of god.[99]

CUL Dd. X. 50:  *Good men and women* these iii days Monday Tuesday and

---

[91]  *Festial*, 149.
[92]  Bodl. MS Douce 108, f. 341r.
[93]  Gonville and Caius College Cambridge MS 168/89, 166.
[94]  Southwell Minster MS 7, ff. 80r–v.
[95]  BL MS Lansdowne 392, f. 66v.
[96]  BL MS Harley 2403, f. 94v.
[97]  BL MS Harley 2420, f. 52v.
[98]  Bodl. MS Hatton 96, f. 299r.
[99]  Dr. William's Library Ancient MS 3, 181.

Wednesday you shall fast and come to church for all we be sinners and none may excuse him from sin.[100]

**Group B manuscripts**

| | |
|---|---|
| Rawlinson 381: | *Good men* these iii days following that is to say Monday Tuesday and Wednesday you shall come to holy church *husband wife and servant* for all we be sinners and need much to have mercy of god that is almighty.[101] |
| University Col. 201: | *Good men* these iii days following that is to say Monday Tuesday and Wednesday you shall come to holy church *husband wife and servant* for all we are sinners and need much to have the mercy of god that is almighty.[102] |
| Trinity College Dublin 201: | *Good men and woman* these three day is following that is to say Monday Tuesday and Wednesday you shall fast and come to holy church *husband wife and servant* for all we be sinners and need much to have mercy of our lord god that is almight.[103] |
| Cosin V III 5: | *Good men* these iii days following that is to say Monday Tuesday and Wednesday you shall fast and come to holy church *husband wife and servant* for all we be sinners and have full much need to the help of god.[104] |
| Harley 2391: | *Good men and women* these iii days following that is to say Monday Tuesday and Wednesday you shall fast and come to holy church *husband wife and servant* for all we be sinners and need much to have mercy of god that is all mighty.[105] |
| Brotherton 502: | *Good men and women*, these three days following, that is to say, Monday, Tuesday and Wednesday, you shall fast and come to holy church, *husband, wife, and child and servant,* for all we be sinners, and need much to have the mercy of god that is almight.[106] |

The second address to the "sinners" who "need the mercy of God" clarifies the salutation "*Good men*" or "*Good men and women*," making it certain that each sermon was directed to male and female alike, or at least male and female married folk, servants, and sometimes children.

Even the Group B manuscripts least inclined toward explicit gender-inclusive language, such as Bodl. MS Rawlinson A 381 and the revised *Festial* manuscripts BL MS Harley and BL MS Royal 18 B XXV, explicitly incorporate women within

---

100  CUL MS Dd. X. 50, f. 92v.
101  Bodl. MS Rawlinson 381, f. 30v.
102  Bodl. MS University College 102, ff. 65r–v.
103  Trinity College Dublin MS 201, f. 25r.
104  Durham Cathedral Cosin MS V III 5, f. 36v.
105  BL MS Harley 2391, f. 33r.
106  Leeds University Brotherton MS 502, f. 19v.

passages discussing pastoral care. Despite rarely employing specific references to women within his salutations, the compiler of Rawlinson A 381 consistently incorporated women in sermons focused on pastoral matters (such as the Nativity of Jesus and the Epiphany sermon). This becomes clear when the language of Rawlinson A 381 is compared with the female-friendly manuscript Bodl. Library MS Gough Ecc. Top. 4. For example, the Gough manuscript contains several instances of male generic and explicit gender-inclusive language within the sermon for the Nativity of Jesus; Rawlinson A 381 emulates each instance of explicit gender-inclusive language, even changing one case of male generic language to explicit gender-inclusive. Gough Ecc. Top. 4 opens the sermon with:

> *Good men and women and christian creatures.*[107]

Rawlinson A 381 echoes:

> *Good men and women.*[108]

Gough Ecc. Top. 4 records:

> *men and women* of good will.[109]

Rawlinson A 381 repeats:

> *men and women* that be of good will.[110]

Gough Ecc. Top. 4 charges:

> By this example *each christian man and woman* should learn to do reverence, and service, and honor this day to this child. Wherefore the third mass of this day is said at midday, in showing that *each man and woman* is held to come and offer of this child and of his mother.[111]

Rawlinson A 381, again, follows with:

> By this example *each Christian man and woman* should learn to do service and honor this day to this child. Wherefore the iii mass of this day is said at midday in showing *each Christian man and woman* is held to come and offer in the worship of this child and his mother.[112]

Gough Ecc. Top. 4 states only:

> for *every man* should do thus for love and not for awe.[113]

Rawlinson A 381 takes one step further, adding:

> and for *each man and woman* should do thus for love.[114]

---

[107]   *Festial*, 21.
[108]   Bodl. MS Rawlinson 381, f. 48v.
[109]   *Festial*, 23.
[110]   Bodl. MS Rawlinson 381, f. 49v.
[111]   *Festial*, 25.
[112]   Bodl. MS Rawlinson 381, f. 50v.
[113]   *Festial*, 25.
[114]   Bodl. MS Rawlinson 381, f. 50v.

Finally, Gough Ecc. Top. 4 records:

> "A child is born to us." A child, he said, and not a man, so that *all men and women* for love should have boldness for to come to him to seek grace.[115]

Rawlinson A 381 follows suit:

> A child is born to us. A child and not a man he said. So that *all men and women* for love should have boldness to come to him to seek grace.[116]

Thus even one of the least gender sensitive *Festial* manuscripts exhibits a reputable amount of concern for women within the language of a pastoral-minded sermon: concern focused on the pastoral responsibilities of male and female parishioners to attend church services regularly, pay proper devotion to the saints, and participate in the sacraments of holy church.

The compilers of BL MSS Harley 2247 and Royal 18 B XXV chose erudition over specific gender-inclusive language. But they still recognized women as ordinary parishioners in need of ordinary pastoral care. The familiar sermon for the Nativity of Jesus addresses men and women explicitly on several occasions, including:

> Thus you may understand how God gives peace, rest and unity to *men and women* of good will and calls all such *men and women his children*.[117]

> giving example to *all men and women* to set little by worldly riches nor by pomp and pride.[118]

> *every Christian man and woman* should learn to do reverence and worship that day to this child, Christ Jesus … so that *all men and women* should for love have boldness to come to him for mercy and grace.[119]

Each of these occasions focused on matters of pastoral care: assuring male and female parishioners that God desired both to be his children and thus both must participate in the sacraments and learn the spiritual lessons taught by their priests. Similarly, the sermon for Corpus Christi explicitly addresses men and women in several instances, including:

> as often as a *man or woman* comes to Holy Church to hear mass and to see Christ's very body, God grants him vii great gifts in his life, and merits.[120]

> that every *man and woman* should remember Christ's passion and by his inward thinking and daily remembering of that precious passion mightily to be armed against the fiend.[121]

---

[115]  *Festial*, 26.
[116]  Bodl. Library MS Rawlinson A 381, f. 50v.
[117]  Ibid., f. 8r.
[118]  Ibid., f. 9r.
[119]  Ibid., f. 10r.
[120]  Ibid., f. 126v.
[121]  Ibid., f. 127v.

and crosses and other images are full necessary to *every man and woman*.[122]

that *every man and woman* should have the more tender remembrance of Christ's passion.[123]

to *every man and woman* that perfectly believe in the sacrament in form of bread.[124]

Again, each of these instances focused on teaching and encouraging male and female parishioners to understand the meaning of the birth, death, and resurrection of Jesus and to participate in the sacrament of the altar. Consequently even the less-than-average gender sensitive *Festial* manuscripts recognize the importance of explicitly including "women" when discussing matters of pastoral significance.

On the one hand, the Group A and Group B manuscripts draw upon the same sermon collection. The overabundance of sensational exempla, which probably played a hand in the popularity of *Festial*, fills each homily just as Mirk intended. Sentences and paragraphs are repeated verbatim, and Mirk's emotionally charged phrases recur continuously. On the other hand, each copy of *Festial* represents the work of individual copyists. These clerics made choices about which sermons they wanted to incorporate, in what order they wanted to arrange them, and how they wanted to use their words. Such decisions certainly were influenced by the version of the text they were copying. As such, we can arrange the *Festial* manuscripts in groups, based on such similarities in the text as dialect, repeated errors, and homily arrangement. Yet, as each of the most complete copies of *Festial* is different, we also know that some choices made by copyists were their own. More than half of the clerics who copied *Festial* manuscripts chose either to keep gender-inclusive language intact from a previous version or to add women into the sermons they were copying. Some even chose both. The Lancashire priest who copied ten *Festial* sermons into Lincoln Cathedral MS 133 inserted the word "*women*" into a phrase that contained only the word "*men*" in other *Festial* manuscripts, thus turning "*good men*" into "*good men and women*."[125] Similarly, the cleric in Southeastern Staffordshire who copied BL MSS Harley 2420 and Harley 2471 seemed so intent on writing women into his sermons that, in Harley 2417, he forgot the word men – directing the sermon salutation only to "*Good women*." This mistake was caught and the word "*men*" was inserted above the line to indicate its usual position.[126] Nonetheless, the point remains clear that many of the clerics who made copies of Mirk's *Festial* were interested in more than compiling sermons; they also wanted the language of those sermons to include women as well as men. Perhaps they hoped by directing their words to the faithful of both sexes, men and women alike would relate better to the words of God.

\*

---

122 Ibid., f. 127v.
123 Ibid., f. 128r.
124 Ibid., f. 129r.
125 Lincoln Cathedral MS 133, ff. 98r–120v.
126 BL MS Harley 2417, f. 67.

In sum, sermons display varying concern for implicit and explicit gender-inclusive language. Some compilations such as *Speculum Sacerdotal* display more comfort in utilizing androcentric and male generic language. Some compilations such as *Middle English Sermons* vary sermon-to-sermon in the employment of male generic, implicit gender-inclusive, and explicit gender-inclusive language. Finally, many of the *Festial* manuscripts incorporate a unique amount of explicit gender-inclusive phrasing, echoing it consistently within salutations and the bodies of sermon text. Yet the compilers of each manuscript persistently included explicit gender-inclusive language in one particular circumstance: when discussing issues of pastoral care. Thus, by specifically including women when discussing the sacraments and when encouraging parishioners to attend church services, sermon compilers recognized their responsibilities to teach, preach, and care for women. Some admitted this more willingly than others. Yet most seemed to realize that "Christ's people" did indeed include "both men and women."

## Chapter 3

# PASTORAL PERCEPTIONS

FROM THE generous acknowledgment of women within some manuscripts to the regular inclusion of women within pastoral discussions of most manuscripts, clerical writers of vernacular sermon compilations recognized female parishioners as an ordinary part of pastoral care – both informing priests how to care for women and informing women how to fulfill their spiritual obligations. But who were the female parishioners to whom clerical writers acknowledged pastoral debt? *Omnis utrusque sexus*, the decree of Fourth Lateran Council, did not imply discrimination against any within the Church's care, male or female. It demanded blanket observance. In practice, however, when clerics penned their sermon compilations and instruction manuals, what types of women did they envision as typical petitioners? Their compassion would have extended to comely maidens, pious matrons, and chaste widows. But how much further would it have gone? Would it have extended to older singlewomen, working women, and those of ill-repute? Or would some women have slipped through the cracks? In short, did clerical writers approach female parishioners as they actually *were* or only as they were *imagined*?

A poignant exemplum from *Festial* sheds light on this matter. A bishop ready to administer the sacrament on Easter Sunday prayed that God would reveal to him the parishioners worthy and unworthy to receive the Host. As the people streamed in the church doors, making their way toward the sacrament table, the bishop realized that his prayer had been granted. Some of the faces he saw appeared red with blood dripping from their mouths; some appeared pitch black; some white as snow; and some fair to behold. Finally, two prostitutes entered the church with faces shining bright as the sun. Marveling at the miracle, yet confused by what he saw, the bishop sought divine assistance. God again responded; this time sending an angel. Those with the bloody faces, the heavenly messenger explained, unrepentantly suffered the deadly sins of envy and wrath. Those with black faces suffered the deadly sin of lechery and had refused to repent. The white faces betokened sinners confessed and shriven; the fair and ruddy faces betokened those of good lives who had yet to fall into deadly sin. The faces of the two prostitutes shone the brightest because they had repented and made sincere vows to forsake their evil lifestyles. "Wherefore God of his mercy has forgiven them their sin, and so clean washed their souls, that they shine thus surpassing all other."[1]

---

[1]  *Festial*, 131–132.

This tale suggests that clerics could view women realistically, even favorably. The miraculous vision made no distinction between the sins of women and the sins of men. Both suffered from envy, wrath, and lechery. Both were portrayed with fair and ruddy faces, illustrating those of good lives.[2] Moreover, the exemplum proclaims two women to be the most worthy parishioners. These two women had professed the most sorrow for their sins; received the most thorough cleansing; repented the most sincerely; and been awarded highest praise for their actions. The author of *Speculum Sacerdotal* enhanced this tale, emphasizing the miraculous changes wrought by God *specifically* within these two women. "And then the bishop said he had great marvel and not only for the changing of the women, for that often happens with good people, but of the mercy and grace of God that not only has released them and withdrawn them from everlasting torment, but that has vouchsafed to give them such a grace and honor."[3]

At the same time, however, this tale also emphasizes women's sexuality. The women who "shone the brightest" represent the worst type of sinners: prostitutes. Whether the female parishioners really sold their bodies, as the *Festial* identification of "common women" suggests, the community perceived them as committing this most degrading sin for women: having sex with multiple partners, possibly for financial gain. Thus the positive portrayal of women as ordinary parishioners fades as the story highlights the negative female quality most feared by clerics: their sexuality. In sum, this two-faced exemplum portrays women as a familiar part of the pastoral process. Yet as one side of Janus smiles at female parishioners, the other side seems to frown.

This chapter examines a similar juxtaposition. On the one hand, it demonstrates that women's dependent status and sexual presence limited clerical vision. Legally and socially, medieval women were identified by their relationships to men – husbands, fathers, or other male household heads – and this carried into the spiritual realm. Women had their own souls, but clerical authors of vernacular pastoral literature could not escape the reality that many women, in the words of *Speculum Sacerdotal*, "be not of their own power."[4] Thus priests understood women as dependent figures. Clerics also understood women as sexual figures, and were seemingly unable to forget the enticing company presented by female bodies. One cleric thought so much about the feminine form that he doodled women with large breasts and long hair in a manuscript margin, labeling them unambiguously "Sirens."[5]

It is this latter topic on which historians customarily have focused: clerical misogyny stemming from obsession with female sexuality. The textbook, *Medieval Worlds: An Introduction to European History 300–1492*, regales its under-

---

2   *Festial*, 132. *Speculum Sacerdotal: Edited from British Museum MS. Additional 36791*, ed. Edward H. Weatherly, EETS original series 200 (London: Oxford University Press, 1936), 123–124. This version of the story indicates that the women, instead of prostitutes, were adulterous wives.

3   *Speculum Sacerdotal*, 124.

4   Ibid., 82.

5   Durham Cathedral Cosin MS V IV 3, f. 11v. M.G. Challis has written, "Depiction of the mermaid [also known as siren] as temptress determined to steal men's souls was a popular myth, and one so lovingly depicted by the *misericord* carvers that one can only surmise that an encounter with these creatures was more to be desired than feared. When shown as temptresses, mermaids would have with them their tools for enticement, the comb and mirror." M.G. Challis, *Life in Medieval England as Portrayed on Church Misericords & Bench Ends* (Nettlebed: Teamband, 1998), 41.

graduate audience with the scathing words of Peter Damian addressed to women:

> I speak to you, o charmers of the clergy, appetizing flesh of the devil, that cast-away from paradise, you, poison of the minds, death of souls, venom of wine and of eating, companions of the very stuff of sin, the cause of our ruin. You, I say, I exhort you women of the ancient enemy, you bitches, sows, screech-owls, night-owls, she-wolves, blood-suckers, … Come now, hear me, harlots, prostitutes, with your lascivious kisses, you wallowing places for fat pigs, souches for unclean spirits, demi-goddesses, sirens, witches, devotees of Diana, if any portents, if any omens are found thus far, they should be judged sufficient to your name. For you are the victims of demons, destined to be cut off by eternal death. From you the devil is fattened by the abundance of your lust, is fed by you alluring feasts.[6]

Damian was condemning women on account of their sexuality, providing teachers and students with a good example of this rampant thread of medieval misogyny. Medieval clerics in the fourteenth and fifteenth centuries continued in the spirit of Damian and wrote prolifically about the dangers of lascivious women. A fifteenth-century Yorkshire priest's notebook defined women as, "man's confusion, an insatiable beast, constant anxiety. A constant losing battle, a house of storms, an obstruction to a man's chastity and the shipwreck of purity, the vessel of adultery, a costly strife, the worst creature, the heaviest weight, a deadly viper, humanity's slave."[7] In fact, misogyny (or at least antiwoman attitudes) so inundates medieval texts that it has become a commonplace subject for many medieval historians. Caroline Walker Bynum has remarked simply, "The misogyny of the later Middle Ages is well known."[8]

Yet the coin has two sides. The voices of known misogynists such as Damian, Jacques de Vitry, and Bernard of Clairvaux scream for attention, and so far they have received it. Softer voices tell a different tale. Ordinary clerics writing in the vernacular tongue spoke less harshly about the women they served. The misogynist attitudes reflected in the Yorkshire notebook lurk in the background, reminding priests of the caution they must exercise around female parishioners. But the words of John Mirk and other clerical authors are more practical than inflammatory, more utilitarian than theoretical. Thus, on the other hand, this chapter demonstrates that clerical writers also regarded women realistically and positively. They defended women from the accusation that, through Eve, women had condemned humankind; they protected women as wives and mothers; and they expanded their view of women beyond traditional marital roles, recognizing even the presence of singlewomen. Janus may have frowned indeed; but, as this chapter reminds us, he also tried to smile.

---

6   *Medieval Worlds: An Introduction to European History 300–1492*, eds. Jo Ann Hoeppner Moran Cruz and Richard Gerbeding (Boston: Houghton-Mifflin, 2004), 274.
7   *Pastors and the Care of Souls in Medieval England*, eds. John Shinners and William J. Dohar (Notre Dame: University of Notre Dame Press, 1998), 156.
8   Caroline Walker Bynum, *Fragmentation and Redemption: Essays on Gender and the Human Body in Medieval Religion* (New York: Zone Books, 1992), 151.

## "NOT OF THEIR OWN POWER"

The dependent status of women complicated how clerics perceived female parishioners, as – legally and socially – many women remained under the authority of men throughout their lives. While sons escaped patriarchal authority after reaching maturity, daughters who married did not. "Covered" by their husbands under most areas of the law, late medieval wives could not legally hold property or be held responsible for business failures or debts. Women (regardless of marital status) were also barred from most public offices and often not considered competent to act as pledges in court. Singlewomen, widows, and other women living without the supervision of men were often regarded with suspicion and sometimes even forced from their own homes into male-headed households.[9] The town of Coventry, for example, ordered in 1492 that "no single woman, being in good health and strong in body to labor within the age of fifty years take or keep from henceforth house or chambers by herself; nor that they take any chamber with any other person, but that they go to service till they be married." In short, the position of women in late medieval England was mostly secondary and usually dependent to that of men. As Judith Bennett has articulated, "In both theory and practice, women came after men in late medieval England."[10]

Sermons, religious literature, and exempla reinforced secular customs about the dependent status of women. The Advent Sunday sermon in *Middle English Sermons* states that, according to the creation order in Genesis, God made "man of the earth and woman of man."[11] When instructing priests how to conduct *Officium Mortuorum* the author of *Speculum Sacerdotal* reminded clerics that church bells should be rung three times for the death of a man, but only twice for the death of a woman. "Why? For she made difference and diversity in that time that she made alienation and parting between God and man. And for the man it is rung thrice. Why? For the man was first created, and the woman was created in

---

9   Ruth Mazo Karras, *Common Women: Prostitution and Sexuality in Medieval England* (New York and Oxford: Oxford University Press, 1996), 19–20. Alice Kettle has similarly found this to be the case for unmarried women in fifteenth-century Lichfield. "If they did not live in the house of their employer, these women seem either to have lived alone or with other women. Such women without husbands were inevitably objects of suspicion, especially if they had received male visitors or had children. Ellen Glyn alias Nurse shared a house with Ellen Wygan; each had a child and was 'badly defamed.'" Alice J. Kettle, "Ruined Maids: Prostitutes and Servant Girls in Later Medieval England," in *Matrons and Marginal Women in Medieval Society*, eds. Robert R. Edwards and Vickie Ziegler (Woodbridge, Suffolk: Boydell Press, 1995), 19–32, at 27. Also, Shannon McSheffrey has recently demonstrated the significant influence of patriarchy on the late medieval city of London, including the control that medieval fathers exerted over the marriage choices of their daughters. Shannon McSheffrey, *Marriage, Sex, and Civic Culture in Late Medieval London* (Philadelphia: University of Pennsylvania Press, 2006). For more information about women in medieval law and society, see: Judith M. Bennett, *Women in the Medieval English Countryside: Gender and Household in Brigstock before the Plague* (New York and Oxford: Oxford University Press, 1987), 27–36, 104–110; Amy M. Froide, "Marital Status as a Category of Difference," in *Singlewomen in the European Past, 1250–1800*, eds. Judith M. Bennett and Amy M. Froide (Philadelphia: University of Pennsylvania Press, 1999), 236–269, at 238–243; Helen Jewell, *Women in Medieval England* (New York: Manchester University Press, 1996), 74–79.

10  Judith Bennett, "England: Women and Gender," in *A Companion to Britain in the Later Middle Ages*, ed. S.H. Rigby (Malden, Mass.: Blackwell Publishers, 2003), 87–106, at 99.

11  *Middle English Sermons edited from British Museum MS. Royal 18 B. xxiii*, ed. Woodburn O. Ross, EETS original series 209 (London: Oxford University Press, 1940, reprint 1987), 316.

man."[12] A popular tale regarding the penance of Adam and Eve portrayed women as spiritually weaker than men and more prone to sin. The version found in *Festial* records how Adam and Eve stood in chin-high water for penance after banishment from the Garden of Eden. Three times the devil appeared to Eve in the form of an angel, persuading her that God was satisfied with her devotion and that she could stop performing penance. Each time Adam ordered her to return to the water. The third time he lost his patience with Eve's weakness. "'Wretched woman, God of his goodness made [you] of one of my ribs to help me; and now you are busy by teaching of the devil afterwards to ensnare me. But think on that; for our former sin stank so in God's nose, that all our offspring shall be infected ... Wherefore though we might do as much penance as all our offspring, it were to little to acquit us to our God." Rebuked by the wisdom of her husband, a meek Eve returned and performed her penance until the end of her life. The story concludes that because of her diligence, she achieved holiness and was able to come "to the joy of paradise, and to the life that ever shall last."[13] This tale reminded parishioners that women needed to remain beneath the authority of men for their own spiritual safety; a lesson that was re-learned each time church bells tolled for a death, as the number rung reminded parishioners that woman came from man and thus should be subordinate to him.

Writers of pastoral handbooks accentuated women's dependent status in the secular world. Mirk's *Instructions for Parish Priests* and the fifteenth-century clerical handbook included in BL MS Sloane 1584 rendered women as less active in the medieval economy than men.[14] Both include queries about economic activities. *Instructions* probes the economic honesty of parishioners within its penitential section. It queries regraters, brewers, millers, and other types of merchants if they have used false measures or weights. Under a discussion of the deadly sin of

---

12 *Speculum Sacerdotal*, 234.

13 *Festial*, 67–68. Although this story does highlight negative stereotypes about women, the point of the story is not so much the weakness of Eve but rather the idleness of Eve which caused her to sin. Unlike other versions of the Fall, Mirk's story "does not spell out as clearly" the sin "attributable to Adam and Eve or the natural weaknesses of the female sex." Christine Peters, *Patterns of Piety: Women, Gender and Religion in Late Medieval and Reformation England* (New York and Cambridge: Cambridge University Press, 2003), 133.

14 Noted by P.S. Joliffe in his *Check-list of Middle English Prose Writings of Spiritual Guidance*, Subsidia Mediaevalia 2 (Toronto: Pontifical Institute of Mediaeval Studies, 1974). BL MS Sloane 1584 was attributed to John Gysborn, Canon of Coverham, in 1782 by Samuel Ayscough. Ayscough described the manuscript as, "The Mynystration of the Dekyn and Subdekyne. Questions and Directions for Confession. Prayers in Metre to the virgin Mary and the Saints. On Hermits Life. Historical account of confession. Account of a miracle, recorded in a book fastened with a chain in the Mynster at Exeter. Prayers to the virgin Mary and the saints." Samuel Ayscough, *A Catalogue of the Manuscripts Preserved in the British Museum hitherto Undescribed: Consisting of Five Thousand Volumes; Including the Collections of Sir Hans Sloane Bart. The Rev. Thomas Birth, D.D., By Samuel Ayscough, Clerk* (London: John Rivington, 1782). *Fasti Parochiales Vol. IV: Being notes on the advowsons and pre-Reformation incumbents of the parishes in the Deanery of Craven*, eds. Norah K.M. Gurney and Sir Charles Clay, The Yorkshire Archaeological Society Record Series 133 (Leeds: Yorkshire Archaeological Society, 1971), does not list a John Gysborn as a canon; however it does list Bro. John Gisburgh as a canon of Coverham for 1521. Very little research has been conducted on the manuscript. What is known is that it was written in the fifteenth century by a member of the Premonstratensians Order, presumably John Gysborn, was formerly owned by Robynett Lyonne, and is clearly a clerical instruction handbook – containing a *Sermo in die Pasche*, a tract on the life of a hermit, a treatises on confession, Rules of the Order for Premonstratensians, and several other entries of a religious nature.

avarice, the penitent is asked if anything has been retained from workmen or if the penitent has beguiled anyone in trade. A third passage under venial sins moves from discussing commercial larceny to agricultural pilfering, questioning if the penitent's animals have been allowed to graze in a field without permission of the field's owner; if the penitent has destroyed the crop of another; if the penitent has stolen ears of corn while walking through a field; and if the penitent has "prone over corn to ride, when you might have gone beside?"[15]

Another contemporary and very detailed pastoral vernacular handbook, BL MS Sloane 1584, makes similar queries. Along with specific directions for the ministrations of deacons and subdeacons and recipes for medicine and cooking, including one to make Eucharist bread, the manuscript contains questions to be used in extracting confessions. It asks if the penitent has plowed any land, "willingly or knowingly," that belonged to another; if the holy days and Sundays have been kept from worldly labor; and if tithes and offerings to Holy Church have been paid.[16] Together the penitential inquiries of *Instructions* and BL MS Sloane 1584 would have helped ferret out cheating parishioners working in both commercial and agricultural pursuits. *Instructions for Parish Priests* even targets the stray passer-by inclined to pinch dinner instead of earning it.

Yet the questions in *Instructions* and Sloane 1584 seem intended for male penitents alone. BL MS Sloane 1584 contains five sections directed to different sorts of parishioners: general penitents, husbandmen, women, servant men or women, and singlewomen. The questions regarding work on Sundays and plowing fields were placed selectively underneath the section for "husbandmen." The only work-related questions directed to women occur in the section for "servant men or women." They concern obedience to masters and tithe payment.[17] Moreover, a later penitential section in the manuscript queries if husbands have provided their families with "food and drink and clothing" – clearly suggesting that the husband was the economic provider – while querying wives only if they have been "obedient to their husband at bed and at board."[18] Despite some variations in the seven extant manuscripts, Mirk also addressed work-related questions in *Instructions for Parish Priests* primarily to male penitents, directing every question concerning commercial and agricultural work to men. Mirk claimed in *Instructions* that men become so wrapped up in their work that they often neglected proper devotion on holy days and Sundays. He also reserved questions regarding false weights and measures used to cheat customers for men.[19] The passage covering the seven deadly sins seems directed toward male penitents as it opens "therefore, son, spare thee not" repeats "son" on several occasions, and relies exclusively on male pronouns. In fact, female pronouns, female categories, and the words, "if she be a woman," appear in *Instructions for Parish Priests* only one more time: under the sin of *luxuria*. Of course, some pastoral literature does place women in the working world. BL MS Sloane 1584 directs penitential questions specifically to female domestic servants, and *Speculum Sacerdotal* states that "women owe for

---

[15] *Instructions for Parish Priests*, 120–123, 135–136, 146–147, quote from Royal MS, 211.

[16] BL MS Sloane 1584, f. 7v.

[17] Ibid., ff. 7v–10r.

[18] Ibid., f. 75r.

[19] This remains consistent regardless of the manuscript. *Instructions*, 120–123, 135–136, 146–147, 200, 206, and 211.

to cease from their works" in holy observance the week after Easter. Yet *Speculum Sacerdotal* categorizes women's work differently from men's work, arguing "it is lawful to men for to till and use works of the earth," but women must cease because, "rural work be more needful than other."[20] This de-emphasis on women's ability to earn their own bread, as well as the classification of women's work as less important than men's, suggests that priests tended to perceive women as needing male providers – helping to tether women as appendages of husbands, fathers, and masters instead of approaching them as autonomous parishioners.

Historical records reveal a contrasting tale. Many women in late medieval England worked in occupations other than tending to their households, earning money both for their families and for themselves.[21] They labored as brewsters, hucksters (retailers), weavers, bakers, tanners, glovers, skinners, traders, dyers, domestic servants, millers, laundresses, shepsters, and, of course, prostitutes.[22] Some women gained success in local land markets; some worked only on the side, earning extra money as spinners or brewsters; and some, such as domestic servants, worked full time "living and laboring in the households of other people."[23] Of course, some of these occupations were extensions of household duties, such as brewing, weaving, and baking. But that does not mitigate the importance of their monetary contributions to household economies, nor does it mean that these occupations would not have encountered the same types of moral challenges as men's occupations. In her study of women and brewing in late medieval and early modern England, Judith Bennett has found that not only did some women in the food and drink trade cheat their customers – such as Alice wife of Robert de Causton of London who used a false measure to sell her ale – but that these women were branded by medieval culture as more likely than men to cheat their customers. "All victualers were suspected of cheating in their trade, and all brewers and alesellers were censured for causing drunkenness and disorder. But brewsters and tapsters suffered from these suspicions more than male victualers, male brewers, and male alesellers," she has argued. "The cultural repertoire of late medieval and early modern England suggested that all the problems associated with brewing – cheating, foul products, disorderly houses, and a host of other uncontrollable disruptions – were caused not by the trade itself but by the presence of women in the trade. Very real anxieties about the trade were displaced in a very unrealistic fashion onto just *female* brewers and *female* alesellers."[24] Hence,

---

20  *Speculum Sacerdotal*, 128.
21  To use the modern description, "worked outside the home," would not be accurate in late medieval England as many jobs, for both men and women, were extensions of the household.
22  For more information about women and work, see: Judith Bennett, *Ale, Beer, and Brewsters*; P.J.P. Goldberg, "Women's Work, Women's Role, in the Late-Medieval North," in *Profit, Piety and the Professions in Later Medieval England*, ed. M.A. Hicks (Gloucester: A. Sutton, 1990), 34–50; Diane Hutton, "Women in Fourteenth-Century Shrewsbury," in *Women and Work in Pre-Industrial England*, eds. Lindsay Charles and Lorna Duffin (London: Croom Helm, 1985), 83–99; Derek Keene, "Tanner's Widows, 1300–1350," in *Medieval London Widows*, ed. Caroline Barron (London: Hambledon, 1994), 1–27; Maryanne Kowaleski, "Women's Work in a Market Town: Exeter in the Late Fourteenth Century," in *Women and Work in Preindustrial Europe*, ed. Barbara Hanawalt (Bloomington: Indiana University Press, 1986), 149–159.
23  Judith M. Bennett and Amy M. Froide, "A Singular Past," in their *Singlewomen in the European Past: 1250–1800* (Philadelphia: University of Pennsylvania Press, 1999), 1–37, at 8.
24  Judith Bennett, *Ale, Beer, and Brewsters*, 137, 132, and 141. Bennett also has found that popular texts (such as *Piers Plowman* and *The Tunning of Elynour Rummyng*) presented alewives as

according to medieval culture, female parishioners needed spiritual guidance about commercial integrity. But since authors of vernacular pastoral literature often excluded women from discussions of the medieval working world, they might not have received such advice as often as their male counterparts.

Discussions of laboring people in pastoral vernacular literature were most likely to appear in sermon stories. Encompassing both exempla, in which the emphasis rests on the moral of the narrative, and saint *legenda*, in which the emphasis rests on the personality of a saint, sermon stories provide ideal windows through which to view pastoral perceptions about medieval life. First, exempla and *legenda* were rooted in reality. The point of sermon stories was to teach parishioners how to behave and what to believe. As such, the narratives providing examples to emulate had to be realistic enough to convince people of their value. "They were meaningful to the listeners because they depicted situations from everyday life," Ruth Mazo Karras has stated. "What people respond to – what they find humorous or interesting, poignant or frightening – varies over time and space, and the compilers and preachers must have chosen their exempla accordingly."[25] One of the most well-known medieval stories verifies the Virgin Birth. According to the tale, a midwife named Salome helped the Blessed Virgin Mary give birth to Jesus. Doubting the plausibility of a maiden conceiving, Salome placed her hand inside the sacred womb. To her surprise she found Mary's virginity quite intact. To her horror she discovered that the ill-gotten knowledge came with a price: her blasphemous arm shriveled.[26] This sermon story combines a well-known biblical account, the birth of Christ, with the familiar medieval figure of the midwife and the familiar medieval test for authenticating virginity. By simply reading the story, a medieval priest would have proven the 1500 year-old Virgin Birth through using standards contemporary to his parishioners. Thus the behavior of the character Salome created a realistic, and doctrinally useful, narrative.

Second, because sermon stories were written, modified, and filtered by clerics, they displayed the world from a distinctly clerical angle. The morals of exempla bolstered vital orthodox teachings, and the dead spiritual helpmates of *legenda* encouraged faith among living Christians. Religious men and women appear frequently in the tales: keeping tabs on local parishioners, admonishing one another, performing the sacraments, experiencing visions of spiritual signifi-cance, and revealing the expertise of the clerical realm. An exemplum in *Festial*'s feast for Corpus Christi provides a vivid example. It records how some clerics doubted transubstantiation (specifically the transformation of wine into blood),

---

especially prone to dishonesty in fourteenth-century England. For example, William Langland describes a brewster in *Piers Plowman* as "breaking almost every possible rule for the production and sale of ale – providing poor-quality ale to the poor, hiding her best ale for preferred customers only, charging exorbitant prices, and measuring with nonstandard cups." Representations such as this "suggested that brewsters would cheat more than male brewers, would temptingly lure men into the gluttonous and sexual sins of alehouses, and would flagrantly resist the rule of men. If alehouses were 'the devil's schoolhouse,' then women were the devil's schoolmistresses – diso-beying men, deceiving them, leading them into both gluttony and lechery, and of course profiting at their expense," 122–144, at 126 and 135. For late medieval court records revealing women engaged in dishonest practices, see Emilie Amt, *Women's Lives in Medieval Europe: A Sourcebook* (New York and London: Routledge, 1993), 184–188 and 203–205.

25 Karras, *Common Women*, 105.

26 *Festial* provides a version of this story, 23.

and a bishop, sorrowing for their unbelief, prayed that God would make the truth known. The final section provides an account of the bishop performing mass: "When he had broken the Eucharist bread "as the manner is, he saw the blood drop down from the host quickly into the chalice. Then he made signs to them that misbelieved, to come and see. And when they saw his fingers bloody and blood run of Christ's body into the chalice, they were horrified that for true fear they cried and said: 'Be thou blessed, man, that has this grace thus to handle Christ's body!'"[27] The graphic detail and personal nature of this depiction suggests first-hand knowledge of this sacred duty. Thus these stories provide a view from the altar, both of clerical actions and clerical perceptions about the men and women they served.

As it was the most popular and prolific orthodox vernacular sermon compilation in late medieval England, not to mention containing more sermon stories than most contemporary sermon collections, *Festial* can be used as an exemplar to measure the type of characters presented within its 110 exempla.[28] On first glance, *Festial* seems to portray a realistic view of the medieval working world. Narrative characters appear as husbandmen, penny-reeves, bailiffs, hired hands, merchants, musicians, chapmen, charcoal-burners, soldiers, thieves, scholars, clerics, and knights. A second glance, however, reveals that few of the working characters are female. The only firm occupations portrayed by women in *Festial* are those of nun and prostitute. Moreover, only one woman *might* be engaged in a legitimate taxable trade: Lasma, the woman who baked the holy loaf for Pope Gregory. But, while she could be a professional baker, the story mentions her as only "working" for Gregory.[29] An account of this same story in *Speculum Sacerdotal* diminishes further the likelihood that Lasma was regarded as a professional baker. Instead of providing the misbelieving woman with a name, as in *Festial*, the exemplum in *Speculum Sacerdotal* identifies her merely as "a housewife."[30] Of course, it cannot be assumed that the term "housewife" in late medieval England carried the same meaning as it does today. Historians such as Judith Bennett and Diane Hutton have established that many women's jobs were extensions of their household duties, as women earned money for their households by selling excess beer and food. Lasma could simply have been one of these women, working from her home. Yet, it is significant that, unlike her male counterparts in exempla, Lasma was not identified as a professional. In fact, women are identified by occupation only six times within *Festial* exempla: twice as nuns, once as abbess, twice as prostitutes, and perhaps once as baker (Lasma).[31]

This assessment is a stark contrast from women living in the Shropshire of Mirk's parents and grandparents. Women were taxed 171 times in Shrewsbury from 1297 to 1336. As "tax charges fell only on those inhabitants who were heads of households engaged in producing or trading in goods," we know that these women worked in legitimate occupations for their livelihood and ran their own households as either widows or singlewomen.[32] Their occupations ranged from

---

27  Ibid., 170–171.
28  See Appendix II for a description of each exemplum in *Festial*.
29  Ibid., 173.
30  *Speculum Sacerdotal*, 39.
31  See Appendix II, nos. 108, 31, 45, and 63.
32  D. and R. Cromarty, *The Wealth of Shrewsbury in the Early Fourteenth Century: Six Local Subsidy*

tanner to butcher, chandler, brewster, spicer, mercer, potter, and trader. Several even possessed livestock. Of course, as Diane Hutton has argued successfully, these female workers were less organized, less stable, and employed in less profitable trades than their male counterparts. Women indeed worked more frequently in regrating, brewing, and spinning than in more lucrative professions such as dyeing, tailoring, and shoemaking.[33] Yet the low status, low pay, and instability of women's work does not negate the fact that women worked consistently in medieval Shrewsbury.

Instead of portraying women as workers, *Festial* most often identified women through the traditional categories of virgin, wife, and mother, depicting the majority of its female exempla characters as mothers, wives, and religious women. Thus, from the Jewish mother protecting her child from her husband to the abbess punished by God for her lecherous mouth, most women in exempla were characterized by their relationship to men (either earthly or spiritual) rather than by self-created work identities (such as merchant or baker).[34] Confined to either the domestic or religious life, female exempla characters also experienced a limited range of motion in *Festial*. Mirk portrayed most of these women in two places: home and church. Of the remaining female characters, only two women traveled (one with her husband and one on pilgrimage) and only four appeared outdoors (three as tormented spirits in visions by men, one as a demon-disguised mistress).[35] Even the wicked woman who masterminded the death of a rich merchant (and ultimately the demise of herself and her husband) never moved. She would tell her husband what to do; he would do it, and report back to her. When they finally met their prophesied doom, she never emerged from the castle that consumed them both when it caught fire and sank into hell. Ironically, one of the more "mobile" female characters was the devil-disguised virgin-princess. According to what she told the bishop, she crept from her house in the middle of the night and sought the bishop to ask for his protection.[36] Yet, despite the ground traveled in between, she still stayed within Mirk's usual settings for women: her home and the church.

Conversely, Mirk depicted his men in much more multi-faceted ways. Male exempla characters, unlike their female counterparts, were most often identified by occupation: at least ninety-nine times in comparison to the mere six times that women were identified by occupation. Male exempla characters worked as thieves, students, charcoal makers, reeves, court officers, servants, soldiers, knights, churchwardens, harpists, merchants, moneylenders, farmers, and kings – as well as husbands, fathers, bishops, priests, and monks. They also were very active. From a priest running through the field, to a charcoal worker sitting by a bonfire, to a little boy on the beach, Mirk envisioned men as more mobile than women. They were pilgrims walking through the countryside, soldiers dying in battle, lepers arguing in the street, sick people journeying to shrines, and students attending classes. Men appeared in Ireland, Italy, France, and Jerusalem, traveling

---

*Rolls 1297 to 1322: Text and Commentary* (Shrewsbury, Shropshire: Shropshire Archaeological and Historical Society, 1993), 35.

[33] Hutton, "Women in Fourteenth Century Shrewsbury," 83–99.

[34] See Appendix II, nos. 79 and 31.

[35] See Appendix II, nos. 8, 72, 34, 101, 102, 104.

[36] Appendix II, nos. 27 and 2.

by foot, horses, and ships. Even Mirk's male monastics were active. While the talkative abbess whispered to her (enclosed) sisters and the virtuous nun prayed within her cell, monks waded in the ocean, visited shrines, traveled to see visions of Mary, and went to the Holy Land.[37] Thus it seems that Mary Flowers Braswell's assessment of Mirk's men as a "noisy, active bunch" is correct.[38] Comparatively, his women were quiet and still.

This rendering of women as significantly less active than their male counterparts presents a skewed portrayal of female autonomy. Late medieval English women survived independently from male authority. Many even flourished. Twice-widowed Isabel Borrey became one of the wealthiest inhabitants of Shrewsbury in the early fourteenth century. As a prosperous merchant she flourished in the international wool trade, owned property throughout Shrewsbury and Shropshire, and financed loans and credit for various knights and lords. She even hosted Edward II at one of her homes in 1322. Although not as affluent, singlewoman such as Agnes le Roo profitably brewed ale in Shrewsbury from 1297 to 1316, along with the proliferation of women documented by Hutton as participating in commercial pursuits.[39] Moreover, women were not confined to domestic and religious spaces. Margery le Wyte traveled from a tavern in Bedford towards Wooten on 10 September 1301. She died trying to break up a fight among her companions. Emma daughter of William the Wiredrawer was arrested in York for wandering around at night after curfew; Margery the Walker took Jon Lok to court in Shrewsbury, 1382, over a debt of 2s. 4d.; and Sibilla Smith of Shrewsbury filled the King's highway with dung in 1400, perhaps protesting her conviction as a common scold.[40] Even Margery Kempe, despite her frequent conflicts with religious authorities, traveled freely throughout England and Europe, making her way from Norwich to Canterbury to the Holy Land and back. Thus working and mobile women would have been nothing new in Mirk's time, as real women participated in the markets of fourteenth- and fifteenth-century England, moving freely throughout village and urban landscapes. The manuscripts of *Festial*, *Instructions for Parish Priests*, and BL MS Sloane 1584, however, present late medieval women as more likely to depend on male providers than make their own way in the world.

## "SIRENS"

Along with sustaining women's traditional dependence on men, clerical authors also maintained the traditional association of women with unbridled sexuality. Durham Cathedral Cosin MS V IV 3 preserves eleven sermons from the Bedfordshire cycle, including one from *Festial*. But unlike the other Bedfordshire manuscripts, the Durham manuscript contains a series of sketches, drawn by the

---

[37] *Festial*, 174, 105, 167, 97, 300, 5, 100, 234, and 302.
[38] Mary Braswell, *The Medieval Sinner: Characterization and Confession in the Literature of the English Middle Ages* (Rutherford, Madison and Teaneck: Fairleigh Dickinson University Press, 1983), 88.
[39] Cromarty, *The Wealth of Shrewsbury*, 35, 44–52, 55–65; Hutton, "Women in Fourteenth Century Shrewsbury," 83–99.
[40] Amt, *Women's Lives in Medieval Europe*, 192 and 73; Hutton, "Women in Fourteenth Century Shrewsbury," 92 and 98.

compiler or doodled by a (perhaps somewhat bored) reader. From the margins leer a caricature of a Jewish man sporting a hat; a man's face; a serpent with what appears to be a woman's head; and "sirens," as the artist himself identified the figures: women with long hair, large breasts, and curling tails.[41] One holds both a comb (a sign of prostitution) and a fish (the sign of a soul ensnared by the devil).[42]

Images of lascivious women appear frequently in parish church woodcarvings. A siren very similar to the ones drawn in the margins of Durham Cathedral Cosin MS V IV 3 appears on a *misericord* in Ludlow St. Lawrence. Instead of a comb and fish, however, she holds a mirror "suggesting vanity."[43] Peter Klein, in his descriptive pamphlet of the woodcarvings in Ludlow, described the mermaid as "symbolic of the fair seductress luring men away with fair words from the path of salvation to their destruction on the rocks of passion." Similar mermaids appear on misericords in Norwich, Ely, Great Malvern, Ripon, Westminster Abbey, Gloucester, Stratford-on-Avon, and Beverly Minster. A different sort of antifeminist carving appears in Ludlow: a harpy. Like the siren, the harpy represents a lascivious woman, "rapacious and craving gratification, who uses her charms to destroy her man."[44] A misericord in Ely Cathedral relays the popular tale of the evil New Testament woman Salome.[45] According to the biblical story, Salome's mother Herodias married her brother-in-law Herod Antipas in first-century Jerusalem. John the Baptist angered Herodias by publicly denouncing this incestuous marriage. One night during a dinner party, Salome enchanted Herod by her graceful, and perhaps seductive, dancing. He granted her one wish, and she (at the suggestion of her mother) requested the head of John the Baptist on a silver platter. Herod regretfully acquiesced. The *misericord* carver depicts the moment in which a kneeling Salome receives the freshly-cut head of John the Baptist. "Given these treacherous images, it is not surprising that women during the Middle Ages were often treated unfavorably under both Church and civil law … If the woman was beautiful, she was likely to be considered all the more dangerous for, in true medieval fashion, beauty in a woman did not necessarily mean simply that she was beautiful but that, perhaps, the beauty hid 'filth beneath the skin.'"[46] With so many depictions of women as evil beasts and sexual temptresses peppering fifteenth-century church woodcarvings, medieval people (including clerics) probably would have considered this association ordinary.

These images of sexually voracious women can be traced repeatedly not only in the woodcarvings of parish churches but also in the texts of pastoral literature. Just as the mermaid wielding the mirror, comb, and fish betrays her lecherous and sinful intentions, emotive warnings about female sexuality run through clerical

---

41    Durham Cathedral Cosin MS V IV 3, ff. 27v, 24v, 26v, and 11v.

42    Challis, *Life in Medieval England*, 41. See also, Juanita Wood, *Wooden Images: Misericords and Medieval England* (Madison: Fairleigh Dickinson University Press, 1999), 30–31.

43    Challis, *Life in Medieval England*, 41.

44    Peter Klein, *The Misericords & Choir Stalls of Ludlow Parish Church* (Birmingham: Ludlow Parochial Church Council, 1986), 3. A harpy is a creature similar to a siren, usually half-woman and half-beast. In this instance, the siren is half-young woman and half-bat.

45    This is not Salome the midwife attending to the Blessed Virgin Mary. This Salome is the stepdaughter of Herod Antipas.

46    Wood, *Wooden Images*, 34. Wood also discusses depictions of Salome and St. John the Baptist, 33–34.

vernacular literature. A sermon found in Bodl. MS Bodley 95 (a sermon compilation related to Shrewsbury School MS 3 and *Middle English Sermons*) states that women adorn themselves for the sole purpose of enticing men to lechery. "Many women use" their dressed-up bodies, decorated with garlands and pearls, "as a mirror of the devil to blind men with and it accords more to a strumpet than to a good woman."[47] Richard of Lavynham's *Treatise on the Seven Deadly Sins* confirms this, arguing women make themselves appear "fair and fresher than nature has granted with nice cheer of looking of going and delectable words drawing men's hearts to folly and to sin."[48] Similarly, the *Book of Vices and Virtues* warns that women dress themselves "with precious apparel for pure vanity and for to do liking and draw folk to sin … and make themselves like fools and not good women."[49] These texts directly link female appearance to the sin of lechery. *Middle English Sermons* solidifies this connection by arguing that the devil employs feminine appearance to ensnare men. A sermon for the First Sunday following Easter alleges that the fiend prowls to regain the souls lost during the devotions of Lent. The time is ripe for him, as parishioners have returned to eating and drinking delicious meals, the weather has turned fair and warm, and women are "nicely arrayed."[50] The sermon for Christmas day drives home the point that women use their sexual attractiveness to deceive men. First, it states plainly that, "much people are steered astray, Ay! and assent to lechery by the nice array of women."[51] Second, it tells the story of Judith and Holofernes. Holofernes was a prince determined to control Israel, but he was thwarted by a widow dwelling in Bethulia. When Holofernes attempted to capture that city, Judith dressed herself alluringly and attracted the attention of the prince. He brought her into his tent for a night of lovemaking, but instead Judith sliced off his head with a sword and thus rescued the city. *Middle English Sermons* ends the account with an unveiled warning. "Lo, sirs, here may you see how that a prince that lacked a great part of the world might not overcome but was destroyed by the nice array and attire of a woman."[52] The androcentric imperative "sirs" seems entirely appropriate for this occasion. The point of the narrative was to warn men against the sexual deceitfulness of women.

*Quattuor Sermones*, a late fifteenth-century pastoral manual often bound with printed versions of *Festial*, states that the attractiveness of women, even women without ill-will in mind, causes the damnation of souls. "Therefore, you women, array not yourself to nicely to be seen of fools though you have no will to sin yourself, for your nice array and countenance been cause of many soul's damnation for the which you shall answer at the high day of doom."[53] It also directs male

47  Bodl. MS Bodley 95, f. 21v.
48  Richard of Lavynham, *A Litil Tretys on the Seven Deadly Sins*, ed. J.P.W.M. van Zutphen (Rome: Institutum Carmelitanum, 1956), 23.
49  *The Book of Vices and Virtues: A Fourteenth Century English Translation of the Somme le Roi of Lorens d'Orleans*, ed. W. Nelson Francis, EETS original series 217 (London: Oxford University Press, 1942), 179.
50  *Middle English Sermons*, 133.
51  Ibid., 234.
52  Ibid., 234–5.
53  *Quattuor Sermones: Printed by William Caxton*, ed. N.F. Blake, Middle English Texts 2 (Heidelberg: Winter, 1975), 31. Based on the English Translation of Archbishop Thoresby's *Lay Folk's Catechism*, *Quattuor Sermones* contained the paternoster, creed, ten commandments, seven sacraments, seven

readers to run away from women to avoid lechery. The apostle Paul, the manuscript claims, ordered people to "flee the occasions" of lechery. "That is to say sight of women, kissing, touching and such other." In this way, the manuscript reminds, "escaped Joseph the sin of his lady when he left his pall or mantel with her and ran away."[54] This biblical story of a male who successfully escaped the entrapment of a lascivious female is followed by the sobering names of three biblical men who succumbed to the wiles of women. David, who destroyed his family and nearly lost his kingdom on account of his affair with Bathsheba; Solomon, who cost his family the kingdom on account of his love for idolatrous women; and Samson, who betrayed his country and himself to the Philistines on account of his love for Delilah. These men serve as solemn reminders that seductive women create chaos and destruction.

Like the woodcuts, pastoral literature regularly voices the presumption of women as dangerous sexually. *Speculum Sacerdotal* argues that spiritually "uncircumcised" people (those trapped in deadly sin) can be identified by their association with "evil women." "They be uncircumcised … that follow the likings and foul sweetness that they feel in strumpets and evil women, and also that array their chambers or beds with flowers, fruits, ointments, or spices for to have the more lust to sin."[55] Similarly, *Middle English Sermons* buttresses this link between fair women and evil, arguing that hypocrites are like the "foul fiend … that appeared to Adam and Eve in Paradise and showed a fair woman's face him to beguile and under that [fair] face there was hid a foul fiend."[56]

Exempla provide further support for this supposition, as sexual sin is the transgression most often committed by female exempla characters. Out of the thirty-four ordinary female exempla characters in *Festial*, twenty-two engaged in some sort of sinful activity.[57] A nun was rebuked for rushing her prayers; two lay women gossiped during mass; St. Katherine reprimanded one woman for leaving her devotions; Lasma doubted the efficacy of the blessed Host; three characters wronged their children; and three committed unspecified evil acts. Sexual temptation, however, proved the Achilles' heel for ten of the twenty-two female characters engaged in sinful activity. Two tempted male characters; one was sorely tempted by a male character; six lived in lecherous lifestyles; and one (a nun) had a dirty mouth that enticed others to lechery.[58] This same pattern repeats itself in *Middle English Sermons*, as seven of the twelve female characters identified by their sinful actions were accused of some sort of sexual sin.[59] *Speculum*

---

deeds of mercy, seven deadly sins, and a passage on contrition, confession, and satisfaction. Caxton printed it 11 times in the late fifteenth century.

54    Ibid., 60.

55    *Speculum Sacerdotal*, 17.

56    *Middle English Sermons*, 294.

57    See Appendix II, nos. 2, 6, 7, 16, 27, 28, 30, 31, 34, 42, 45, 49, 63, 78, 94, 96, 101, 102, 104, and 108, for the female characters engaged in sinful activity. Thirty-four is the number of ordinary individual, not-saint female exempla characters (I excluded the Blessed Virgin Mary, Eve, and the two female saint characters Elizabeth and Katherine, see nos. 4, 5, 16, 18, 19, 21, 23, 33, 36, 37, 39, 76, 77, 79, 80, 85, 86, 94, 108, and 110). Approximately fifty-five individual female exempla characters (excluding groups of people, such as the thousand-plus mothers in no. 10) appear in the 110 exempla of *Festial*.

58    See Appendix II, nos. 2, 6, 31, 34, 45, 78, 101, 102 and 104.

59    BL M Royal 18 B XXIII contains ten exempla portraying sinful female characters, although only eight of these were published in *Middle English Sermons*. The exempla may be found: f. 49r, f. 73r,

*dotal*, however, takes the prize for stereotyping women, as eight of the nine female exempla characters identified by their sinful actions were portrayed as engaging in lecherous activity.[60]

Moreover, as far as clerical authors were concerned, the lustfulness of women was not confined to prostitutes. It was a fault of *all* women: daughters, wives, widows, nuns, and prostitutes. The author of *Speculum Sacerdotal* clarifies this point, incorporating within his exempla lecherous female characters from each of these walks of life. First, he relays a story of a daughter who became pregnant out of wedlock and then lied about the father of her child: "the "daughter of a rich man," who "had changed her flower of virginity for the seed of a lemon." When her friends and family angrily pressed her for the name of the father, she accused a deacon. The child itself exonerated the victim by speaking through the power of the Holy Spirit, "The deacon is chaste and holy, and he never fouled his body with no woman."[61] Second, he relays the story of a lustful wife who murdered her brother-in-law. The woman burned with passion for her husband on Easter morning. He refused her, as married couples were to abstain from sex three day before receiving the sacrament as well as abstaining during the 40 days of Lent, and left to attend church services. Able to think only of quenching her lust, the wife tried to seduce her brother-in-law. The young man, aghast at the request of his brother's wife, also refused her. The woman became incensed with desire and anger, grabbed a sword and smote off his head. When her husband returned, she accused him, saying, "Lo, all this I have done you have made me to do."[62] Third, he relays the story of a widow who, among other crimes, intentionally seduced clergymen. Because the widow literally sold her soul to the devil, the devil made her promise to deprive the poor of alms, interrupt prayers in church with her chattering, refuse to confess her sins, and tempt clerics to sin sexually. She was saved from hell by the penance of her faithful son.[63] Fourth, the author of *Speculum Sacerdotal* tells of a nun who succumbed to sexual desire and eventually became a prostitute. Devoted to the service of the Blessed Virgin Mary, the nun was enticed by the sensual words of an attractive young man. Abandoning a life of chastity for immorality, she plunged from nun to mistress to prostitute. After fifteen years she returned broken and destitute to the abbey, only to find that the Blessed Virgin Mary had fulfilled her duties during her absence and no one suspected the sinful life she had been living. She repented and lived a godly life in the convent.[64]

The moral of these stories was simple: women from all walks of life – daughter, wife, widow, and nun – were sexually traitorous, unable to bridle lust and desire. A final exemplum from *Speculum Sacerdotal* explains the reasoning behind this paradigm. A wife was required to attend the dedication of an oratory for Saint Sebastian. The night before the service, however, she burned with lust for her

---

and the printed edition 216, 62, 148, 154, 161, 183, 216, 219. The sexually sinful female characters may be found: f. 73r and the printed edition 148, 154 (this is perhaps the only questionable inclusion, as the woman is accused of staring at men in church instead of concentrating on her prayers), 161, 183, and 219.

60  *Speculum Sacerdotal*, 39, 42, 94, 123, 127, 202, 218, and 227.

61  Ibid., 218.

62  Ibid., 128. This exemplum also highlights the contradictions of the marriage debt. For further discussion, see below, 77–78.

63  Ibid., 226–227.

64  Ibid., 202–203.

husband and he (seemingly with little resistance) yielded to her desire. When the relics had been carried into the church the next day, an evil spirit entered the weak-willed and sexually impure woman. Her neighbors tried to help by taking her to sorcerers, but she soon worsened when a legion of demons captured her body. Finally her friends brought her to a bishop who prayed for her until the devils released their grip on her soul. "And therefore, dear friends, you may perceive and know by this relation what crime and peril it is for to incline to lusts and lechery in such holy times." Married couples, the exemplum reminds, should take abstinence during holy times seriously. Even though husbands and wives are required to pay the marriage debt, husbands should remember that "woman has no power of her body, but the man has."[65]

This explanation for women's lasciviousness, "woman has no power of her body," also provided husbands, at least, with a convenient excuse for indulging in sex: they had to succumb to protect their wives. The fictional sexually deprived woman who killed her brother-in-law implicated her husband in the sin because, if he had given up his body in the first place, the murder would never have occurred. Thus the exemplum reports him sharing equally in the penance of his wife.[66] This story fits well with medieval teachings about the marriage debt. Both husbands and wives were required to pay the conjugal debt (submit to sex) whenever their spouse requested. The concept stemmed from the teachings of St. Paul (1 Corinthians 7:1–4) and was thought to protect married couples from committing more serious sins. For example, if the husband from the first exemplum had submitted to his wife's request, they would only have committed the sin of sex during a holy time instead of the far greater sins of attempted incest and murder. Yet, at the same time, the second exemplum suggests that when the husband acquiesced to the sexual demands of his wife, they still committed a serious sin which resulted in the demonic possession of the woman. Hence the dilemma of the marriage debt: if a spouse refused the debt it could lead to even greater sin (such as adultery, incest, and murder), yet if they rendered the debt, it still could lead to great sin (if committed during holy times or in holy places) with extreme consequences (such as demonic possession).

Unfortunately medieval pastoral literature provides little help in clarifying the contradictions of the conjugal debt, but – in a fashion similar to the exempla from *Speculum Sacerdotal* – it does emphasize the responsibility of husbands to render the marriage debt in order to protect their wives from more serious sin. *Quattuor Sermones* orders husbands not to make commitments of abstinence against the will of their wives, or else they would be held responsible for the sin of their wives: "for the wife has no power of her own body but the husband. And if the man abstain him from his wife by such wise without the will of his wife and she give him no leave he is cause of her sin."[67] Of course, *Quattuor Sermones*, along with *Speculum Sacerdotal*, briefly notes that wives owe the same courtesy to husbands: "and the wife is in the same case if she do the same to her husband." Yet the two sex-deprived exempla characters used by *Speculum Sacerdotal* were tellingly female. Moreover, the phrase "for the wife has no power of her own body, but

---

[65]   Ibid., 94–95.
[66]   Ibid., 127–128.
[67]   *Quattuor Sermones*, 44.

the husband" reverberates throughout the manuscripts while St. Paul's original addendum to this phrase in 1 Corinthians 7:3, "likewise the husband does not rule over his own body, but the wife does," is absent.[68]

"Woman" in sermons and clerical handbooks was not synonymous with sexual sin, but the two were close associates. When priests wrote about lechery, female parishioners came frequently to mind. Again, the words of Adam to Eve in *Festial* seem to echo the thoughts of medieval men, secular and regular alike: "Wretched woman, God of his goodness made [you] of one of my ribs to help me; and now you are busy by teaching of the devil afterwards to ensnare me."[69]

## EVE, MARY, AND AGNES LE ROO

All was not lost. While identifying women as dependent figures and emphasizing their sexuality, clerical authors of vernacular pastoral literature defended women from the accusatory image of Eve, offered protection and concern for women in their roles as wives and mothers, and recognized the existence of women outside of traditional marital roles. Clerical perceptions of women were not balanced; but neither were they one-sided.

To begin with, authors of pastoral literature excused women from the sin of Eve through the grace of Mary. This line of defense began with St. Paul in the first century. "For it was Adam who was first created, and then Eve. And it was not Adam who was deceived, but the woman being deceived, fell into transgression. But women will be preserved through the bearing of children if they continue in faith and love and sanctity with self-restraint," he stated in the New Testament epistle 1 Timothy 2:13–15. Clerical authors followed in Paul's footsteps, arguing that Eve was indeed at fault for the downfall of humanity, but that she was redeemed when Mary gave birth to Jesus. The author of *Speculum Sacerdotal* explained this in a sermon for the Nativity of Jesus. "Right as the devil by his crafty serpent incited the woman Eve for to taste the old apple, the which woman after steered her husband for to taste the same, through which tasting all the

---

68 Dyan Elliott has noted the interesting link between the privileging of men in interpretations of the marriage debt and the emphasis on women's bodies as belonging to their husbands. "The emphasis on the debt, intertwined with a seemingly benign paternalism, corresponds with cannon lawyer's growing precision about the husband's dominance and the dramatic increase in his control over his wife's person – an influence that eddied out into property law. This trend is inseparable from the concomitant emphasis on the wife's submission and unquestioning obedience. Certain authorities, such as the Dominican Raymond of Penafort, even justified the wife's acquiescence to the husband's quasi-sinful orders, arguing that, in obeying the husband, she was obeying God. Thus, in the high Middle Ages, the wife was remorselessly rendered *sub virga*: a phrase usually translated as 'under the rod of the husband,' signifying his rule, but which can also be translated as 'under the penis.'<l>" Of course, she also has noted that not all clerics subscribed to the idea of women as more lustful than men and that some assumed husbands to be sexual aggressors rather than their wives. Dyan Elliott, "Bernardino of Siena versus the Marriage Debt," in *Desire and Discipline: Sex and Sexuality in the Premodern West*, eds. Jacqueline Murray and Konrad Eisenbichler (Toronto: University of Toronto Press, 1996), 168–200, at 173 and 178–179. For more on the marriage debt, see: Elizabeth Makowski, "The Conjugal Debt and Medieval Canon Law," *Journal of Medieval History* 3 (1977), 99–114; James A. Brundage, "Sexual Equality in Medieval Canon Law," in *Medieval Women and the Sources of Medieval History*, ed. Joel T. Rosenthal (Athens: University of Georgia Press, 1990), 70–72.

69 *Festial*, 68.

world was lost, right so God showed unto a woman … the blessed Virgin Mary, that she should conceive a child the which should restore redemption and health to mankind." The sermon for Saturday before Easter emphasizes the significance of Christ appearing first to women after his resurrection, despite women being "of feebler and lesser kind." Because death entered the world through a woman, Christ appeared first to women to illustrate that salvation also came through the feminine sex. "And Christ did it for this reason, for it behooved that beginning of our reconciliation were showed to the world by a woman, right as the beginning of our death entered the world by a woman."[70]

This theological absolution carried practical implications for both male and female parishioners. Superficially, pastoral literature portrayed medieval women as caught between the competing images of Eve and Mary. As Christine Peters explains: "At one extreme was the figure of the Virgin Mary, embodying female virtues, and at the other the figure of Eve, symbolizing the disastrous consequences of female weakness and justifying women's inferiority and subordination."[71] Historians such as Alcuin Blamires, Penny Schine Gold, and Joan Ferrante (to name a few) have tackled this infamous dichotomy, both verifying its saturation of medieval culture and debating its actual impact on real men and women.[72] Joan Young Gregg, in her examination of medieval exempla, has even argued that the competing images of Mary and Eve were institutionalized by the Church to support their "misogynistic agenda." Because "the obverse figure to Marian veneration, and the female against whose sexuality and mortality Mary's physical intactness shone even brighter, was Eve, acknowledged in both theology and popular religion as the 'bad mother,' the first sinner who transmitted her transgression to the rest of the human race," the images of Mary and Eve presented real women with "a model that supported the church's misogynistic agenda. For while women could pray to Mary, repent of their sins because of her, and model their behavior on hers, they could never achieve her unique perfection as both mother and maid."[73] Sermon compilations and pastoral guides from fifteenth-century England seem less inclined toward this "misogynistic agenda" and more inclined toward – as Larissa Taylor has noted – stressing "the dignity of woman and her equal role in Christian life."[74]

On a theological level, clerical authors did not exonerate Eve. But, on a prac-

---

70  *Speculum Sacerdotal*, 6 and 115.

71  Christine Peters rightly argues that this juxtaposition of Eve and Mary "often leads to oversimplified conclusions based on the mistaken view that the nature and importance of this polarity was unchanging." In reality, "The familiar stereotype of Eve, enshrined in the idea of pit and pedestal, was a long way from the complex views offered to the late medieval laity." Peters, *Patterns of Piety*, 130 and 151.

72  *Woman Defamed and Woman Defended: An Anthology of Medieval Texts*, eds. Alcuin Blamires and Karen Pratt (Oxford: Clarendon Press, 1992); Penny Schine Gold, *The Lady and the Virgin: Image, Attitude, and Experience in Twelfth-Century France* (Chicago: University of Chicago Press, 1985); Joan Ferrante, *Woman as Image in Medieval Literature* (New York: Columbia University Press, 1975).

73  Joan Young Gregg, *Devils, Women, and Jews: Reflections of the Other in Medieval Sermon Stories* (Albany: State University of New York Press, 1997), 106.

74  Larissa Taylor, *Soldiers of Christ: Preaching in Late Medieval and Reformation France* (New York and Oxford: Oxford University Press, 1992), 157. Patricia Ranft has also discussed the positive attitudes toward women in sermon literature in her *Women and Spiritual Equality in Christian Tradition* (New York: St. Martin's Press, 1998), 195–211.

tical level, neither did they allow the shame that Eve brought on the female sex to adversely affect women. A sermon for Easter day in *Middle English Sermons* serves as case in point. It argues that God loves women and chose them expressly as vessels both for destruction and restoration, and thus men should never despise women on account of Eve's sin.

> Look now what messengers that Jesus has made of his resurrection. These iii women knew his private [affair] and showed and told that he was arisen from death to life. Lo, to them that were sorrowful and in will to [for]sake their sin, to them he showed his private [matters]. By women he sent for these words, for he entirely loved them. Through a woman we were lost, and through a woman we found comfort again; through a woman entered death, and through a woman came in again everlasting life. A woman brought Adam into much pain, and therefore Our Lady amended that was amiss, that woman should not be ashamed in that that she made Adam trespass. Therefore through Christ Adam was amended, for no man should have woman in contempt, for it is no wisdom to despise that God loves.[75]

Clerical authors also refused to allow men the privilege of excusing their sin as Adam did, claiming "the woman made me do it." Worcester Cathedral MS F 10 prohibits male parishioners from using the seed of Eve as an excuse for sin.

> For many men, when they come to shrift where they should accuse themselves, they excuse themselves and accuse other folk. For they say, "Sir I have sinned in pride, I have sinned in gluttony, I have sinned in lechery, but truly it was not my fault but all the fault was of the woman's seed." And a lie falsely, it is nothing so, but it is his own wretchedness and his own unrepentance.[76]

This principle is upheld in the story from *Festial* about the adulterous woman and her knighted lover. The knight's tormented ghost attempts to minimize his guilt, and therefore maximize pity for his plight, by claiming that each night for penance he slew and burned the woman for "she was cause of my sin." Yet he also suffered pain for his crime, as in his own words, "I ride here on a fiend like a horse, and this saddle burns hotter than any earthly fire; and thus we shall do till we are helped by some good man."[77] Women might be considered weaker than men, through fault of their mother Eve. But, according to the pastoral guides that priests used, men ultimately were responsible for their own actions.[78]

Moreover, pastoral literature protects women's roles as wives and mothers, expressing both concern and admiration.[79] Clerical authors understood that

---

[75] *Middle English Sermons*, 137.

[76] *Three Middle English Sermons From the Worcester Chapter Manuscript F. 10*, ed. D.M. Grisdale, Leeds School of English Language Texts and Monographs 5 (Kendal: Printed by T. Wilson for Members of the School of English Language in the University of Leeds, 1939), 45.

[77] *Festial*, 292.

[78] Christine Peters has noted that, "This tempering of stereotypes with notions of contextualized responsibility was a feature of catholicism throughout the medieval period, but in the later Middle Ages the movement away from rigid gender stereotypes, and judgements based upon them, was given a further stimulus." Peters also recognizes that exempla employed by Mirk emphasize male responsibility as well as female culpability. Peters, *Patterns of Piety*, 151 and 148–151.

[79] Although many women became mothers outside of matrimony, Mirk also valorized marriage, commending it as a sacred ceremony approved by God as holy. In his marriage sermon, for example, he stated that marriage was created because, "It is not good a man to be himself [alone]."

marriage could place women in precarious positions, leaving them at the mercy of neglectful, or even tyrannical, husbands. Penitential questions reveal attempts by clerics to enlighten husbands about harmful behavior within their marriages. *Instructions for Parish Priests* pointedly queries if a husband has been too self-absorbed and slothful to notice the needs of his wife and family. "Have you been sluggish and slow to help your wife and your family of such as they had need to?"[80] Similarly, BL MS Sloane 1584 and BL MS Cotton Vespasian A XXV investigate whether a husband has approached his wife and children with meekness, providing them with adequate food, drink, and clothing. "And [if] he be a man the priest shall ask him if he have by way of meekness born him to his wife and his children and has served them food and drink and clothing."[81] Raising the severity of the questions a notch, the author of Cambridge St. John's College MS S 35 inquired into the sexual faithfulness of a husband. Questions following a section on lechery ask the husband if his wife has reason to suspect him or speak evil of him.[82] The author of BL MS Sloane 1584 approached the subject directly. "Have you broken your wedlock with any woman besides your wife?"[83] Finally, authors of pastoral handbooks attempt to curb domestic arguments and violence. Statements within St. John's College MS S 35 warn parishioners not to cause wrath between husbands and wives, while a question in *Instructions for Parish Priests* asked if a male penitent had quarreled or had strife with his family or with his wife.[84] Although such queries might not have prevented marital problems, they at least indicate clerical awareness of domestic stresses and clerical concern for protecting the family structure.

Mirk's admiration for women in childbirth reflects his overall attitude toward women: they were real people deserving of pastoral care and concern. In his sermon for the Circumcision of Jesus, he encouraged parishioners to "think, how grievously he pained his mother in her birth-time in so much, that it is God's high miracle that she escaped to live."[85] Similarly the sermon for the Nativity of Mary states that "it is wonder that she is not all broken and bruised limb-to-limb in her birth-time." Mirk's focus on the physical pains of motherhood seemed to heighten his awareness for the potential pastoral needs of mothers. Childbirth – despite improved standards of living during the later Middle Ages – was a hazardous affair. Fully cognizant of the dangers awaiting them, pregnant women attempted to protect themselves as best as they could, seeking assistance from friends and

He also compared marriage to the Trinity, writing that Adam was the first person of the Trinity, Eve the second, and the person they became together the third. While this reverence of marriage was good for married parishioners of both sexes, it was especially good for women – validating their traditional familial role. Of course, within the same sermon, Mirk also noted that the priest read more over the woman than the man because the "woman guilted more than Adam." *Festial*, 289–293.

80   *Instructions for Parish Priests*, 131 and 203.
81   BL MS Sloane 1584, f. 75.
82   Cambridge St. John's College MS S 35, f. 39 v.
83   BL MS Sloane 1584, f. 7v.
84   Cambridge St. John's College MS S 35, f. 11v. *Instructions for Parish Priests*, 145 and 210.
85   Medieval Church tradition usually judged (in a literal interpretation of the Genesis account) the hardships of childbirth as a punishment for Eve's sin and consequently regarded the birth process as a shameful event. Carole Rawcliffe, "Women, Childbirth, and Religion in Later Medieval England," in *Women and Religion in Medieval England*, ed. Diana Wood (Oxford: Oxbow, 2003), 91–117, at 91–92.

midwives, saints such as the Virgin Mary and Margaret – who had requested that God allow her to help "women that call to her in time of travailing of child, that she might be sound delivered, and the child come to Christendom" – and from their priests, who could act as both spiritual counselors and minor medical practitioners.[86] A pregnant Margaret Paston even requested that her husband wear a ring set with the image of St. Margaret (presumably to help protect her as well as to remind him to pray for her sufferings) while he was away.[87]

Sensitive to women's fears, Mirk reminded priests to be especially attentive to the needs of pregnant women and women in labor.

> Women that be with child also,
> You most them teach how they shall do,
> When their time is near to come.
> Bid them do this all and some:
> Teach them to come and shrive them clean,
> And also housel [receive Eucharist] them all at once
> For dread of peril that may be-fall,
> In their travailing that shall come.[88]

He understood that expecting mothers might not survive the birthing process and wanted to insure their souls were properly shriven – just in case. Moreover, for the women who did survive, Mirk carefully explained the purification ceremony in *Festial*, and (supplementing the *Legenda Aureau's* purification sermon) advised mothers of the reasons for churching and ecclesiastical rules that forbade sex (for a certain amount of time) after the birth of a child. Once again reflecting a concern for women, Mirk clarified to priests that husbands would share equal guilt in breaking this rule. If "she has been at his bed before (the purification ceremony)," he wrote, "she must take her penance and he, both."[89]

Nor was Mirk alone with his concern for mothers. *Quattuor Sermones* recommends that "each woman before her travail of child [should] come to church and take shrift and housel [receive Eucharist]." This was for two reasons, as the passage explains. First it would help protect the child in his mother's womb, keeping the mother from "heaving and shoving, great travail and falling and all other mischief that should take the child's life and so be lost body and soul." Second it would protect the mother in case she did not survive the birthing process, cleansing her soul of sin to make her ready for the afterlife.[90] It also orders that parishioners should pray for "all the women that been in Our Lady bonds and with child in this parish or in any other that God send to them fair deliverance, to their children right shape, name and Christendom, and to the mothers purification."[91] The author of BL MS Sloane 1584 expressed concern that mothers-to-be not accidentally, and certainly not intentionally, harm the babies growing in their wombs.

---

86  Rawcliffe, "Women, Childbirth, and Religion," 92–103. See also: Peter Biller, "Childbirth in the Middle Ages," *History Today* 36 (1986), pp. 42–49. Mirk records this statement about St. Margaret, in his sermon dedicated to her, *Festial*, 202.

87  Rawcliffe, "Women, Childbirth, and Religion," 101.

88  *Instructions for Parish Priests*, 71–72.

89  *Festial*, 56–60, and 59.

90  *Quattuor Sermones*, 37.

91  Ibid., 88.

The manuscript queried specifically if pregnant women had ingested any meat or drink that potentially could harm unborn children. The author also protected pregnant women (and the children they carried) from the sexual advances of men, asking if men had lain with women in such a way as to terminate their pregnancies, and even questioning husbands if they had pursued sex with their wives regardless of the women's health. As this latter statement falls directly after the former, it could suggest that the women's sickness stemmed from pregnancy. Of course, some of the clerical concern expressed for pregnant women served to protect the unborn children, both physically and spiritually. Yet some of the concern also served to protect the women themselves.[92]

Finally, along with redeeming Eve and expressing concern for wives and mothers, the authors of pastoral handbooks expanded their perception of women beyond the traditional virgin, wife, and widow. They also incorporated single-women, female parishioners who did not conform to traditional marital roles, within their visual framework. Just as historians today have defined singlewomen as sexually mature, not-yet-married (life-cycle singlewomen) or never-married women (life-long singlewomen) who made up as much as one-third of the adult female population in late medieval England, contemporary authors of pastoral literature recognized the existence of these same women.[93] Some women were married; some were widowed; some were virgins; some were daughters; some were prostitutes. And some were simply single.

To begin with, women flourished as both life-cycle and life-long singlewomen in fourteenth- and fifteenth-century England. Maryanne Kowaleski has estimated that England contained "fairly large concentrations of singlewomen (roughly 30–40 percent of the adult female population) in the later Middle Ages."[94] Supporting her argument, fourteenth-century poll tax returns from Shropshire reveal that singlewomen would have been nothing new in Mirk's time. Ninety-six different not-married women appear in the local subsidy rolls from Shrewsbury, 1297–1322. As only heads of households could be taxed, we know that these were either widows like Isabell Borrey, who inherited a flourishing trade from her rich merchant husband, or singlewomen like Agnes le Roo who ran their own households and businesses.[95] Perhaps an exception to this was Juliana, servant

---

92  BL MS Sloane 1584, 8r–10r. For a discussion of clerical attitudes towards women, marriage, and childbirth in Latin pastoral manuals, please see: Peter A. Biller, "Marriage Patterns and Women's Lives: A Sketch of a Pastoral Geography," in *Women in Medieval English Society 1200–1500*, ed. P.J.P. Goldberg (Phoenix Mill, Stroud, Gloucestershire: Sutton, 1997), 60–107.

93  Judith M. Bennett and Amy M. Froide, "A Singular Past," in their *Singlewomen in the European Past*, 2. "The term 'singlewomen' encompasses both women who would eventually marry and those who never would. Some adult women lived and worked as singlewomen for five, ten, fifteen years or more, and then married. It is useful to think of these women as *life-cycle singlewomen*, for they lived single only for the years between childhood and marriage. Other women might have expected to marry while they were young but, for a variety of reasons, never did. For these *lifelong singlewomen*, the single state was a permanent one."

94  Maryanne Kowaleski, "Singlewomen in Medieval and Early Modern Europe: The Demographic Perspective," in *Singlewomen in the European Past*, eds. Judith M. Bennett and Amy M. Froide (Philadelphia: University of Pennsylvania Press, 1999), 38–81, at 64.

95  Cromarty, *The Wealth of Shrewsbury in the Early Fourteenth Century*, 35. "Tax charges fell only on those inhabitants who were heads of households engaged in producing or trading in goods ... The women taxed were those only who were heads of households through widowhood or as single women ... Altogether, in the ten subsidy rolls, there were 96 individuals of whom almost half

of Thurstan de Pichford, who ran a prosperous enough brewing trade to attract the attention of the sub-taxers in 1306 and 1309. Her identification as servant suggests that she might not have been a household head, perhaps living under the authority (and roof) of her master Thurstan de Pichford. Yet she was taxed individually for such goods as brassware and household utensils which could very well indicate that she lived on her own.[96] With little doubt, however, Agnes le Roo lived much of her life as a self-supporting singlewoman. First taxed in 1297 for 6s. of malt and 3s. of clothes, brassware, and household utensils, Agnes worked as a successful brewer for at least nineteen years, her business peaking in 1309 when her total taxed goods amounted to 41s. 2d.[97] If she entered the trade as a young women, perhaps in her late teens or early twenties, Agnes would have been well into her late thirties or early forties by 1316, the last time she appears in the records.

Agnes le Roo was not alone. The Shrewsbury subsidy documents specify nineteen of the ninety-six women taxed to be widows. Of the remaining seventy-seven women, some also were widows whom the sub-taxers never identified in the tax listings. For example, Isabel Borrey was never identified as a widow although other records clearly show that she was.[98] Cordelia Beattie has found similar discrepancies in the 1379 poll tax returns for Lynn, Norwich. Although the taxers seemed to clearly identify women as *vidua*, *puella*, or *solute*, Beattie has argued that because the term "*solutus* encompasses widowers and young unmarried men, *solute* is probably also an umbrella category." A woman identified as *solute* might also be (and sometimes irrefutably was) a widow. "Women were labeled as *vidua* or *puella* when marital or familial status was seen as more important than their work to their identities," Beattie has explained. "When women's work identities were considered more pertinent, though, the converse happened: a precise marital status was not considered crucial and the umbrella term *solute* was used."[99] The Shrewsbury subsidy rolls do not provide an exact parallel to the poll tax returns examined by Beattie, as the term *solute* was never employed. Women were identified as daughter, such as "Edith, daughter of William le Hyne," in 1297; as widow, such as "Cecily, widow of Stephen Russel," in 1309; as servant, such as

appear once only. Re-marriage is probably the main reason for this." D. and R. Cromarty identify Agnes Le Roo as an "unmarried wom[a]n with relatively large-scale brewing" business.

96   Ibid., 90 and 103. In 1306 Juliana is identified as "Juliana le Servant," and taxed for malt, clothes, brassware, oats, wheat, and household utensils totaling 40s. 6d. She was taxed again in 1309, this time with the identification of servant of Thurstan de Pichford. Her goods totaled 25s. 4d.

97   Ibid., 1297, 83. In 1306 her malt, clothes, brassware, firewood, pigs, and household utensils were assessed at 20s. 10d., 90. 1309, 102. In 1316 she was assessed for the last time, her goods totaling 15s., 121.

98   Ibid., 55, 96, 107, 117, 120. Twice-widowed Isabel became one of the wealthiest inhabitants of Shrewsbury, acting as hostess to Edward II in 1322. She was taxed in 1306 for goods totaling 104s. 4d.; in1309 for goods totaling £7 10s.; in 1313 for goods totaling 50s.; and in 1316 for goods totaling 100s. Juliana le Pottere is another woman (or women?) who is identified ambiguously. First taxed in 1306, her malt, clothes, brassware, wheat, rye, oats, and household utensils totaling 40s. 8d., 98. Then another woman with a similar name, Juliana le Pottare, was taxed in 1309 with goods totaling 12s. 6d., 100. In 1313, Juliana is taxed again, this time identified as Juliana, widow of Peter le Pottere, and taxed for goods totaling 30s., 110. Another Juliana le Potter is identified as widow of William le Potter in 1316, with goods totaling 30s., 118.

99   Cordelia Beattie, "The Problem of Women's Work Identities in Post Black Death England," in *The Problem of Labour in Fourteenth-Century England*, eds. James Bothwell, P.J.P. Goldberg, and W.M. Ormnrod (York: York Medieval Press, 2000), 1–19, at 7.

"Juliana, servant of Thurstan de Pichford," also in 1309; or simply listed by their name, such as "Agnes le Roo."[100] Yet the principle found in the 1379 Lynn poll tax returns could still apply. "It is not always possible to distinguish single women from widows in the tax documents. As the subtaxers were not consistent in using the formula 'widows of x', external evidence – and that relatively thin – has to be relied upon to confirm their marital status."[101] Just as external evidence confirms Isabell Borrey's status of widow, external evidence has also confirmed the status of never-married (or at least not-yet-married) singlewomen, such as Agnes le Roo, Alice Hagerwas, Edith le Hyne, and perhaps even Emma de Kent.[102] The lay subsidy rolls may sometimes fail to distinguish between widows and single-women. But they reveal that some women were indeed single and that none of these known singlewomen achieved the financial security of widows like Isabell Borrey. Isabell ranked among the wealthiest in Shrewsbury, while known single-women always remained in the lowest two rankings for wealth.[103]

Singlewomen also flourished in late medieval law codes, although – instead of being lumped with widows as they often were in economic records – they were sometimes indistinguishable from prostitutes. Evidence presented by Ruth Mazo Karras reveals fifteenth- and sixteenth-century English towns linking single-women with prostitutes in their attempts to control sexual immorality. Oxford banned all "bawds, whores, and incontinent women" from a circumference of ten miles around the university in 1461.[104] Bawds and whores would have referred to professional prostitutes and pimps, while incontinent women would have embraced sexually-active (or at least suspected sexually-active) singlewomen. By combining these three types of women in the same phrase, the governors of Oxford might have been making a not-so-gentle connection: unchaste single-women should be considered the same as whores. Only by containing them under the authority of male household heads did governors think they could regulate the liminal sexuality of these not-married women.[105] Similarly, P.J.P. Goldberg

---

100 Cromarty, *The Wealth of Shrewsbury*, 88, 101, 103, and 102.

101 Ibid., 65.

102 Alice Hagerwas was identified as an unmarried woman through outside sources. Ibid., 35. She appeared in the tax records in 1306 with goods totaling 12s. 2d., 92. Edith le Hyne was identified as the daughter of William le Hyne in 1297, and taxed for goods totaling 9s., 88. Emma de Kent appeared alongside Agnes le Roo in 1306 with goods totaling 42s., 91, and in 1309 with goods totaling 33s. 4d.,102. As malt was listed as her first taxable item, as it also was with Alice Hagerwas and Agnes le Roo, it suggests that she was a brewer, 48.

103 Ibid., 64–65.

104 Karras, *Common Women*, 19.

105 Marjorie McIntosh provides further evidence for this fear of singlewomen and for the association of singlewomen with illicit sex. "A few Elizabethan towns described more fully their reasons for concern with independent women. In Southampton, jurors reported in 1579 that 'there are in this town diverse young women and maidens which keep themselves out of service and work for themselves in diverse men's houses,' but three years later they said more precisely that 'within this town there be sundry maid servants that take chambers and so live by themselves masterless and are called by the name of char women, which we think not meet nor sufferable.' Similarly, jurors in Manchester first ordered in 1588 that 'no single woman, unmarried, shall be at her own hand, to keep house or chamber within the town of Manchester.' The following year they progressed to a wonderfully explicit statement of the core reasons for distress: 'Whereas great inconvenience is in this town, in that single women being unmarried, shall be at her own hand, to keep house or chamber within the town of Manchester.' The following year they progressed to a wonderfully explicit statement of the core reasons for distress: 'Whereas great inconvenience is in this town, in that single women being unmarried be at their own hands, and do bake bread and exercise

has noted that the use of "single women" within the provisions of the South-wark brothel customary also encompassed prostitutes – although, instead of as a "euphemism for prostitute" (as Karras has argued), it was "a conscious assertion within a legal document of the independent status of the women who worked in the stews vis-à-vis the stewmongers who managed them."[106] Despite different interpretations about why the term "single women" was employed, however, the end result is the same: English law recognized singlewomen, but often within the context of prostitution.

The authors of Latin pastoral literature also obscured the identity of single-women. Early medieval penitentials confine singlewomen to the categories of virgin, widow, and young girls. The seventh-century *Penitential of Theodore* specifically records the female partners of fornicators as *only* virgins and married women (who were the partners of not-married men, hence fornication instead of adultery).[107] It mentions no others. Likewise, the seventh-century *Penitential of Columban* and the ninth-century *So-called Roman Penitential* both explain forni-cation as between a laymen and "women who are free from the bonds of matri-mony, that is, with widows or girls."[108] Latin handbooks from the later medieval period fare little better. After examining the fourteenth-century clerical handbook *Fasciculus Morum*, Ruth Mazo Karras has concluded that it contained no concep-tual space for unchaste singlewomen. "There is no place for a singlewoman who is no longer a virgin. The only category for her is either concubine, a term that indi-cates the domestic partner of a priest, or meretrix, which would conflate her with the commercial prostitute." She comments that the definition of simple fornica-tion "implies some degree of recognition of singlewomen (and widows) as sexual beings," but "where the texts went into more detail about fornication, listing the possible partners with whom the sin might be committed, it becomes clear that the sexually active singlewoman was viewed in quite narrow terms – indeed, defined as a prostitute."[109] Sharon Farmer has found similar results in her study of thirteenth- and fourteenth-century Parisian clerics. Because they viewed women through a marriage prism, these priests ignored and sometimes even denied the existence of females who violated their ideology that all women should live under the control of men. Humbert of Romans, for example, discussed singlewomen only within the categories of servant and prostitute, and, like his counterparts Jacques de Vitry and Gilbert of Tournai, classified women by their sexual status – as virgins, wives, and widows. Thus ordinary singlewomen working in Paris

---

other trades, to the great hurt of the poor inhabitants having wife and children; as also in abusing themselves with young men and others, having not any in control of them, to the great dishonour of God and evil example of others.'" Marjorie K. McIntosh, *Controlling Misbehavior in England, 1370–1600* (Cambridge: Cambridge University Press, 1998), 111.

106 P.J.P. Goldberg, "Pigs and Prostitutes: Streetwalking in Comparative Perspective," in *Young Medi-eval Women*, eds. Katherine J. Lewis, Noel James Menuge, and Kim M. Phillips (New York: St. Martin's Press, 1999), 172–194, at 185.

107 *Medieval Handbooks of Penance: A Translation of the Principal Libri Poenitentiales and Selection from Related Documents*, trans. and eds. John T. McNeill and Helena M. Gamer (New York: Columbia University Press, 1990), 184–185.

108 Ibid., *Penitential of Columban* (quote) 254, article 16; *Roman Penitential* 303, article 16.

109 Ruth Mazo Karras, "Sex and the Singlewomen," in *Singlewomen in the European Past*, eds. Judith M. Bennett and Amy M. Froide (Philadelphia: University of Pennsylvania Press, 1999), 127–145, at 129.

slipped through the cracks of acceptable society and, consequently, could not receive much-needed charity.[110]

In short, singlewomen who did not fit into traditional female categories of virgin, wife, and even widow existed in late medieval England. Although medieval law and Latin pastoral literature failed to recognize the reality of these single-women, some writers of Middle English pastoral literature did: distinguishing life-cycle and life-long singlewomen from prostitutes, domestic servants, widows, and young girls. This acknowledgement of singlewomen as a distinct social category reveals that some clerical writers in late medieval England were able to view their unattached female parishioners in a more pragmatic, even if not more approving, light.

BL MS Harley 2250 contains an ordinary definition of fornication in its tract on vices and virtues: "fornication ... is between single man and single woman that be neither trothplight to wedlock nor have a vow to chastity and it is a deadly sin for if a man died in this sin without shrift or repentance he should have perforce the pain of hell without end."[111] Although not repeated verbatim, this explanation of fornication as occurring between single people proliferates in Middle English pastoral manuals. British Library MS Sloane 3160 records that "simple fornication is a trespass between single man and single woman."[112] British Library MS Harley 211, also known as *A Litil Tretys on the Seven Deadly Sins by Richard Lavynham*, states that, "simple fornication is trespass between single man and single woman."[113] *The Book of Vices and Virtues* describes the first branch of lechery "of man and woman that be not bound by a vow, nor by marriage, nor by order, nor by religion, nor by other ways."[114] And, in *Quattuor Sermones*, William Caxton printed the explanation of pre-marital sexual sin as a "deadly sin done fleshly between single man and single woman against the love of God and the teaching of Holy Church."[115] This definition of fornication, then, is commonplace. Yet it also articulates the existence of singlewomen who were neither virgins, nor prostitutes, nor widows. Merely by their inclusion, the words "single woman" suggest that clerical writers of Middle English pastoral literature recognized the existence of not married women among their parishioners.

Several fourteenth- and fifteenth-century vernacular texts differentiate single-women from prostitutes. Some of the clearest examples come from discussions of the seven deadly sins. The Midland compiler of BL MS Additional 37677, a

110  Sharon Farmer, "'It Is Not Good That [Wo]man Should Be Alone': Elite Responses to Single-women in High Medieval Paris," in *Singlewomen in the European Past, 1250–1800*, eds. Judith M. Bennett and Amy M. Froide (Philadelphia: University of Pennsylvania Press, 1999), 82–105.

111  BL MS Harley 2250, f. 103r. The manuscript is clearly a pastoral manual, compiled between 1477 and 1500 by a Thomas Masse and containing versified English homilies, an abridged version of the *Speculum Christiani*, versified lives of the saints, extracts from *Festial*, and an English tract on vices and virtues including the ten commandments.

112  BL MS Sloane 3160, f. 17r. This manuscript also appears to be a pastoral manual, written in the fifteenth century and containing a collection of homilies, medical recipes, and a tract on the seven deadly sins.

113  Richard of Lavynham, *A Litil Tretys on the Seven Deadly Sins*, 22. Lavynham was a member of the Carmelite order at Ipswich, prior at Bristol, and later a doctor of theology at Oxford. Some docu-ments speculate that he also was confessor to King Richard II. Fourteen manuscripts preserve his treatise; thirteen of which were written in fifteenth-century hands, xviii–xlix.

114  *The Book of Vices and Virtues*, 44.

115  *Quattuor Sermones*, 59.

fifteenth-century pastoral manual containing a loose translation of the *Somme le Roi*, explicitly describes the first degree of lechery as between a single man and woman who were neither married nor vowed religiously; the second degree was with a common woman, or – as we would say – prostitute.[116] Although only separated by a few words, the "woman that stands single" in the first degree is clearly distinguishable from the "common women" in the second degree. In fact, the passage states that sex with a common woman was a more perilous sin than sex with a singlewoman, leaving no doubt that the clerical writer considered these two women to be different.[117] BL MS Harley 2250 makes a similar distinction, recording that impudence (a branch of the deadly sin pride) was like a "common woman or a common lecher ... not ashamed of their lechery, or other spouse break [adultery] as a monk, as a friar, priest, or nun, single man, or single woman, or in any other degree."[118] Again, the separation of common lecher and common woman from single man and single woman suggests an understanding that these identifications should not be conflated.

*A Myrour to Lewde Men and Wymmen*, another English version of the *Somme le Roi*, expanded its descriptions of singlewomen and common women further, giving another reason as to why these women should be differentiated.

> Simple fornication that is between single man and single woman, that neither of them is bound to marriage nor to chastity by vow, nor professed to no religion. And doing this deed is deadly sin. The second degree is between a single man and a common woman that proffers her wretched body to sell. This sin is worse and fouler and more like the devil than that other, for it may bring a man into much more peril. For such a woman may perhaps be a wife or a woman of religion, or has had to do with father, brother or other near kin to him that has to done with her; for such one forsakes no man.[119]

Communities knew singlewomen not to be married or vowed religiously and, given the close quarters in which neighbors lived, perhaps even knew their romantic partners. Thus committing lechery with a singlewoman was a lesser sin as it was probably the *only* sin being committed. A common woman, however, could be anyone – a disgraced wife, runaway nun, clerical concubine, or secret lover of one's brother or cousin. Sleeping with her could compound the sins of lechery and prostitution with the sins of adultery, sacrilege, and even incest. Although priests made these distinctions among women primarily to help in their administration of penance to male penitents, they show that late medieval

---

116 BL MS Additional 37677, f. 77r. W. Nelson Francis remarked that "the translator seems to have been not too sure of his French ... he seems also to have worked from a MS. Of the *Somme* of a tradition different from and inferior to that of the other versions." *Book of Vices and Virtues*, xxxiv. In other words, the compiler of Additional 37677 created a copy of *Somme le Roi* rather different from the original and other versions of the text. Clearly a clerical manual, the manuscript also contains a treatise by Richard de Wethershed, Archbishop of Canterbury 1229–1231, a sermon attributed to master Richard Alkartoun, a sermon preached by Thomas Wimbledon at Paul's Cross in 1388, an anonymous sermon on John VI, a sermon attributed to John Wycliff, and several other entries of a theological nature.

117 BL MS Additional 37677, ff. 76r–77r.

118 BL MS Harley 2250, f. 93r.

119 *A Myrour to Lewde Men and Wymmen: A Prose Version of the Speculum Vitae, ed. from B.L. MS Harley 45*, ed. Venetia Nelson, Middle English Texts 14 (Heidelberg: Winter, 1981), 165.

English priests understood clear differences between the woman who was single and the woman who was common.

So why did pastoral vernacular literature from the fourteenth and fifteenth centuries make distinctions between singlewomen and prostitutes that law codes and Latin pastoral literature were not willing to make? At least part of the answer lies in the nature of the documents. Officials created ordinances such as those passed in Oxford and Coventry to eliminate sexual misconduct: from the one-night stand, to the habitual love affair, to prostitution. Thus the unchaste singlewoman was no different from the prostitute as they both participated in extra-marital sex. Sexual sin was sexual sin, and distinctions only muddied the water. In contrast, clerical instruction handbooks were created to help priests ferret out the details concerning sin so that they could administer penance correctly. John Mirk declared in his *Instructions for Parish Priests*:

> For often you must penance give
> Both to men and to women ...
> Therefore by good discretion,
> You must in confession
> Enjoin penance both hard and light.[120]

Whether priests dealt hard or light penance to incontinent women was contingent on exactly who the women were and why they committed the sin. Even Mirk made it clear that unchaste women could not always be equated with prostitutes. After asking the female penitent the degree of the man with whom she had sinned:

> kin or single, or any spouse,
> Or what degree of religion,
> Or whether it were against her will,
> Or whether she assented fully there-till,
> Or whether it were for covetry.

Mirk understood that women committed sexual sins for different reasons. Sometimes they were raped.[121] Sometimes they had sex for commercial gain. And sometimes women simply consented to having sex outside of marriage, which Mirk considered a lesser sin than prostitution. Thus it was necessary to make a distinction between the independent brewster who confessed to sleeping with her single neighbor and the woman who made a living from offering her body to anyone who would pay for it, as the first would receive less penance than the second.[122]

This need to gather as much information possible about penitents and their sins encouraged clerics to clarify distinctions among their female parishioners even further. Several manuscripts deconstruct the word "single," differentiating singlewomen from more women than prostitutes. BL MS Additional 37677 records that the first degree of lechery occurred between single people "not married nor ordered of religion"; the second degree occurred with a prostitute;

---

[120]  *Instructions for Parish Priests*, 108.
[121]  Ibid., 141. Mirk's language implies this association between rape and sexual sin.
[122]  Ibid., 141.

the third degree with a widow; the fourth degree with maidens; and the eleventh and twelfth degrees with secular women of religion and regular women religious. By being so specific in its description of the different degrees of lechery, the manuscript separates singlewomen from prostitutes, widows, maidens, and any women who had taken a religious vow.[123]

The medieval world considered virginity a valuable commodity. Men marrying virgins could guarantee the parentage of children; and women who remained virgins received highest accolades from the medieval church. Richard of Lavynham recorded in his rendition of the seven deadly sins that, "the state of wedlock is good. The state of widowship is better. But the state of maidenhood is best of all." As such he stressed that it was indeed a great sin to "rob a woman the flower of her maidenhood be she secular or regular."[124] Yet, by accentuating the sin of fornicating with a virgin, Lavynham made an interesting revelation: he considered maidens different from singlewomen. Simple fornication occurred between single man and single woman; spouse-breaking when married men and women had sex with those other than their spouses; ravishing when a man led "away another man's daughter without his will and knowing"; and violation of maidenhood when a man had sex with a virgin. Violation of maidenhood did not occur during simple fornication – indicating that Lavynham did not equate "single woman" with virgin.[125] Of course, some singlewomen certainly could have been virgins. The terms were not mutually exclusive. But not all singlewomen were virgins, and Richard of Lavynham understood this. The writers of vernacular pastoral literature considered some singlewomen to be simply single – not widowed, vowed, common, or even virgin. Cambridge St. John's College MS S 35 summed up these distinctions well in its description of women with whom a male penitent might sin sexually: "with any single woman, wife, widow, with any of your kin, or any of your ghostly children, or with any religious woman, or with any other that has vowed chastity, or with any strumpet or any unknown woman that you knew not of what degree she was, single, wedded, or religious."[126]

BL MS Sloane 1584 even distinguishes singlewomen from domestic servants. It also provides evidence that at least one clerical author distinguished singlewomen on their own merits. Instead of confining singlewomen to penitential questions concerned primarily with the degrees of male sin (and thus focused on men), Sloane 1584 provides singlewomen with their own category, separate from other parishioners.[127] It first directs questions to all penitents (although with a male generic slant), asking if they have been proud of riches and dignity, lived in adultery with any man's wife or daughter or servant, paid tithes and offerings unto holy church, killed or held ill will toward any man or woman, oppressed any poor man, or closed any land in any pasture.[128] Then the questions became more specific, directed to a husbandman, a woman, a servant man or woman, and a singlewoman.[129] Without speculating on why these particular

---

[123] BL MS Additional 37677, f. 77r.
[124] Richard of Lavynham, *A Litil Tretys on the Seven Deadly Sins*, 24.
[125] Ibid., 22–24.
[126] Cambridge St. John's College MS S 35, f. 5v.
[127] I am grateful to Judith Bennett for noting this important distinction.
[128] BL MS Sloane 1584, f. 7r.
[129] Ibid., ff. 7r–10r.

penitents were chosen, it is quite remarkable that three of the four categories contain women. Also remarkable is that a domestic servant woman was separated from the singlewoman, just as the singlewoman was separated from the married woman. Obviously the author of the manuscript considered these women to be different enough to need individual attention.

Some of their differences were reflected in his questions. He asked the woman if she had obeyed her husband at all times as she was required and if she had sinned fleshly with any man other than her husband, or sinned fleshly with her husband when she was in childbed. Such questions would not have applied to not-married women. Likewise, he asked the servant man or woman if they had defamed their master or mistress or caused them any harm; and to the "Single woman" the author of Sloane 1584 inquired if she had pledged to be the wife of any man. Interestingly, the only mention of whoredom or prostitution comes not under the questions to singlewomen or domestic servants, but under the section addressed to women generally.[130] Just as important as the questions asked are the questions *not* asked. Unlike the categories of "women" and "domestic servants" (who lived under the authority of husbands and masters), singlewomen were not asked if they had taken vows of fasting or pilgrimage. As both of these vows would have impinged on marital and customary obligations (such as the conjugal debt), the simple fact that singlewomen were not asked these questions underscores the assumption that they were considered autonomous individuals. By the nature of the questions asked and the questions that remained unasked, the author seems to have considered singlewomen as different from wives, female domestic servants, and perhaps even prostitutes.

But this acknowledgement of singlewomen did not equal a complete under-standing of whom these women might be. The author of Sloane 1584 recognized singlewomen, but he saw them through a familiar lens as sexually lascivious and dependent on men. First, the author of BL MS Sloane 1584 seemed to assume that singlewomen were sexually licentious. Six of the ten questions asked single-women concerned sexual matters. Had they made any contract with any man to be his wife? Had they sinned in lechery with any man single or wedded? Had they drunk any drink that they should not consume with child? Had they desired to sin with any man privately in their heart? Had they made themselves prettier in their appearance with any garment more for the pleasing of young men than of god? And had they washed their face with any waters or herbs to make themselves more fair?[131] Because it did not specifically ask these women about prostitution, as so many other pastoral manuals did, it seems likely that the author did not consider these particular singlewomen to be prostitutes. But his probing into their sexual habits indicates his disapproval (and attempted discouragement) of their sexual experimentation outside of marriage.

Second, even though he seemed to assume autonomy, he simultaneously seemed to assume that singlewomen did not earn money. To husbandman, women, and domestic servants he asked four identical questions concerning their relationship with holy church: had they made any solemn vow of fasting or pilgrimage, had they had any vomit or casting at Easter or any time of the year (did they inad-

---

130  Ibid., ff. 8v–10r.
131  Ibid., ff. 9v–10r.

vertently regurgitate a consecrated host, which was sacrilege), had they paid their tithes and offering, and had they done their penance that their holy father had charged them. Yet to singlewomen he asked only if they had any vomit or casting at Easter or any other time of the year and had they done their penance as their holy father had given them. They are the only group not asked about tithing, perhaps because the author assumed they had no income on which to tithe.

Third, the manuscript could suggest that the "Single woman" was a not-yet-married girl rather than a never-married woman or widow. Part of this stems from the failure of the author to inquire about their tithing. Women who headed their own households and ran their own businesses would be expected to pay their dues to holy church. Young girls living at home and waiting for marriage might have had any income they generated subsumed under that of their household head. Part of it also stems from the assumption that the men they attempted to attract would be young. Have you made yourself more attractive in clothing at anytime "more for pleasing of young men then of god?"[132] Young single girls, the author of BL MS Sloane 1584 seemed to assume, would want the attention of young single men so that they perhaps could get married.

Yet, despite its limited portrayal of singlewomen, the careful delineation made by BL MS Sloane 1584 is significant because it shows clerical understanding of the complexities of women's lifecycle stages. Instead of simply virgin, wife, or widow, the categories of women multiplied in Middle English pastoral literature. Some certainly were virgin, married, and widowed; but, as this manuscript – along with Mirk's *Festial*, his *Instructions for Parish Priests*, St. John's College MS S 35, *Quattuor Sermones*, BL MS Harley 2250, BL MS Additional 37677, BL MS Sloane 3160, BL MS Harley 211, *The Book of Vices and Virtues, A Myrour to Lewde Men and Wymmen* – shows, women were also single, common, servile, daughter, religious, and vowed.

Moreover, although confining most of their discussions of singlewomen to areas of sexual sin, clerical authors did not present singlewomen as any more sexually problematic than other women. The manuscripts implicated all women, single and married, virgin and widowed, as possible participants in lechery. Although the author of BL MS Sloane 1584 focused on sexual matters in more than half of his questions to singlewomen, this proportion is the same as in the questions addressed to wives and other women, as nine of their seventeen questions concerned sexual matters. Both singlewomen and women were asked if they tried to make their clothes more pleasing to men, if they washed their faces to make themselves more attractive, if they attempted abortions through drink, and if they had committed lechery. Singlewomen were not asked such explicit questions as the other women: if they had displayed their breasts openly to tempt anyone to sin, or if they had envied any woman who was more fair or better loved than they were.[133] Singlewomen committed sexual sins just like their married counterparts; but their sins were no worse. Only prostitutes and virgins received stiffer penance for lechery.

---

132    Ibid., ff. 9v–10r. Of course, as it is surprising that widows are not mentioned within these discussions of women, I cannot rule out the possibility that the clerical author intended them to be included in this singlewomen section. However, evidence (as mentioned above) does suggest that the section refers primarily to not-yet-married women.

133    Ibid., ff. 8r–10r.

Thus the authors of Middle English pastoral literature acknowledged that many female parishioners were not married. Some of these women certainly were prostitutes. Some were domestic servants; some were widows; some were young virginal maids. And some were simply single. They headed their own households, ran businesses, participated in the parish social life, went to church, and had romantic relationships. The particulars of these women's lives are often difficult to see, obscured by their relative absence from the records. But what we do know is that some priests recognized their existence. They recognized that singlewomen lived in parishes throughout England and needed pastoral care just like other female parishioners. Most importantly, however, clerical authors of vernacular pastoral literature recognized that singlewomen were a distinct social category; different from prostitutes, widows, maids, and even domestic servants. Priests might not have approved of how these singlewomen lived; but their disapproval did not equal dismissal.

\*

Janus both smiles and frowns. Clerical authors of vernacular pastoral literature perceived female parishioners through bifocal lenses. On the one hand, they saw women as dependent on men and associated with sexual licentiousness. On the other hand, they saw female parishioners unfettered by the sin of Eve, worthy of protection and admiration in their roles as wives and mothers, and not confined to the traditional categories of virgin, wife, and widow. When combined, these dual images produced dual results. These manuals offered priests a more realistic image of the female parishioners they served, but they also warned of the challenges inherent in caring for women.

## Chapter 4

## PASTORAL CARE

CLEARLY authors of pastoral vernacular literature recognized their responsibility to women. They understood that "Christ's people" included both men and women; they perceived the women they served in a somewhat realistic light; and, as this final chapter demonstrates, they attempted to offer women proper pastoral care. At the same time, female parishioners presented priests with unique challenges that complicated the pastoral care process.

John Mirk's *Instructions for Parish Priests* illustrates these points well. First, it recognizes women as ordinary parishioners who required ordinary pastoral care. Twice Mirk stressed that priests should impress upon both men and women the need for confession. In the introduction, he wrote:

> Thus you must also often preach,
> And your parishioners carefully teach:
> When one has done a sin,
> Look he lie not long therein,
> But immediately that he him shrive [confess],
> Be it husband, be it wife,
> Lest he forget by Lenten [Easter] day,
> And out of mind it go away.[1]

Later, under a section entitled *De modo audiendi confessionem*, Mirk reiterated that priests must be prepared to care for male and female penitents.

> Now I pray you take good heed,
> For this you must necessarily know,
> Of shrift [confession] and penance I will you tell ...
> For often you must penance give
> Both to men and to women.[2]

Second, Mirk encouraged priests to exercise special caution with women,

---

[1]  *John Mirk's Instructions for Parish Priests: Edited from MS Cotton Claudius A II and Six Other Manuscripts with Introduction, Notes, and Glossary*, ed. Gillis Kristensson, Lund Series in English 49 (Lund: Gleerup, 1974), 71–72. These highlighted passages from *Instructions* are discussed in greater detail within the chapter.

[2]  Ibid., 108.

because of their sexuality. He warned priests about fraternizing with questionable women.

> Women's service you must forsake,
> Of evil fame lest they you make,
> For women's speech that are shrews,
> Turns often away good intentions [manners].

When female parishioners came for confession, Mirk directed priests to:

> Look her face that you not see,
> But teach her to kneel down beside you,
> And somewhat your face from her you turn."[3]

He also portrayed women as problematic penitents who required extra sensitivity and encouragement during confession. "But when a woman comes to you," *Instructions* records, make sure that you do not upset her by moving around too much, or spitting, or kicking,

> Lest she suppose you make that fuss
> For loathing that you hear there,
> But sit you still as any maid
> Till that she has all said.[4]

Finally, Mirk suggested that the dependent status of wives complicated how priests could perform pastoral duties. Warning priests of the "need to be wise," Mirk recommended that:

> If a wife has done a sin,
> Such penance you give her then
> That her husband may not know,
> Lest for the penance sake
> Woe and wrath between them wake [arise].[5]

This advice served to protect women, yet it also forced priests to exercise special caution when tending to the spiritual needs of female parishioners.

Like Mirk's *Instructions for Parish Priests*, the authors of other pastoral vernacular handbooks and sermon compilations recognized women as ordinary parishioners deserving of ordinary care. Yet they simultaneously cautioned priests about female parishioners. In both the instructions they gave on how priests were to care for women and the exempla they shared about pastoral situations involving women, they rendered female parishioners as problematic. Women's sexuality threatened clerical purity; women's behavior frustrated the process of pastoral care; and women's dependent status complicated how priests administered penance. Moreover, exempla routinely depict female parishioners as prone to conceal sin from their confessors, circumvent clerical authority, and doubt sacerdotal power.

---

3  Ibid., 70 and 113.
4  Ibid., 113–114.
5  Ibid., 154–155.

Thus, from the clerical perspective presented in pastoral literature, women were ordinary parishioners who posed extraordinary problems for priests.

## THE ORDINARY CARE OF FEMALE PARISHIONERS

Clerical authors of pastoral vernacular literature recognized that women – just like their male counterparts – were normal parishioners deserving of normal pastoral care. The authors of these guides stressed that women and men had similar confessional and penitential needs. The second vernacular sermon contained in Worcester Cathedral MS F 10 begins with the words "*Christian people*," and offers advice on how Christians can be delivered from the prison of deadly sin. "Truly I read that we do right as the children of Israel did, gather us together right as we be now at this time and pray to God heartily and meekly, that He will of His high goodness bring us out of this mischief and disease that we be in." The use of gender-inclusive language within the sermon emphasizes how all parishioners suffered from the seven deadly sins and needed to cleanse themselves of these sins. Gluttony, for example, "makes a *man or a woman* not only blind bodily, but also ghostly." The sermon author ordered both men and women to emulate the example of Christ and, instead of living sinfully, to live chastely and meekly because, "cleanness [chastity] makes a *man or a woman* beautiful of birth in bodily beholding" and "meekness makes a *man or a woman* gracious and ghostly in goodness of living."[6] Thus the author made certain that audiences knew the sermon principles applied to all parishioners, regardless of gender.

Because women sinned as readily as men, authors of pastoral guides addressed both men and women in penitential questions used to ascertain which of the ten commandments and deadly sins had been transgressed. Some authors emulated the formula of earlier Latin penitentials: using "man" to refer to both sexes. Richard of Lavynham did precisely this. "*Vainglory* [a branch of Pride] is when a *man* boasts of himself greatly," he explained, continuing: a "covetous *man* is likened to a hedgehog," "a *man* that is comely indignant and angry. fierce and malicious is likened to the wolf," "the envious *man* likened to the hound," a slothful "*man* which is given to this vice is likened to the ass," and "Right so a glutton delights *him* so greatly in sweet food and delicious drink that *he* is not ashamed to go where *he* may soonest find sweet morsels and devour that other *men* have sore travailed for." The discussion of lechery begins in a similar manner, "A lecherous *man* is likened to a hog or to a swine." But, unlike within the previous discussions, the manuscript specifically states women as committing this sin. "Also if a *woman* make herself through curious attire and by craft to seem fairer and fresher than nature has granted. with nice cheer of looking of going and delectable words. drawing men's hearts to folly and to sin."[7] Thus the text does not forget about female parishioners, yet Richard of Lavynham failed to take either the space or

---

6   *Three Middle English Sermons From Worcester Chapter Manuscript F. 10*, ed. D.M. Grisdale, Leeds School of English Language Texts and Monographs 5 (Kendal: Printed by T. Wilson for Members of the School of English Language in the University of Leeds, 1939), 22–23, 30, and 43.
7   Richard of Lavynham, *A Litil Tretys on the Seven Deadly Sins*, ed. J.P.W.M. van Zutphen (Rome: Institutum Carmelitanum, 1956), 2, 5, 10, 13, 15, 19, and 23.

the time to explicitly include women within discussions of six of the seven deadly sins. Only when turning to lechery did he intentionally include women.

Other pastoral manuals are more gender inclusive. Instead of confining women to discussions of sex, the compiler of St. John's College MS S. 35 regarded women as ordinary sinners who committed the same sins as men. The phrase *man or woman* flourishes ubiquitously within the text, leaving little doubt that the clerical compiler regarded male and female parishioners as equally capable of error. Both men and women drank too much, slandered one another, took God's name in vain, bore false witness, coveted, and – of course – engaged in illicit sexual activities.[8] Shrewsbury School MS 3 reflects a similar outlook: women and men erred in identical ways. The fiend, the manuscript records, drags the souls of both male and female parishioners into the wretched depths of gluttony, drunkenness, manslaughter, and lechery. Consequently both men and women should cleanse their souls during the holy time of Lent.[9] The compiler of Bodl. MS Bodley 110 found it so important that male and female parishioners understood their sinful nature, that he opened his treatise on penance reminding every "*man or woman*" that they both can be "bound in deadly sin."[10] Likewise, the compiler of Durham Cathedral MS V IV 2 seemed so convinced that women trespassed in the same ways as men that he recorded the words of the ten commandments as applying specifically to female parishioners. Personalizing the ninth and tenth commandments for each penitent, he wrote, "I shall not covet my neighbors wife, nor his daughter, nor his servant … *I shalt not covet my neighbors husband nor his son nor his servant* … I shalt not covet my neighbors ox nor his ass …" Without even a pause, this clerical compiler transformed the biblical male neighbor into either a man or a woman.[11] When priests read such pastoral guides as these, they were consistently reminded that female parishioners presented as likely candidates as male parishioners to commit the seven deadly sins and break the ten commandments.

Because women sinned in the same ways as men, they needed God's grace as much as men – grace delivered in the accessible form of the seven sacraments. Pastoral manuscripts explicitly include female parishioners in discussions about sacramental ministrations. Bodl. MS Bodley 110 contains a detailed (and explicitly gender-inclusive) description of the sacraments, failing only to mention female parishioners during discussion of ordination, a rite reserved for males: "the fifth sacrament is [ordination] that belongs to *men* of holy church."[12] But the compiler of Bodley 110 included women when discussing the other sacraments. For example, the manuscript states that the second sacrament is "that each christian *man and woman* is to bring their children as soon as they may" (or at least by the time they are five years old) for confirmation.[13] In a vein very similar to that of Bodley 110, *Quattuor Sermones* informs priests and parishioners that both men and women need the sacraments. "The fourth thing that you should know God by is the seven sacraments of Holy Church which be ministered to the

---

8   St. John's College Cambridge MS S. 35, ff. 3v–15v.
9   Shrewsbury School MS 3, ff. 54r and 40v.
10  Bodl. MS Bodley 110, f. 134v.
11  Durham Cathedral Cosin MS V IV 2, f. 134v.
12  Bodl. MS Bodley 110, f. 161r.
13  Ibid., ff. 160r–v.

*people* of persons and priests that have power thereto. Of the which the first five, that is baptism, confirmation, shrift, housel, and anointing, are every *man and woman* held to do in pain of cursing in certain time, as the law orders." To make sure the point is not lost, the text reiterates in each section discussing these five sacraments that they are needful for male and female parishioners alike. *Quattuor Sermones* explains that mothers and fathers share in responsibility for insuring the baptism and confirmation of each of their children. "To this is every christian *man and woman* bound to bring their children as soon as they may." For penance (or shrift), the text emphasizes that "every *man and woman* is bound immediately as they can reasonably know at twelve years every year to be clean shriven at least once at their own curate."[14] Similarly, for the "holy sacrament of the altar" it states that "every *man and woman* bound by the law once a year as at Easter if he be fourteen years of age and have discretion to receive it when they be with shrift and penance made clean of their sins." This sacrament is so important that *Quattuor Sermones* adds that those who neglect to receive Christ's body regularly will be cast from the church, unless they have a reasonable excuse. Moreover, parishioners who partake of consecrated bread unworthily will be damned. Finally, *Quattuor Sermones* turns to extreme unction. Although introducing this sacrament with male-generic (or perhaps androcentric) language, "The fifth sacrament is anointing of sick *men*," the text references both men and women as needing the service, "so that this sacrament may be given as often as needed to every *man and woman* that be in point of death."[15]

The sacraments of Eucharist and confession concerned clerics the most. As canon law required parishioners to partake of these annually, rather than once in a lifetime, these were the sacraments most often performed by priests and most often received by parishioners. They were also the sacraments most often discussed in clerical manuals. *Instructions for Parish Priests* emphasizes that priests must impress on male and female parishioners the importance of confession.

> Thus you must also often preach,
> And your parishioners carefully teach;
> When one has done a sin,
> Look he lie not long therein,
> But immediately that he him shrive [confess],
> *Be it husband, be it wife,*
> Lest he forget by Lenten day,
> And out of mind it go away.[16]

Bodl. MS Bodley 110 encourages "each *man and woman* as soon as they can" to seek the "third sacrament" of "shrift or penance."[17] BL MS Sloane 1584 likewise reminds that, "every *man and woman* owe by the law to be shriven once in the year." Thus around Easter time curates should ordain a private place "but somewhat dark or else clothe it with cloth about" and cover his "visage that the peni-

---

14  *Quattuor Sermones: Printed by William Caxton*, ed. N.F. Blake, Middle English Texts 2 (Heidelberg: Winter, 1975), 36.
15  Ibid., 36–42.
16  *Instructions for Parish Priests*, 70–71.
17  Bodl. MS Bodley 110, f. 160v.

tent see him not in the face ... both *men and women* ... that the penitent be not ashamed to tell him his sin."[18] The manuscript author also explained that after confession, male and female parishioners each should receive Eucharist: "every *man and woman* that be here present which this day should come to god's board to receive his pained body the blissful sacrament of the altar kneel down devoutly upon one your knees with meekness in heart and contrition for your sins and say after me like as I shall tell you."[19]

Finally, the text inquires if each of four groups of penitents – husbandmen, women, servant men and women, and singlewomen – have participated in various sacraments, especially the two annual sacraments. To husbandmen, it asks: "have you drunk any time on the Sunday before you have heard mass or gospel and taken holy water and holy bread have you done your penance that you have taken before time of your ghostly father in time of lent ... have you had any vomit or casting at Easter when you have received your housel." The question is similarly posed to servant men and women: "have you made any solemn vow of fasting or pilgrimage have you had any vomit or casting at Easter or any time of the year ... have you kept your fasting days and holy days as you are bound ... have you done your penance that you were charged with by your ghostly father to do." To the singlewomen it asks: "have you had any vomit or casting at a Easter or any other time of the year have you done your penance as your ghostly father and you were agreed at all times."[20]

Like the copiers of Mirk's *Festial*, clerical authors of vernacular pastoral manuals understood that women required the sacraments just as did their male counterparts, and they explicitly incorporated male and female parishioners into the language of their texts. Worcester Cathedral MS 172 contains a startling example of this. Opening with a discourse on clerical behavior, the manuscript soon turns to a treatise on "ghostly temptations." Just as in St. John's College MS S. 35, the phrases "good *men and women*," "a *man or a woman*," and "every *man and woman*" flourish throughout. In one instance, the manuscript relays instructions on how parishioners obtained God's grace through the seven sacraments. "Therefore every *man and woman* ... ask mercy and forgiveness of all your sin and make you lowly to the sacraments of holy church and then you owe to believe that there be forgiven and that you been received into the grace of god." In addition to the gender inclusive phrase *man and woman*, the compiler of Worcester Cathedral MS 172 also employed gender inclusive pronouns. "And if a *man or a woman* may prove in his heart as very sorry and though *he or she* think when *he or she* bidden their beads or cries to god mercy that he does all against heart in for all that should *he or she* not deem *him or her* graceless for whoso that would have very sorrow for his sins" will indeed receive the mercy of God.[21] For the author of this manuscript, the gender inclusive pronouns *he* and *she* complemented the consistent usage of *man and woman*. The author seemed to understand that women were distinct parishioners who had to be distinguished

---

[18] BL MS Sloane 1584, f. 69r.

[19] Ibid., ff. 50r–v.

[20] Ibid., ff. 74–10r. One question during the domestic servants section clearly refers only to men, as it asks if the penitent has asked any woman to be her husband.

[21] Worcester Cathedral MS 172, ff. 33v–34v.

textually from their male counterparts. Female parishioners were commonplace; but female parishioners were also different from men.

## THE EXTRAORDINARY PROBLEMS OF FEMALE PARISHIONERS

Pastoral authors explicitly recognized that women were among the parishioners to whom priests ministered, but they also emphasized that female parishioners were different from their male counterparts. By accentuating women's sexuality, portraying women as especially reluctant penitents, and highlighting the complications stemming from women's dependent status, the clerical compilers of sermons and pastoral handbooks presented women as challenging parishioners whose pastoral needs sometimes stumped their priests.

To begin with, clerical compilers of vernacular pastoral literature accentuated the sexuality of women. Discussions of the seven deadly sins in BL MS Additional 37677, BL MS Sloane 3160, and Bodl. MS Douce 60 include women primarily within the context of sexual misconduct – regardless of under which umbrella sin the discussion takes place (such as pride).[22] BL MS Sloane 1584, despite its separate sections on wives and singlewomen, devotes more than half of its questions for women to seduction, lechery, and abortion.[23] Similarly, in Durham Cathedral Cosin MS V IV 3, the sirens inked in the margins of sermons that had nothing to do with either women or sex suggests the mind of at least one cleric was pondering women as both sexually desirable and sexually dangerous.[24]

*Instructions for Parish Priests* continues this special attention to women's sexuality. In addition to warning priests about fraternizing with questionable women,

> Women's service you must forsake,
> Of evil fame lest they you make,
> For women's speech that are shrews,
> Turns often away good intentions [manners],

Mirk underscored the presumed lasciviousness of women by focusing on their sexual sins. While men committed a variety of sins within Instructions – from stealing, to fornicating, to forsaking the Sabbath, women were almost exclusively associated with sexual sin. Out of the thirty times Mirk specifically discussed women within *Instructions*, three of the discussions concerned baptism, seven concerned husbands and wives and issues of marriage, three concerned parenthood, one concerned consanguinity, five concerned confession and penance, one concerned the sinners condemned in the *Great Sentence*, and ten concerned sexual sin. Moreover, when discussing the seven deadly sins, the only time Mirk directly addressed female penitents was within *luxuria*. This is also the only time Mirk discussed female earnings, asking if the sexual sin committed by female penitents was for covetousness "of gold or silver, or anything of his," and if so then the sin

---

22 BL MS Additional 37677, ff. 62r–84r; BL MS Sloane 3160, ff. 2r–23r; Bodl. MS Douce 60, ff. 213r–228v.
23 BL MS Sloane 1584, ff. 7r–10r.
24 Durham Cathedral Cosin MS V IV 3, f. 11v.

was double and required more penance. With a third of his discussions about women focused on lechery, it is not surprising that Mirk's recognition of working women was of prostitutes.[25]

What is surprising is that – even though the penance for women's sexual sin was "much more" for prostitution – the text does not indicate that penance lessened for rape.[26]

> And if she be a woman,
> Bid her tell, if she can,
> Of what rank the man was
> That sinned with her in the case,
> Kin or single or any spouse,
> Or what rank of religious,
> Of whether it was against her will,
> Or whether she consented fully there-till
> Or whether it was for covetousness
> Of gold or silver, or anything of his,
> Then the sin double were,
> And needed penance much more.

Although it is difficult to know exactly what Mirk meant by this, it could suggest that women who chose to commit fornication or adultery were considered *no more sinful* than women who were forced to have sex "against her will." Of course, Mirk's lack of elaboration about the penance assigned for fornication, adultery, and rape make an assessment of his attitude toward female culpability difficult. But it does seem telling that, considering the amount of concern and attention otherwise expressed for women, Mirk's *Instructions* does not express concern about the crime of rape nor remarks that the penalty for a woman who had sex "against her will" should be lessened.[27] Thus this passage might indicate that women were considered guilty for sexual sin – regardless of the circumstances.

---

[25] *Instructions for Parish Priests*, 70, 71–2, 97; 78, 80, 89, 122, 130, 145, 155; 76, 121, 160; 77; 71, 108, 113, 115, 148; 104–107; 70 (the "evil fame" seems to imply sexual indiscretion), 79–80, 110, 118, 124, 139, 140, 141, 143, 149–150; 142–143; 141.

[26] Ibid., 141.

[27] Rape was a major felony in England, articulated in the 1285 second Statute of Westminster as: "It is provided that henceforth if a man ravishes a married woman, a maiden, or other woman, without her consent before or afterwards, he shall have judgement of life and limb; and likewise where a man ravishes a woman – married woman, maiden, or other woman – by force even though she consents afterwards, he shall have the judgement before stated if he is convicted at the king's suit, and there the king shall have his suit." As quoted by Corinne Saunders in *Rape and Ravishment in the Literature of Medieval England* (Cambridge: D.S. Brewer, 2001), 60–61. Legally, then, women were not considered guilty when raped, but – as Corinne Saunders has demonstrated – the legal definition of rape was complex and this complexity persisted in religious texts. Canon law focuses more on the status and value of female victims than on the question of consent, while some fourteenth-century Middle English pastoral literature asserts that "neither maidenhood nor its rewards are lost in rape," emphasizes the sin of rapists, and even highlights the trauma of female victims. Saunders, *Rape and Ravishment*, 87, 116–119. This sympathetic attitude towards female rape does not appear in the literature I examined, and indeed, in some respects, late medieval sermons, exempla, and pastoral handbooks might better reflect the progression noted by Kim M. Phillips: that attitudes toward women proceeded from bad to worse throughout time in medieval rape narratives. "The process from the bleeding body, to the deflowered body, to the absent body, sketches the outlines of a complex picture of decline for women under the common law," Kim M. Phillips, "Written on the Body: Reading Rape from the Twelfth to Fifteenth Centuries," in *Medieval*

Ruth Mazo Karras, in her study of John de Bromyard's fourteenth-century Latin writings, has found evidence suggesting that clerics did indeed consider women culpable when raped. "In Bromyard's view even women who were raped were guilty of sexual sin. In one tale a woman chargers her attacker with rape; the judge tells the defendant to take the plaintiff's money from her. She fights for it tooth and nail, and he is unable to seize it. The judge then declares that if she had fought for her chastity as fiercely as she did for her money, she would have been able to keep it. Bromyard classifies the story under lust, implying that the woman's own desires prompted her to invite the rape."[28] Exempla discussing rape are rare in pastoral vernacular literature, but the tales that do exist underscore Bromyard's attitude – namely, that women shared in the guilt of their rapists. For example, an exemplum from the *Gesta Romanorum* (including a Middle English version) narrates the adventure of a knight who rescues a damsel in distress from her ravisher. Yet, after he carries the woman home to his castle (with the intent of marrying her), he finds himself betrayed when she brings the rapist into the castle with her and locks the knight out of his own house. At the very least, the tale emphasizes the potential treachery of women. Because it portrays the woman as preferring the rapist over the knight, it also could imply that the woman enjoyed the attentions of the rapist and was (at least eventually) complicit in his plans.[29] Another exemplum found in Shrewsbury School MS 3 tells of a young girl sexually abused by her father. The story emphasizes the guilt of the father as it states, "there was a man that had ado with his own daughter bodily." But the story also emphasizes the guilt of the daughter, as it tells how she was rebuked by her mother for the incest, flew into a rage when her father stopped his sexual advances (suggesting to a medieval audience that she was complicit), murdered him, and then became a prostitute.[30] In short, when rape and sexual assault was discussed in the literature of John Mirk and Middle English sermon stories, it was not presented as a crime against women. It was presented as sexual sin, and depicted women as sharing in the guilt.[31]

In addition to portraying women as especially lascivious, compilers of pastoral vernacular literature emphasized the dangers that women's physical bodies posed to celibate priests.[32] Exempla portray women as intent on seducing clerics. John

---

*Women and the Law*, ed. Noel James Menuge (Woodbridge, Suffolk: Boydell Press, 2000), 125–144, at 144.

28    Ruth Mazo Karras, *Common Women: Prostitution and Sexuality in Medieval England* (New York and Oxford: Oxford University Press, 1996), 109.

29    *The Gesta Romanorum*, ed. Sidney J.H. Herrtage, EETS extra series 33 (London: Oxford University Press, 1932), 219–221.

30    Shrewsbury School MS 3, ff. 59v–60r. *Jacob's Well* narrates a similar version of this story. *Jacob's Well: An English Treatise on the Cleansing of Man's Conscience. Edited from the Unique MS about 1440 A.D. in Salisbury Cathedral Part 1* (all published), ed. Arthur Brandeis, EETS original series 115 (London: Kegan Paul, Trench, Trubner & Co., 1900), 172–173.

31    The only time women are exonerated from rape is when they fight against their attackers. For example, *Jacob's Well* records the story of the "faithful wife" who tried to escape ravishers by swimming away. Two men pursued her by boat, and dragged her into the boat with them. She exclaimed, "she was wife truly wedded, and she would not be false to her husband; rather she would take her death." She broke away from the men and jumped into the sea. The boat capsized from her leap, drowning the two men. The good wife, however, escaped to dry land, "for her true love in matrimony, by grace of god." *Jacob's Well*, 54.

32    "Total avoidance [of women] was hardly practical, however, for the many types of religious males populating the medieval landscape whose duties as confessors, spiritual advisors, parish workers,

Mirk, in his sermon for the feast day of St. Andrew, tells of a bishop who had devoted himself to serving St. Andrew and of a devil who had decided to thwart this bishop "out of purpose." The devil only began to succeed, however, after he had disguised himself as a beautiful woman and requested that the bishop hear his confession. "[E]ver when the bishop looked on her, him thought her so fair that he was so tempted upon her, that he had nigh forgotten himself." After the bishop listened to the devil-disguised-female-penitent's confession, he casually suggested that she have dinner with him. The devil slyly refused on the grounds that "men would have suspicion of evil." Perhaps disappointed, the bishop then promised that they would dine with many other people as well so that there "shall be no suspicion of misdeeds." Yet every time he looked upon her, the bishop lusted for her within his heart, and soon forgot his devotion to St. Andrew. Thus this story tells of a pious and devoted cleric who lost his way on account of his desire for a beautiful female penitent seeking pastoral care. If he had continued to succumb to her temptations, the exemplum implies, he could have lost his soul. Lucky for him, St. Andrew had pity on his plight and disguised himself as a pilgrim to rescue the bishop from the seductive demon.[33] *Alphabet of Tales* relates a similar narrative. A monk of "great abstinence" became prideful about his holiness, and so the devil came to tempt him. Choosing the likeness of a beautiful woman, the devil came to the monk's den and called out that she was afraid and needed a place to rest for the night. "Sir," she said, "it is now near night, and I beseech you let me lie to tomorrow in a corner of your den, so that wild beasts slay me not and eat me." The monk had compassion on the woman and brought her inside. "And with her fair speech and her sweet words, she smote his heart into a lust and a liking … So this monk was so tempted with her, that he raised and took her in his arms and kissed her, and thought to have done his lust and liking with her." The woman then transformed into an ugly demon, slipping from his embrace as a choir of demons surrounded him, singing, "O! you monk, that was so extolled in heaven, how deep now you are drowned in hell!" The monk then fell into despair and eventually died in "wicked living."[34]

From this distinctly clerical viewpoint, fear of women's sexuality and of the feminine body seems understandable (even if not condonable). The text of Bodl. MS Bodley 95 rails against women dressing seductively and acting as temptresses.

> Many women bend in her waist and put out the breast and many use wide colors to seal her white breast with garlands and pearls and enticing of her head as a mirror of the devil to blind men with.[35]

---

pilgrims, and the like brought them into intimate rather than merely casual acquaintance with women. The celibacy of these men, so central to their calling, was thus at continual risk, and exemplum after exemplum turns on cases of church officials low and high who succumbed to temptation." Joan Young Gregg, *Devils, Women, and Jews: Reflections of the Other in Medieval Sermon Stories* (Albany: State University of New York Press, 1997), 102.

33  *Festial*, 9–11.

34  *Alphabet of Tales: An English 15th Century Translation of the Alphabetum narrationum of Étienne de Besançon. From Additional MS. 25, 719 of the British Museum*, ed. Mary Macleod Banks, 2 parts, EETS original series 126 (London: Kegan Paul, Trench, Trubner & Co., 1904–1905), 90–91.

35  Bodl. MS Bodley 95, f. 21v.

The language it uses parallels advice from Proverbs, warning men from the wiles of prostitutes.

> This is to say take thee no heed to woman's deceit for the lips of a common woman [are] as a dripping honey comb and more shining than oil is her throat but the last of her is bitterer than wagmote and her tongue is sharp as a double edged sword. Her feet go unto death and her steps perish into hell.[36]

The author of BL MS Harley 2250 used an Old Testament story to directly connect this perception of women as sexually-dangerous to the dire implications of breaking clerical chastity, and therefore defiling sacerdotal purity. During a discussion of *luxuria*, the manuscript states it is sacrilege when monks, friars, priests, and deacons, "and others that have bound you [yourself] to chastity and to do god's service in cleanness of body when they turn you [yourself] to lechery … and receive god's body on the altar without shrift or taking of penance may be afraid when god will take vengeance on you." The manuscript then states that God struck dead "in holy scripture whosoever touched the house that the tables were in that the Old Testament were written on [the ark of the covenant]." The section concludes, "he that touches god's own body unworthily may be sore afraid."[37] The lesson is obvious: sex made priests unworthy of their sacred duties and the potential punishment for being unworthy was death.

Exempla throughout medieval Europe emphasize the dangers, both physical and spiritual, of priests succumbing to the wiles of women. One tale told of a lecherous priest who failed to confess before performing mass. He was carried off and devoured by demons. Another priest after having sexual relations with a woman had his mass interrupted by a heavenly being who snatched the host from his hands and struck him down. A third lecherous priest stumbled and fell on the way to the altar. Similarly, a plethora of stories tell of priests guilty of sexual sin

---

36  Ibid., f. 84r. Proverbs 6:23–6 states, "For the commandment is a lamp and the teaching is light; and reproofs for discipline are the way of life to keep you from the evil woman, from the smooth tongue of the adulteress. Do not desire her beauty in your heart, nor let her capture you with her eyelids. For on account of a harlot one is reduced to a loaf of bread, and an adulteress hunts for the precious life." Proverbs 7:6–27 contains a longer indictment. "For at the window of my house I looked out through my lattice, and I saw among the naïve, and discerned among the youths a young man lacking sense, passing through the street near her corner; and he takes the way to her house, in the twilight, in the evening, in the middle of the night and in the darkness. And behold, a woman comes to meet him, dressed as a harlot and cunning of heart. She is boisterous and rebellious, her feet do not remain at home; She is now in the streets, now in the square, and lurks by every corner. So she seizes him and kisses him and with a brazen face she says to him: 'I was due to offer peace offerings; today I have paid my vows. Therefore I have come out to meet you, to seek your presence earnestly, and I have found you. I have spread my couch with coverings, with colored linens of Egypt. I have sprinkled my bed with myrrh, aloes and cinnamon. Come, let us drink our fill of love until morning; let us delight ourselves with caresses. For my husband is not at home, he has gone on a long journey; he has taken a bag of money with him, at the full moon he will come home.' With her many persuasion she entices him; with her flattering lips she seduces him. Suddenly he follows her as an ox goes to the slaughter, or as one in fetters to the discipline of a fool, until an arrow pierces through his liver; as a bird hastens to the snare, so he does not know that it will cost him his life. Now therefore, my sons, listen to me, and pay attention to the words of my mouth. Do not let your heart turn aside to her ways, do not stray into her paths. For many are the victims she has cast down, and numerous are all her slain. Her house is the way to Sheol, descending to the chambers of death."

37  BL MS Harley 2250, ff. 103r–v. II Samuel 6:6–7 contains an example of a man who touched the ark of the covenant and was immediately struck dead.

who discovered the host vanishing from their sight when they tried to perform mass, impart Eucharist to parishioners, and administer extreme unction.[38] This idea of women and sex as occupationally hazardous to priests persists within Middle English pastoral literature. *Alphabet of Tales*, for example:

> tells of a priest of Saint Peter church … how on a day when he had said his mass and laid down the sacrament on the altar, when he should take it again he could not find it, not all the other people that helped him to seek it. Wherefore witty men that knew him supposed that angels had taken it from him, and translated it into heaven, that he that was a lecherous priest should not receive it unto his damnation; for it was not unknown that he had a mistress in the town and held her openly.[39]

Similarly, *Speculum Sacerdotal* records the story of a priest who refused to give up his mistress. One night after visiting her, he fell off a bridge and drowned. Demons and angels fought for his soul until finally the Blessed Virgin Mary intervened and gave the incontinent priest one more chance. He awoke to find himself alive and immediately forsook his mistress.[40] Thus, according to a variety of exempla, lecherous priests were punished for their sins. Sometimes the punishments proved physically fatal; sometimes the punishments merely undermined sacerdotal power, preventing priests from performing mass; and sometimes punishments were both physically and spiritually damning, such as the case of the priest devoured by demons.

Evidence from visitation records reveals other consequences faced by those suspected of sexual sin who worked in the clerical profession: those in major orders, minor orders, and even those in the gray areas between minor orders and the laity. The vicar choral George Upton was disciplined by the dean of Salisbury in 1405 for incontinence with Isabel Walyssch. He was forced to "stand as last of the choristers and abjure on pain of paying 20s. to fabric."[41] Similarly, the vicar choral John Harnham was disciplined for fornication with one Christine in 1409. He was forced "to stand in choir at services as last of choristers in penitential manner; warned on pain of 20s. not to frequent city nor eat in his house but in common hall with his fellows, who may testify to his conduct."[42] The commissary at Broadway threw the book at chaplain John Jonson in 1498, after he was found guilty of keeping Joan Garrard in the rectory with him and fathering two children by her. They ostracized John from his diocese for ten years, on pain of excommunication, and forbade him from celebrating mass during the next twelve months.[43]

This last punishment faced by chaplain John Jonson was potentially the most damaging to clerics in priestly orders, as it stripped them of sacerdotal authority.

[38] Frederic C. Tubach, *Index Exemplorum: A Handbook of Medieval Religious Tales* (Helsinki: Suomalainen Tiedeakatemia, 1969), 208–212.

[39] *Alphabet of Tales*, ed. Banks, 462.

[40] *Speculum Sacerdotal: Edited from British Museum MS Additional 36791*, ed. Edward H. Weatherly, EETS original series 200 (London: Oxford University Press, 1936), 42–45.

[41] *The Register of John Chandler, Dean of Salisbury, 1404–17*, ed. T.C.B. Timmins, Wiltshire Record Society series 39 (Devizes: Wiltshire Record Society, 1984), 137.

[42] Ibid., 158.

[43] *The Register of John Morton II*, ed. Christopher Harper-Bill, The Canterbury & York Society, vol. 78 (Woodbridge, Suffolk: Boydell Press, 1991), 149.

Sermon 42 in *Middle English Sermons* quotes John Chrysostom that a priest's power exhibited "at the altar working the mystery of the blessed Sacrament" is greater than that of Elijah when he called forth divine fire during his struggle with the priests of Baal. Moreover, "not only this mystery is given to priests, but over all this they have power to open and shut the gates of heaven, the which power neither archangel nor angel might never attain."[44] Because of this great power, proved by the miracle of the altar, "there is none earthly power equal to the power of priesthood ... the power that priests have, it perishes heavens, it attains to man's soul and makes it both free and bound, quick and dead." Imbuing priests with spiritual and temporal power that, according to clerical authors, set them above kings and angels, the miracle of mass was indeed an inimitable privilege – the loss of which severely undermined clerical authority. Perhaps this explains why the vicar of Remmesbury, after he was suspended from performing "the divine services" in 1409 for committing adultery with three different women, ignored the injunction against him and continued performing mass.[45] In addition to divine retribution (as suggested by exempla) and the humiliation of public denouncement, then, clerics suspected of sexual immorality also risked losing their spiritual authority.

Hence clerical authors who complained about women's seductive clothing and railed against temptresses could have been acting in part from a concern for self preservation. This attitude also could explain why clerical authors viewed their guilty brethren so tolerantly: they perceived priests as on the defensive, fighting against an assault of temptresses. The text of *Speculum Sacerdotal* prescribes the year-long penance for priests who fornicated once with a woman: saying seven Psalters each month, each week reciting the three disciplines, and each day reciting the seven psalms with seven genuflections. The penance steadily increased for each time fornication occurred, cresting with those clerics involved in long-term sexual relations with married women. Penance, of course, lessened for priests who had enough self-control not to consummate their lust. "And he that kisses a woman without will or heart of fornication to be done, let him have iii disciplines for his evil example. And he that kisses a woman with will of trespass, let him have x disciplines with as many 'Miserere Mei, Deus.' And he that kisses [and] in his kissing ejects out his seed, let him therefore sustain xv disciplines." Penance also lessened for priests seduced by lecherous women. "If any do fornication of adultery with a woman through sudden chance, all by the woman's steering and not of his own purpose or deliberation, then is much less penance for to be enjoined unto him then such as we spoke of before."[46] *Instructions for Parish Priests* simply recommended clerics avoid the company of questionable women, so as not to tarnish their reputations, and suggested that confessors avert their eyes specifically from female penitents.[47]

This desire to protect themselves from immorality, not to mention the perception of women as culpable for sexual indiscretion, could have interfered with

[44] *Middle English Sermons edited from BM MS. Royal 18 B xxiii*, ed. Woodburn O. Ross, EETS original series 209 (London: Oxford University Press, 1940), 281.

[45] *The Register of John Chandler*, 101.

[46] *Speculum Sacerdotal*, 87–89.

[47] *Instructions for Parish Priests*, 79 and 113. The author of *Jacob's Well* specifically states that the sight of women can indeed cause sin. *Jacob's Well*, 159.

clerical obligations to care for women. Peter Biller has commented in his survey of Latin pastoral manuals that: "The dangers of confession becoming the occasion of sexual entanglement is reflected in warnings which are commonplace in the instructional literature: the priest was to avoid looking at the woman and to hear confession in a place where both can be seen. Even with modest and chaste confessor and penitents, the difference of gender could still make things awkward."[48] John Mirk provides a clear example of this awkwardness of gender in the instructions he gives for confessing penitents. With a man, the priest was to instruct him "to kneel down on his knee" and then (after already speaking with the penitent), "over your eyes pull your hood, And hear his shrift with gentle heart." With a woman, however, the priest was first to make sure he did not "see her face," then to instruct her "to kneel down beside you," and finally to "turn your face a little away from her" throughout the confession. If taken literally, Mirk's advice distanced priests from the women they served. Similarly, St. Paul's advice in *Quattuor Sermones* to flee women's company was incompatible with what priests acknowledged they must do: provide female parishioners with proper counseling and spiritual care.[49]

Priests were concerned about the perception of sexual immorality and advised one another to take precautions when dealing with women. *Middle English Sermons* relates the story of a hermit who rescued his sister from prostitution and then set out with her to journey home. Understanding the negative connotations involved in a cleric traveling alone with a woman (regardless of their sibling relationship), this hermit called out to his sister when they met travelers along the road: "For God's love, sister, withdraw you and go another way; for these folk will else say that you are my lemon [mistress], and you go [in] my company." His sister meekly obeyed, withdrawing to a safe distance away from her brother. After the travelers had passed, the hermit called to his sister, but she did not respond. He went searching for her and found her dead, her feet bloody from the treacherous road.[50] According to sermon context, the point of this story was to both demonstrate that true repentance could save the worst of sinners (the prostitute) and encourage parishioners to hurry with their confession and repentance "for to lie in sin long, it is great peril" because death could come at any moment. Yet, the story also depicts a cleric safeguarding himself from the suspicion of sexual immorality.

Nonetheless, even though "hostility toward sexuality could easily shift into hostility toward women," as Ruth Mazo Karras has commented, pastoral vernacular literature is less antiwoman than one might expect.[51] As we have already seen, clerical authors perceived women as ordinary parishioners – explicitly incorporating them within their texts – and urged priests to fulfill their pastoral obligations to women. An exemplum from *An Alphabet of Tales* accentuates these points. In the story, a woman in need of council presents herself to St. Augustine. He neither looked on her nor answered her, and she assumed that "he would not behold a woman's face" because of his holiness. Sadly, she went away. But the next

48  Peter Biller, "Confession in the Middle Ages: Introduction," in *Handling Sin: Confession in the Middle Ages*, eds. Peter Biller and A. J. Minnis (York: York Medieval Press, 1998), 1–34, at 13.
49  *Instructions for Parish Priests*, 109–113; *Quattuor Sermones*, 60.
50  *Middle English Sermons*, 148–149.
51  Karras, *Common Women*, 103.

day, she had an epiphany during mass that St. Augustine had been meditating on the joys of the Trinity during her visit. So she went to him again, and this time he spoke with her and listened to her problem and gave her "his best council."[52] In short, St. Augustine treated this woman as an ordinary parishioner despite the conventional wisdom that holy men should "not behold a woman's face." Similarly, a fifteenth-century exemplum from *Middle English Sermons* tells of a priest who went to extraordinary lengths to help a particularly dangerous female parishioner: a prostitute who specialized in seducing clergy. "Where she knew any holy man in a country, thither she would go and would not leave till that she had tempted him to sin with her." Yet, despite the danger she posed to clerical celibacy, the curate of her local church actively tried to reform her. When she passed his church one day, he spoke to her, begging her to leave her sin and confess. She refused. Finally the priest tricked her into confessing by hiring her to say prayers: "'I pray you for my love, go into the church and say 5 Ave Maria's before the image of Our Lady.' 'No, Peter, I will not,' said she; 'go thyself.' Then the priest said to her, 'Go and say this with good devotion, and I shall give thee 40d.'" The woman complied, and (after the image of the Blessed Virgin came miraculously to life) she became overwhelmed by her own guilty conscience. She ran from the altar, fell before the priest, and begged for confession. He tried to take her to a private place, but she insisted she had sinned openly and thus would confess openly. But before she could finish her shrift, sorrow for her sin overcame her, and she fell to the ground dead. Her sins had beleaguered her literally to death. Yet, because of the priest's concern, she died repentant and an angel came from heaven and carried her soul to "the bliss that ever shall last."[53] This exemplum reveals the sexual hazard that women posed to priests; it also reveals the pastoral concern of a priest for the soul of a wayward woman.[54]

Female sexuality was not the only problem associated with women. Pastoral vernacular literature also portrays women as difficult penitents – hazardous to meet with, challenging to assign penance to, and prone to not completing their confessions. Although the Archbishop of York was not speaking about confession, his cry of exclamation when the troublesome Margery Kempe appeared before him a second time might indeed have reflected the feelings of some priests when confronted with the equally troublesome aspects of caring for female parishioners: "What, woman, are you come again? I would fain be delivered of you."[55]

In general, confession comprised one of the most complicated aspects of pastoral care. On the one hand, it was difficult for priests. They were responsible for convincing their parishioners of the necessity of confession, asking the right

---

52 *Alphabet of Tales*, EETS original series 126, 70.
53 *Middle English Sermons*, 161.
54 It must be noted that priests also posed a sexual hazard for female parishioners. Women could and were sexually harassed by male clerics. Some certainly also were raped. Yet the evidence for this book stems from the clerical perspective. Thus it reveals the clerical perception of women as sexual hazards to clerics rather than the other way around. I am expanding this work to include women's perspective on pastoral care as well as the clergy's perspective. But that discussion will take place in my future scholarship.
55 Margery Kempe, *The Book of Margery Kempe: The Text from the Unique MS Owned by Colonel W. Butler-Bowdon*, ed. Sanford Brown Meech with prefatory note by Hope Emily Allen and notes and appendices by Sanford Brown Meech and Hope Emily Allen, EETS original series 212 (London: Oxford University Press, 1940), 131.

questions to insure that parishioners remembered all their sins, safeguarding the privacy of confession so that parishioners would feel comfortable revealing their sins, assigning appropriate penance so that sins could be absolved without over-burdening or overwhelming the penitents, and making sure that they did not accidentally reveal confessions, either intentionally or unintentionally. Further-more, they were expected to do all this within a very short amount of time: a few days during Holy Week.[56] Alexander Murray has remarked, "A day spent hearing confessions could thus be exhausting." He then quoted a Carthusian monk, "he knew no more 'dangerous or difficult work' than the hearing of confessions."[57] A passage in *Jacob's Well* reinforces how critical it was for priests to conduct confession properly, comparing confession and penance to a well "scoop" which removes the water of sin from the soul. "If the scoop of penance be broken, that is, if the shrift be parted, some to a priest and some to another for shame, or if you be shrive(n) of some sins, and of some sins not shriven, then the scoop is broken, and ... the water of curse falls again into the pit of your conscience through the broken scoop of your broken penance."[58] If penance was not conducted properly and penitents did not fully confess their sins, the whole process was wasted (just as drawing water with a hole-in-the-bucket is wasted effort) and the parishioner remained, as *Jacob's Well* describes it, "cursed as ever was Judas or Pilate." It was the priest's job to make sure that this did not happen. Mirk likewise emphasized the critical nature of the priest's role in hearing confession and assigning penance in his *Instructions for Parish Priests*:

> Wherefore you need to be wise,
> For, forsooth, great need it is,
> Lest you do ought on madness,
> And so send all to the devil;
> Better it is with penance slight,
> In-to purgatory a man to put,
> Then with penance over-much,
> Send him to hell.[59]

On the other hand, confession was also difficult for parishioners. They were the ones who had to trust their most intimate transgressions to a priest. By itself, this was a difficult task. The text of BL MS Sloane 1584 urges male and female parish-ioners to overcome their embarrassment about revealing their sins and to make full confessions: "if any of you know himself in any deadly sin which paraventure he dare not be shriven of for shame ... be it *man be it woman* and spare not for no rebuke of the people for ... better it says for to fall in danger of man's power than in god's for man may no more do but hurt your body by word or by deed but god

---

56  Tentler, *Sin and Confession*, 82–88. Although he is not writing about England, W. David Myers provides a good picture of late medieval/early modern confession in his '*Poor, Sinning Folk*': *Confession and Conscience in Counter-Reformation Germany* (New York: Cornell University Press, 1996), 27–60.

57  Alexander Murray, "Counseling in Medieval Confession," in *Handling Sin: Confession in the Middle Ages*, eds. Peter Biller and A.J. Minnis (York: York Medieval Press, 1998), 63–78, at 75. Some parish-ioners confessed more frequently than this, such as Margery Kempe. But, in general, most parish-ioners confessed only once a year during Lent.

58  *Jacob's Well*, 65.

59  *Instructions for Parish Priests*, 155.

may hurt your both body and soul and put them into the fire of hell without end therefore fear not for no shame."[60] Logistics further complicated the difficulty of confession. The confessional booth was a sixteenth-century invention and, since most ordinary parishioners waited to confess until the last few days before Easter and since ordinary confessions took place in public and semi-public places(such as the parish church), absolute privacy would have been difficult. Some evidence suggests that priests rigged up curtains or tried to hold confession in sheltered corners of the church, while the popular exemplum (narrated in the introduction to *Pastoral Perceptions*) about the priest who could see the sins of his penitents suggests that confession during Lent was organized by gender – with men confessing first, and then women. These precautions, if implemented, could have afforded some privacy and alleviated some jitters about confessing with members of the opposite sex, but they would not have shielded parishioners from nosy neighbors, casual passer-bys, or intentional interlopers.[61] Most confessing penitents would have been in the visual range (or at least the curtain behind which they stood), and sometimes in the auditory range, of their peers – jostling one another in the queue as they awaited their turns.[62] A further complicating factor stemmed from the priests themselves: some were untrustworthy. Although priests should not have revealed confessions, evidence suggests they sometimes did. An exempla from the *Alphabet of Tales* tells of a "rich housewife that had done many horrible sins." She was ashamed to confess them until finally she sought a young priest and "shrove her unto him of all her sins." The inexperienced priest, instead of confirming her guilt and assigning penance, "was loathe to displease her, and counseled her to fulfill the lust and the liking of her body." The woman was (understandably) surprised by this advice and refused to do it. This upset the priest, and in revenge, he disclosed her sins to "any man and defamed her."[63] Visitation records indicate that the actions of this fictional priest occurred in the real world. Chaplain Thomas Bourton was accused of being a "habitual gossip and causes quarrels between parishioners"; rector Stephen Froggemere publicized the confession of John Smith; and the chaplain of Wokingham, within a litany of charges, was accused of revealing the confessions of his parishioners.[64]

In short, confession was a difficult business. Women made it more difficult. To begin with, because many women lived under the authority of male household heads and because women were female, all men working in the clerical profession had to be aware that private meetings with female parishioners were subject to misinterpretation. *Speculum Sacerdotal* speaks about men who "find a cleric

---

60  BL MS Sloane 1584, ff. 49v–r.
61  BL MS Sloane 1584, ff. 69v–70v; *Festial*, 132. See also, Ann Eljenholm Nichols, "The Etiquette of Pre-Reformation Confession in East Anglia," *The Sixteenth Century Journal* 17:2 (1986), 145–163, for a discussion about the visual evidence of confession provided by seven sacrament fonts.
62  Although discussing Germany, Myers comments on confession are still applicable: "Routinely, when Christians made their confessions, other members of the congregation watched, and perhaps hoped to overhear. The penitent had little chance of anonymity. The congregation could also witness refusals to confess, arguments between penitent and priest, denials of absolution, or even excessively lengthy confessions. As a result, distinctions between 'private' and 'public' penance do not adequately describe the late-medieval situation, which was, curiously, both." Myers, '*Poor, Sinning Folk*,' 52.
63  *Alphabet of Tales*, EETS original series 126, 126–127.
64  *The Register of John Chandler*, 35, 25, and 93–94.

against reason with his wife, mother, sister, or daughter" and "violently smite" the cleric.[65] Maurice Tyler, a rector in the deanery of Salisbury, fueled the flames of concern about relationships between women and priests when he was caught alone with two women in 1405. He confessed to sexual immorality with one of the women, Margaret from Yevele, but he denied the charge of misconduct with an unnamed servant woman from Shirbourne.[66] Of course, acceptable meetings between women and priests, concerning pastoral issues such as confession and penance, most certainly were the norm. But even with innocent motives, a woman and a cleric found huddled in an alcove or interacting outside the walls of parish churches raised suspicion – regardless of the cleric's status. The dean of Salisbury, for example, warned vicars choral John Sangere, William Blundell, and Richard Coke respectively in 1405 not to meet women "in suspect places," "in close or in other suspect places," nor to take "different women to his house in close."[67] In the same manner, the vicar John Wellys was forbidden to meet one Denise Sturyes "in suspect places or receive her in his house on pain of £10."[68] Ostensibly because of previous problems, harsh measures were implemented against the canons in Repton to insure that suspicion would not cloud their relationships with women. "They should never henceforth have open or clandestine conversation with any woman within the bounds of the house, unless they had previously obtained express licence from the prior, on pain of incarceration for seven days for the first offence, twenty days for the second offence, one month for the third offence, three months for the fourth offence, the penalty thereafter increasing at the prior's discretion."[69] Even clerics testing the authenticity of Margery Kempe's devotional weeping made sure to take some children along with them as they accompanied Margery to an isolated chapel.[70] Moreover, it would have been difficult to tell the difference between a cleric comforting a distraught female penitent and a cleric engaged in improperly touching a woman, especially if the cleric had previously been accused of sexual impropriety. Perhaps this is what happened to Alexander Champion, a vicar in the deanery of Salisbury, who, in 1412, was charged by five different men with multiple crimes of sexual immorality.[71] Indeed, Champion might have been guilty of committing adultery with Walter Luyde's wife and John Shifford's wife, of carrying on a two year affair with Alice, wife of William Burton, of sustaining a seven year affair with John Forst's wife, of frequently impregnating his concubine in Salisbury, and even of soliciting female parishioners during confession at Lent. Then again, he might also have been as innocent as he claimed – guilty of nothing more than attempting to befriend and provide pastoral care to female parishioners.

The dependent status of wives also complicated pastoral care – impinging on how priests assigned penance. Because a wife "be not of her own power," priests had to be especially careful about dispensing penance so as not to accidentally

---

65   *Speculum Sacerdotal*, 82.
66   *The Register of John Chandler*, 23.
67   Ibid., 136–137.
68   Ibid., 77–78.
69   *The Register of John Morton II*, 108.
70   *The Book of Margery Kempe*, 200–201.
71   *The Register of John Chandler*, 119. "In Lent he solicited wives and servant girls," a footnote reads, "The context suggests that this was done at confession."

reveal the sins of their married female penitents.[72] *Speculum Sacerdotal* states in its homily *On Penance*, "if a woman have trespassed in adultery and dare not fast for her husband should not hold her suspect, it is our counsel that she receive the fasting that is worthy for adultery, but let her eat … that she be not in no suspect of her husband."[73] Just make sure, the text continues, that she does not eat to full-ness on those days, only enough to allay suspicion. Mirk concurs with this advice in his *Instructions for Parish Priests*.

> Now take heed what I you relate,
> If a wife has done a sin,
> Such penance you give her then
> That her husband may not know,
> Lest for the penance sake
> Woe and wrath between them wake [arise].[74]

Clerical literature consistently cautions priests to avoid creating strife between husbands and wives. The compiler of St. John's College MS S. 35 reiterated that penitents should not create strife or discord between any man and woman, but especially not between a man and his wife.[75] Because standard penance was often assigned for certain sins, a husband who discovered the penance of his wife might also discover the sins she had committed. By assigning penance carelessly, priests might reveal (albeit inadvertently) private confessions that could instigate marital discord and harm the women entrusted in their care.

In addition to highlighting the difficulties caused by the sexuality and dependent status of female parishioners, clerical authors also rendered the behavior of female parishioners as frustrating the pastoral care process. John Mirk portrayed women in his *Instructions* as overly sensitive to inattentive and impatient confessors.

> But when a woman comes to you …
> Still as stone there you sit,
> And keep you well that you not spit.
> Cough you not then if you please,
> Nor wring you not with your legs,
> Lest she suppose you make that fuss
> For loathing that you hear there,
> But sit you still as any maid
> Till that she has all said.[76]

Mirk seemed to think that careless clerical behavior adversely affected female penitents – perhaps scaring them or shaming them into not completing their confessions. Margery Kempe's account about the confessor who "was a little too hasty and began sharply to reprove her before she had fully said what she intended, and so she would no more say for aught he might do" seems to substantiate Mirk's fear. To counter the problem – and hopefully avoid an aftermath like that of

---

[72]  *Speculum Sacerdotal*, 82.
[73]  Ibid., 77.
[74]  *Instructions for Parish Priests*, 154–155.
[75]  St. John's College Cambridge MS S. 35, f. 11v.
[76]  *Instructions for Parish Priests*, 113–114.

Margery Kempe's – Mirk implored priests to stay quiet and still throughout the confession so as not to scare or upset their female penitents.[77]

Margery Kempe's behavior highlights another characteristic that Mirk associated with women: a tendency to not complete confessions. Sermon 34 in *Middle English Sermons* underscores the importance of full confessions, stating that, "You must look that you tell all your sins and leave no deadly sin behind, for and [if] you do for that sin you go to hell."[78] Sermon 31 of *Speculum Sacerdotal* concurs with this advice, "And let it not be confessed of one sin only but of all, for he that has many sins and leaves them all except one, he may be likened to him that is bound with many chains and breaks them except one, the which is strong and suffice to hold him still ... So of him that has many crimes of sins, if he leave all except one, that one is cause of his damnation."[79] To be sure, reluctance about confessing sins would have been a problem faced by all parishioners – male as well as female. John Mirk's story about the evil chapman who refused to confess even when solicited by Jesus attests to this fact. Yet a passage from *Instructions for Parish Priests* associates women particularly with concealing sins from their confessors:

> And when she stops and says no more,
> If you see she [still] needs teaching,
> Then speak to her in this fashion,
> And say "take you good advice,
> And what manner thing you are guilty of,
> Tell me boldly and make no mockery.
> Tell me your sin, I you pray,
> And spare you not by no way.
> Hesitate you not for no shame,
> Perhaps I have done the same,
> And very probably much more,
> If you knew all my distress."[80]

Mirk's unambiguous language suggests that he believed women would be especially reluctant about revealing some sins to priests, and so he concluded the section with advice about how priests could loosen women's tongues. A myriad of reasons could explain the reticence of female penitents, from fears about eavesdropping husbands and neighbors to fears about gossiping priests. But one reason stands out: female penitents were embarrassed to share intimate sins with a masculine clergy.[81] It seems telling that exempla emphasizing women's reluc-

---

77 *The Book of Margery Kempe*, 6–9.
78 *Middle English Sermons*, 183.
79 *Speculum Sacerdotal*, 121.
80 *Instructions for Parish Priests*, 113–114. The Royal manuscript clearly associates this problem only with female parishioners, 196–197. Mirk did encourage male penitents some during confession, 144, but he never assumed men would stop confessing (like he did with women). He also spent less time encouraging men then he did women. For further discussion of the Royal manuscript, see my article, "Gendering Pastoral Care: John Mirk and his *Instructions for Parish Priests*," in *Fourteenth Century England*, vol. IV, ed. J.S. Hamilton (Woodbridge, Suffolk: Boydell Press, 2006), 93–108.
81 Of course, this fear might also be combined with the others – women might have feared priests gossiping to their husbands. For example, one Middle English version of the *Gesta Romanorum* tells of a Lady who committed murder, confessed, and commenced with her penance. Her confessor,

tance to confess often involve sexual sin. *Festial*, tells of the woman who called out to Jesus in despair because she had committed the sin of lechery. A voice from heaven absolved her because, presumably, she had been unable to confess this sin to her priest.[82] Similarly, *Jacob's Well* relays the narrative of a Roman lady who became pregnant by her son. She was so ashamed that after the child was born, she killed it and threw away the body. "But always, in her heart, she was sorry, and always prayed god of mercy, and did sharp deeds of penance, and made restitution of her wrongs, save she durst not be shriven of her cursed sin, for shame."[83] Finally she was accused by a demon, and so "with full sorrow of heart and weeping," she was forced to confess her crimes of incest and murder to a priest. Whatever the reason for the reticence of female penitents, however, Mirk's advice depicted women as overly sensitive to impatient confessors and prone to concealing sins from their priests. To help clerics overcome these challenges, he taught priests to be especially careful in how they responded to female penitents and to be especially adept at extracting confessions from unwilling participants.

Exempla mirror Mirk's assumptions about female penitents, portraying them as prone to concealing rather than confessing their sins. An *Alphabet of Tales* tells of a "rich housewife" who had committed many horrible sins. "She had great sorrow for them in her heart, and yet she would never shrive her of them."[84] BL MS Harley 1288, a fifteenth-century exempla collection in Latin and English that contains *Festial* narratives, relays at least three stories about penitents concealing sins from priests or being too ashamed to confess certain sins – including one woman who, after hiding a great sin during confession, went home and hanged herself. In each case, the distraught penitent was a woman.[85] Likewise, one Middle English version of the *Gesta Romanorum* contains three stories encouraging parishioners to make full confessions and not conceal their sins: the first tells of the woman with a hand stained by the blood of Christ, which will not wash away until she makes full confession; the second tells of a crucifix that curled its toes away from a woman attempting to kiss them, until she had made full confession; the third tells of a pious woman rebuked by a saint for not making full confession.[86] In a final example, sermon 34 of *Middle English Sermons* addresses good living, penance, and confession. The narrative that it uses to illustrate the necessity of full confession is that of a priest who sang masses and did good deeds for seven years for the soul of his mother, which he confidently assumes would go to heaven because of her good deeds. She appeared to him in a dream as a horrible and ugly shadow, confessing: "I am perpetually damned ... For when that I was first wedded I did adultery in my youth, and for shame I would never shrive me thereof and so suddenly I died without confession. And therefore I am damned without end." The sermon concludes, "by this you may well see that if you leave any deadly sin within you for shame, and is not willing to shrive you thereof,

---

however, betrayed her crimes to her husband, who ripped open her clothes to see her penitential hair shirt (as proof of her guilt). Heaven intervened on her behalf, and the hair shirt disappeared from her body in a cloud of white smoke. *Gesta Romanorum*, 394–396.

82  *Festial*, 26.
83  *Jacob's Well*, 67.
84  *Alphabet of Tales*, ed. Banks, 126–127.
85  BL MS Harley 1288, ff. 34r, 35v (repeated 37v and 39r), 36v (very similar in 40r).
86  *Gesta Romanorum*, 393–394.

and if you so die without doubt you go to hell."[87] Like so many others of her sex, this female exemplum character was condemned because she had been ashamed of a sexual sin and concealed it instead of confessing it. Women would not have been alone in concealing sins from priests. But, according to their depiction in exempla, they were especially likely to do so.

Whereas Mirk gave advice about how to loosen the tongues of female penitents, some exempla suggest another option: that Jesus himself could assume the role of priest and motivate taciturn women. BL MS Royal 18 B XXIII tells the story of a woman caught in deadly sin who avoided confession. Concerned about this woman's spiritual state, her confessor visited her and encouraged her to confess. It was to no avail. Shortly thereafter Jesus appeared in a vision to the unrepentant woman and bade her place her hand in the wound on his side. She complied and touched the heart of Christ. Jesus explained that she should be no more ashamed to reveal her heart to him as he had been to reveal his heart to her. The woman then awoke, distraught with blood dripping from her hand. In a scene reminiscent (to modern readers) of Shakespeare's Macbeth, this female parishioner found she could not wash away the damned spot. Embarrassed, she covered the tell-tale bloodstain with a "cloth." It was not until she attempted to receive Eucharist that a vision of a fair lady appeared to her priest and revealed that the woman was in deadly sin, hiding proof of her guilt with the cloth. Ripping the cloth from her hand, the priest forced exposure of the sin.[88]

A similar tale appears in *Festial*.

> I read of a woman that had done a horrible sin, and might never, for shame, shrive her thereof. And oft, when she came to shrift, she was in purpose forto have been shriven; but ever the fiend put such a shame in her heart, that she had never grace to cleanse her thereof. Then, on a night, as she lay in her bed, and thought much on that sin, Jesus Christ came to her and said: "My daughter, why will you not show me you heart, and shrive you of that sin that you live in?" "Lord," said she, "I may not, for shame." Then said Christ: "Show me you hand"; and took her hand, and put it into his side, and said, and drew it all bloody out: "Be you no more ashamed to open you heart to me, then I am to open my side to you." Then was this woman grieved of the blood, and would have washed it away; but she might not, by no way, till she had shriven her of that sin. Then, when she was shriven, immediately the hand was clean as that other.

A priest takes part in this exemplum, despite his nominal role, as the text specifically states the woman went to a priest and confessed her sin.[89] Yet, in both stories, the priest is not the impetus for confession. Each woman confesses only after Jesus intercedes, forcing, literally, their hands. A third exemplum carries this scenario one step further, removing the human cleric from the sacrament of penance and confession. In the tale, a woman became overwhelmed by her own sinful life. "I read of a woman that was fouled with the sin of lechery, and almost fell into despair." After comparing herself to the perfect life of Jesus, she knew herself unworthy of paradise, and deserving the pains of hell. At last, however, she

---

[87] *Middle English Sermons*, 183–184.
[88] BL MS Royal 18 B XXIII, f. 51v. Ross omitted this exemplum from *Middle English Sermons*.
[89] *Festial*, 90 and 95. A very similar tale also occurs in *Middle English Sermons*, 216–217.

remembered the childhood of Christ. "Wherefore she cried to Christ praying him for his childhood that he would have mercy on her, and forgive her her sin and her trespass." A voice from heaven, presumably that of Jesus, responded: declaring her sins forgiven. "Your trespass is forgiven you."[90] Thus Jesus usurped the role of an earthly confessor, hearing the woman's confession and providing absolution.

In short, these three exempla suggest that female penitents were prone to conceal sin from their confessors and prone to require divine assistance to complete their confessions – sometimes through bypassing clerical authority. These gendered trends persist throughout medieval exempla.[91] First, as previously discussed, exempla depict female characters as especially prone to concealing sin from priests. In Mirk's *Festial*, exemplum characters that conceal sin or are ashamed to confess sin are almost exclusively female.[92] Although some exempla do attribute these characteristics to male penitents, these narratives occur less frequently and many times the reasons given for a man's failure to confess are different from those given for women. A narrative in *Jacob's Well* tells of the "obstinate" sinner who knew he had sinned but refused to confess. "I may no sorrow have. I may not shrive me. I may have no will to make amends," he said. "Grace is gone from me. For, when I might have done penance, then would I not, and now, though I would, I may not. I have be[en] so long in my cursed sin, without very repentance; therefore, now have I no grace to be in will to do penance, nor to ask mercy, for the doom of damnation is soon upon me."[93] This man chose not to confess because he was stubborn and believed his actions had already damned him. Conversely, female exempla characters – such as the woman absolved by a voice from heaven – want to confess but are too ashamed to reveal their sin. This juxtaposition of defiant male penitents with fearful female penitents permeates medieval exempla. The narratives Mirk retold about the evil chapman and the woman with the bloody hand exemplify this well. The woman is repentant and sorrowful, eventually persuaded to overcome her fear and confess. The chapman, however, is obstinate even after Jesus appears to him and begs him to confess. The man defiantly refuses, claiming he does not believe Jesus will show him grace, and Jesus responds by flinging blood (or a bit of his flesh, depending on the version) in the chapman's face. The gendered responses of these exempla characters perhaps suggested to clerical readers that they should approach male and female penitents differently. Persuasion, for example, seemed futile with male exempla penitents, whereas female exempla penitents needed to be cajoled, coerced, and sometimes threatened to uncover their concealed sins.

---

[90] *Festial*, 26.
[91] Judy Ann Ford also has discussed many of these exempla, but she reads them mostly within the context of lay agency and Lollardy. Judy Ann Ford, *John Mirk's Festial: Orthodoxy, Lollardy, and the Common People in Fourteenth-Century England* (Cambridge: D.S. Brewer, 2006), 32 and 44–45 (as well as throughout). Albert R. Elsasser has found that most of Mirk's exempla have long histories, extending to the twelfth and thirteenth centuries. For example, the story of the embarrassed woman (as Ford has called it), can be found in at least three manuscripts that predate *Festial*: the mid-thirteenth-century Odo of Cheriton's *Fables*, the late thirteenth-century *Speculum Laicorum*, and the late fourteenth-century BL MS Cleopatra CVIII. Albert R. Elsasser, "The Exempla of Mirk's *Festial*," Ph.D. diss., Princeton University, 1924, 97–98.
[92] Men in *Festial* sometimes refuse to confess sin (such as the evil chapmen), but they are not portrayed as hiding sin or described as too ashamed to confess their sin. See Appendix II.
[93] *Jacob's Well*, 21–22.

Second, exempla also depict women as inclined to circumvent sacerdotal authority. One famous story tells of a woman unable to attend mass on the feast day for the Purification of the Virgin Mary. Sad and discouraged, she fell asleep, only to find herself attending the feast in heaven, accompanied by angels, saints, the Virgin Mary, and Jesus as substitute priest. Thus, when she was unable to attend an earthly service, God provided a divine one.[94] Variations of other stories popular throughout medieval Europe tell of women who likewise bypassed the traditional parochial route, such as the woman who received Eucharist directly from the hands of heaven (as the host flew into her mouth without assistance from the priest) and the woman for whom angels celebrated mass when her chaplain was unavailable. Such tales, according to Miri Rubin, "often centre on questions of authority, the women being blessed by communion which obviates parochial routine and its limitations ... These were the stories which could feed the suspicion and rumor about religious women, that they did not recognize sacerdotal mediation or parochial discipline."[95] Mirk's stories about the woman who placed her hand in the side of Jesus and the woman absolved by a voice from heaven fit nicely into this genre. Ashamed of their sin, both women (at least initially) shirked the traditional clerical route and found absolution through divine intervention.

Third, in addition to circumventing clerical authority, female exempla characters are also depicted as doubting sacerdotal authority. Three Middle English exempla illustrate this point well. In the first exemplum (as told in Shrewsbury School MS 3), a woman is tempted "with the sin incredulity." When it came time for her to receive the Eucharist at Easter, she spit the host into a handkerchief, carried it home, and hid it in a chest. Shortly thereafter, she opened the chest to find a "full fair child" hanging on a cross with "wounds all bleeding." Crying out in surprise at this sight, the woman found herself quickly surrounded by nosy neighbors who sent for a priest. The priest, recognizing the sacrilege that the woman had committed, lifted up the cross with child and turned to face his now-penitent parishioner. She confessed her sin of disbelief, cried out to God for forgiveness, and was rewarded with the child shrinking miraculously back into the form of bread.[96] CUL MS Ff. 2. 48 contains a similar story, except this time the doubting female buries the bread in her yard instead of hiding it in a chest. This wife of a pious knight "believed nothing in the mass that very god was in form of bread," records the manuscript. When it came time for her to take mass, she hid the holy bread in a kerchief, carried it home, and buried it under a pear tree. All was well until the knight invited a bishop to Christmas day dinner. In the midst of the feast, a squire brought attention to a fair sight in the knight's yard – a pear tree blossoming with red and white flowers in the middle of winter. The bishop went to see this strange tree, and found a bleeding child. Realizing that her sin had been discovered, the woman confessed to the bishop, saying, "I have grieved my god in word and deed." Miraculously the child reverted back to the Host, and the bishop then administered the consecrated bread to the penitent

---

94 *Festial*, 60–61.
95 Miri Rubin, *Corpus Christi: The Eucharist in Late Medieval Culture* (Cambridge and New York: Cambridge University Press, 1991), 120–121.
96 Shrewsbury School MS 3, f. 54v.

woman.[97] In a third exemplum (as told in *Festial*) Gregory the Great saw Lasma, the woman who had baked the Eucharist bread, laughing during mass. "Lasma," he said, "why smiles you, when you should have taken God's body?" The woman responded that she had made the bread with her own hands, so how could it be God's body? Grieved by her doubt, Gregory asked the people to pray with him that Lasma might believe. "And when they had prayed, Gregory went to the altar, and found the host turned into raw flesh bleeding; which he took and showed this woman. Then she cried and said: 'Lord, now I believe.'"[98] *Speculum Sacerdotal* also records this story, but omits the name Lasma, referring to her only as a housewife. Despite these differences, the woman still explained her laughter in the same manner: "I hear you say that the bread which I made with my hands is God's body."[99] She was similarly rebuked and witnessed the miraculous transformation of the bread she had baked into the bleeding flesh of Jesus. Again, she fell to her knees in repentance.

Doubting sacerdotal authority would have been a critical problem for priests, who derived much social and religious status from their unique ability to perform the miracle of mass. BL MS Sloane 1584 states that penitents should sit below the priest's hand during confession "for the priest sits there in god's stead." It also reminds readers that, "we owe to be shriven to a priest for unto them almighty god gave power to bind and to loose."[100] Representing Jesus on earth, priests authenticated their divine authority – the ability to hear confessions, forgive sins, and bind and loose in heaven and in hell – through their ability to transform ordinary bread and wine into the actual body and blood of Christ. For parishioners to doubt this miracle was a serious sin. *Quattuor Sermones* records that for "Lewd men and women to dispute of this sacrament is utterly forbidden, for it is enough to them to believe as Holy Church teaches them."[101] Perhaps even more serious than the consequences for parishioners were the implications such doubt could have for priests. BL MS Royal 18 B XXIII argues that the office of the priest is so holy that not even angels are able to attain it and that the supreme manifestation of this divine position was the miracle of the altar. "Truly this miracle is heavenly and wonderful that God … [who] sits in heaven upon his Father's right side, in time of sacrifice is contained in the priest's hands."[102] If the bread and wine failed to become the body and blood of Christ, something was seriously wrong. Either the sacrament was false, or the officiating priest – for whatever reason – lacked the power of God.

Yet women, according to exempla, were prone to not believing in this sacerdotal power. Miri Rubin has recognized this gendered trend in her study of *Corpus Christi*, writing: that "Women feature prominently" in tales focused on "the doubts of simple folk, the doubts and errors of those who were misguided by an alleged simplicity, who wished to believe and simply could not. These tales repeated questions about worthy reception, of the dilemma of those who wished to receive, and yet did not properly believe that they were receiving the very body and blood of

97   CUL MS Ff. 2. 38, f. 54.
98   *Festial*, 173.
99   *Speculum Sacerdotal*, 39.
100  BL MS Sloane 1584, ff. 65v and 20v.
101  *Quattuor Sermones*, 42.
102  *Middle English Sermons*, 280.

Christ, and therefore attempted to rid themselves of the host."[103] In addition to the stories already told, Frederic C. Tubach references several more tales and their variations in which a woman rejected the host as bread, a woman who spit the host into her hand because she doubted its efficacy, and even a woman who, tempted by the devil into disbelief, tests the host in her oven by baking it. When she hears a baby boy screaming and sees a vision of the Virgin Mary removing her son from the burning coals, the woman cries out for forgiveness.[104] Similar tales do reveal both men and women failing to take the sacrament of receiving the Eucharist seriously. For example, Shrewsbury School MS 3 tells the tale of two women (one rich, one poor) embroiled in a feud. Their parish priest refused to give them the consecrated host until they reconciled, so the poor woman publicly asked the rich woman for forgiveness. Because of the public arena, the rich woman acquiesced publicly, but privately did not forgive the woman. After both women had knelt at the Lord's board, the poor one thanked the rich one for her change of heart. Spitefully the rich woman than cursed the poor one, crying that she had tricked both her and the priest and lied about extending forgiveness. No sooner had the words crossed her lips, the rich woman tripped, fell down the church steps, and died. Then, before all the people in the churchyard, her breast opened up and the host that she had just received flew out. The priest gathered up the sacred bread and bore it inside the church with great reverence, leaving the sacrilegious body of the woman lying in the dirt.[105] BL MS Sloane 1584 records a similar exemplum, except this time the lackadaisical penitent is a man and instead of falling down the church steps after receiving housel unworthily, he is struck by lightning, his body reduced to a pile of ashes.[106] Thus, according to these stories, both male and female exempla characters partake of the consecrated bread unworthily. Yet, also according to exempla, the outright rejection of the bread as the body of Christ is a characteristic peculiar to women.[107]

Hence, exempla speak loudly about gendered perceptions of female parishioners, depicting women as especially inclined to conceal sins, circumvent clerical authority, and doubt sacerdotal power. According to this portrayal of female parishioners, priests would have had to work extra hard both in extracting confessions from female penitents as well as convincing female penitents of their sacred authority.

*

---

[103] Rubin, *Corpus Christi*, 121; Shrewsbury School MS 3, ff. 55v–56r. This story is also told in *Middle English Sermons*, 62. BL MS Sloane 1584, ff. 47v–48v.

[104] Tubach, *Index Exemplorum*, 207–211.

[105] Shrewsbury School MS 3, ff. 55v–56r. This story is also told in *Middle English Sermons*, 62.

[106] BL MS Sloane 1584, ff. 47v–48v.

[107] This is, of course, based on the exempla I have examined. Interestingly enough, the men who do doubt the Eucharist are priests (from my examination, male doubters are never lay men). *Festial* records one of the rare occasions that men are portrayed as doubting the Eucharist miracle. But these are not male parishioners; they are priests. And they do not doubt the bread; they doubt the wine, as Mirk recorded, they believed not "that Christ shed his blood in the mass." The bishop prayed for their disbelief to be cured, and a "drop of blood ran from the host into the chalice." Amazed the clerics cried, "We believe now fully that this is very God's body and his blood that drop there into the chalice." *Festial*, 170–171.

To conclude, female parishioners deserved pastoral care, a need recognized by clerical authors. Yet these ordinary parishioners presented extraordinary challenges. Women's physical presence threatened clerical purity; women's behavior, dependent status, and sexuality complicated the administration of pastoral care; and women's depiction in exempla as prone to conceal sin, circumvent clerical authority, and doubt sacerdotal power suggested that they required especially proactive participation from their priests. Clerical authors perceived the pastoral care of women as challenging. But it was a challenge they had to face on a daily basis. Thus the exempla portraying Christ as a substitute confessor might have been as comforting to priests as it was comforting to women – for if a priest stumbled over the difficulties involved in caring for a woman, perhaps Jesus himself would pick up the slack.

# CONCLUSION: GENDERED LESSONS

This book opened with an exemplum about a Devonshire priest who diligently set out to deliver extreme unction to a dying woman. He faced many challenges in this task, but succeeded in vanquishing a demon, witnessing a miracle of the consecrated host, and fulfilling his pastoral duties to a female parishioner. The tale ends with the priest going home, praising God for the marvelous events that had occurred.[1]

I would like to end this book by relaying the conclusion of a similar, but more somber story that I introduced in the fourth chapter, *Pastoral Care*. Shrewsbury School MS 3 contains the tale of a young girl whose father sexually abused her as a child. The mother discovered the illicit affair and the father shunned his daughter. When the young girl, now very emotionally confused, "saw her father have no use of her," she flew into a rage, murdering him in the night. Immediately thereafter she ran away to another country and became a prostitute, or "common woman" as the text specifically reads. Yet haunted by the guilt of her livelihood, her former incestuous relationship, and the murder of her father, she stumbled into a local church one day where a devout cleric was preaching. The sermon focused on "the mercy of our lord and how ready he is to grant mercy to sinners and they will ask it." Overwhelmed by her guilt, the penitent prostitute threw herself at the feet of the preacher, pouring out her crimes and begging forgiveness. "I pray you give me penance for my sins for I trust fully in the mercy of our lord," she cried.

Instead of responding to this impassioned plea, however, the cleric paused. We can almost see the look of bewilderment on his face. "[S]eeing the great and horrible sins that the woman had done and because that he should preach again at after noon," the priest told her that her penance and absolution would have to wait. "Abide here still unto my service be done at after noon and then I shall give you penance," he said, further charging her to wait in "contrition and sorrow" until he could meet with her.

This penitential session never occurred. The woman became so distraught over her sins that her "heart burst," and she died "as the people were gathered again for to hear the service." The priest, after discovering her death, became concerned as he had neglected to provide her with penance and absolution. Thus he immediately ordered his congregation to "kneel down and pray heartily to our lord that he would have mercy on the sinful woman's soul." Probably to the great relief of the cleric, a voice responded from heaven, telling the people to leave their praying "for she is in heaven and may pray for you."[2]

---

[1]  *Festial*, 173–174.

[2]  Shrewsbury School MS 3, ff. 59v–60r. Like most exempla, this tale is repeated by many other manuscripts – including the *Gesta Romanorum*. In this version, the priest specifically prays to God to forgive him "of his negligence, that he gave her no penance." *The Gesta Romanorum*, ed. Sidney J.H. Herrtage, EETS extra series 33 (London: Oxford University Press, 1932), 390–392.

To fifteenth-century parishioners, this exemplum reinforced traditional Church teachings that true contrition and repentance could redeem the most lost of souls. For the purposes of this study, however, the significance of the exemplum is somewhat different. While this particular tale tells of a woman's redemption, it also tells about a priest who neglected to provide proper pastoral care to a female penitent.

These two exempla encapsulate the argument of this book. On the one hand, priests with cure of souls were committed to providing for the spiritual needs of their female parishioners. The fictional priest of Devonshire exemplifies this well. He acknowledged the dying woman as an ordinary parishioner; accepted his obligation to provide her with proper pastoral care (which in this instance was extreme unction); and dedicated himself to fulfilling his promise that she would receive God's body before she died. Similarly, clerical authors of vernacular pastoral literature recognized their obligations to teach, preach, and care for women. By their own hands, they explicitly directed text discussing pastoral matters to female parishioners, reminding both their clerical readers and the people they served, that women deserved pastoral care just as their male counterparts. They also accepted their obligations to care for women, outlining practical ways that priests could help meet the needs of female parishioners. Finally, they perceived their female parishioners in a relatively realistic light, understanding that women had pastoral needs different from those of men and acknowledging the different life stages of female parishioners. Some even thought so much about the needs of women that they recognized their lifecycle stages and differentiated singlewomen from the traditional categories of virgin, wife, and widow.

Yet, on the other hand, priests also approached female parishioners cautiously, as did the fictional priest of Shrewsbury School MS 3. Uncertain about how to provide such a sinful penitent with proper penance (and perhaps also shocked by her sins), he stalled, placing his clerical obligation to provide mass over his clerical obligation to care for a soul in need. Because she was truly contrite for her sins, the woman received absolution *not* from the priest, but from God who acted *despite* the priest instead of through him. Similarly, clerical authors of vernacular pastoral literature approached female parishioners cautiously. For them, women's physical presence threatened clerical purity; women's behavior in the confessional, dependent status, and sexuality frustrated the pastoral care process; and the depiction of women in exempla as prone to conceal sin, circumvent clerical authority, and doubt sacerdotal power suggested that priests needed to be especially proactive when caring for the needs of female parishioners. Thus, in both the instructions they gave on how clerics were to care for women and the exempla they shared about pastoral situations involving women, clerical authors rendered female parishioners as problematic.

In short, this study contends that clerical authors of Middle English pastoral literature taught their audiences to think differently about women and men. Sometimes such gendered lessons were helpful. Priests reading John Mirk's pastoral literature would have learned that women were important parishioners who needed to be addressed specifically in their sermons and not overlooked when they administered sacraments. They also would have learned that married women had pastoral needs different from those of singlewomen; that pregnant women had pastoral needs different from those of widows; and that their status of wives affected the penance they could receive. By their own writings, then, many late medieval English clerics acknowledged the important role that female parishioners played in their ministry and professed concern about the quality of care they received.

Sometimes, however, such gendered lessons were also harmful. By focusing so much on the distinctiveness of women, clerical authors branded female parishioners as problematic. They depicted female parishioners as especially ashamed about revealing sensitive confessions, therefore making the confessor's job more difficult as he attempted to unearth concealed sins. They realized that the dependent status of women complicated the pastoral care process (such as how to assign penance). They even portrayed female parishioners as cynical about sacerdotal powers. Most damning, however, clerical authors continued to uphold the medieval tradition of obsessing about female sexuality – perhaps encouraging priests to consider female parishioners as guiltier than their male counterparts when it came to sexual sin. In these respects, the literature designed to help priests serve women better only seems to have widened the gap between them.

In the end it seems priests were neither misogynist villains nor saintly heroes. They were men attempting to fulfill their spiritual obligations to parishioners. Because this study has focused on prescriptive literature written by and for clerics, it has presented only the clerical point-of-view. It would be injudicious to move unproblematically from the advice, sermons, and exempla in these guides to the actual actions of priests and the responses of the women for whom they cared. But it would be equally problematic to seal off this practical literature and pretend that its effect was limited to books and readers. No priest likely followed the suggestions of John Mirk and his peers to the letter, but many priests read and copied their sermon compilations and pastoral handbooks, and some doubt-less shaped their work according to the advice. Thus it is indeed significant that authors of vernacular pastoral literature persisted in both their characterization of women as difficult parishioners and in their attempts to recognize women as ordinary parishioners who deserved ordinary pastoral care. While it is difficult to forget that the repentant prostitute in the exemplum from Shrewsbury School MS 3 died after a priest neglected her immediate request for penance and absolu-tion, we must not forget that the dying woman from Devonshire received Eucha-rist one last time because of the tenacity of another priest. In the real world of late medieval England, evidence from pastoral vernacular literature suggests that neither of these women would have been alone.

## THE MAJOR MANUSCRIPTS OF MIRK'S *FESTIAL*[1]

M.F. Wakelin, Susan Powell, and Alan Fletcher have made notable contributions to cataloguing and describing manuscripts containing the sermons of John Mirk.[2] But these descriptions are scattered throughout a variety of articles and dissertations. Drawing on this previous scholarship and on my own examination of each manuscript, this appendix provides a unified list of the major *Festial* manuscripts.[3] It also helps to clarify further distinctions between the Group A and Group B manuscripts and provides transcriptions of the two prayers and the prologue. Finally, it contains a brief introduction to the minor manuscripts of Mirk's *Festial*.

### British Library MS Cotton Claudius A II[4]

*Description*: Fifteenth century, 1425–50. 158 folios. Manuscript written in several different hands and includes 74 *Festial* homilies (the most in any extant version, ff. 1v–123v) and *Instructions for Parish Priests* (ff. 127r–152v). It includes the usual prayer and prologue and – as Wakelin remind us – the relatively rare homilies on St. Winifred, St. Alkemund, the death of Nero, and the Lord's Prayer. The sermons begin with First Sunday in Advent and end with Dedication of a Church. As Wakelin noted, the compilers of this manuscript clearly were concerned with pastoral needs. This collection would have provided readers with all the necessary information to conduct everyday duties such as baptism and confession; weekly duties such as preaching; and a calendar to remind them of upcoming feasts and celebrations (ff. 152v–153r). This is also the oldest and most complete version of *Festial* (although not the original text), and thus has been used as a basis of comparison for the remaining manuscripts. Wakelin identified it linguistically as coming from northeastern Shropshire (near Lilleshall Abbey and the Staffordshire border), the probable area of original composition.[5] The prayer and prologue it contains, f. 1v, follow:

---

[1] I have appended this list of manuscript descriptions to help clarify the case study of Mirk's *Festial* in the chapter *Pastoral Language*.

[2] The manuscript descriptions often reiterate what Wakelin, Powell, and Fletcher have also found, but I have examined each separately to verify their accuracy. Descriptions of all the manuscripts may also be found in: Martyn F. Wakelin, "The Manuscripts of John Mirk's *Festial*," *Leeds Studies in English* n.s. 1 (1967), 93–118; Alan Fletcher, "Unnoticed Sermons from John Mirk's *Festial*," *Speculum* 55:3 (1980), 514–522; Alan Fletcher and Susan Powell, "The Origins of a Fifteenth-Century Sermon Collection: MSS Harley 2247 and Royal 18 B XXV," *Leeds Studies in English* 10 (1978), 74–96; Susan Powell, "A Critical Edition of the *Temporale* Sermons of MSS. Harley 2247 and Royal 18 B. xxv," Ph.D. diss., University of London King's College, 1986. I have based my dates for the manuscripts on the works of Wakelin, Powell, and Fletcher.

[3] I was unable to view Trinity College Dublin MS 201 in person (obtaining only a microfilm), and thus it is not included in this list. However, as it only contains 36 *Festial* sermons, it hovers somewhere between the major and minor manuscripts.

[4] Description of this MS found in Wakelin, "The Manuscripts of Mirk's *Festial*," 95; and Carl Horstmann, *Altenglische Legenden Neue Folge* (Heilbronn, Germany: Gebr. Henniger, 1881), cxiii–cxvii.

[5] See Wakelin's "Tentative Localisations of the Dialects of Manuscripts of Mirk's Festial" map, in his, "The Manuscripts of John Mirk's *Festial*," 103. Powell notes that Wakelin derived many of these localizations from suggestions by Professor Angus McIntosh. Powell, "A Critical Edition of the *Temporale* Sermons," Part II, Appendix 8, 90.

**The prayer (Prayer I):** God maker of alle thyng/ be at oure be gynnyng/and ȝef us alle hys blessyng/ and bryng us alle to a good endyng amen/

**The prologue:** By myne owne febul lettrure Y fele how yt faruth by/othur that bene in the same degre that hauen charge of/ soulus and bene holdyn to teche hore pareschonus of alle/the principale festus that cometh in the ȝere schewyng/home what the seyntus sofferden and dedun for Goddus/loue so that they schuldon haue the more deuocion in God/ dus seyntys and with the better wylle com to the chyrche/ to serue God and pray to holy seyntys of her help. But/for mony excuson ham by defaute of bokus and sympul/nys of letture therfore in helpe of suche mene clerkus as I am/ my selff, I have drawe this treti sewyng owt of Legenda/Aurea with more addyng to. So he that hathe lust to study/there in, he schal fynde redy of alle the principale festis of the ȝere a schort sermon nedful for hym to techym and othur/for to lerne and for this treti speketh alle of festis I wolle/and pray that it be called a festial the whyche be gynnyth / the forme sonday of the aduent in worschup of God of al/le seyntis that ben wryten there in.

## FIRST RECENSION OF GROUP A MANUSCRIPTS

Three of these four manuscripts contain the prayer (Prayer I) as preserved in BL MS Cotton Claudius A II. Furthermore, again like BL MS Cotton Claudius A II, two contain the homily for St. Alkemund and three contain an extra sermon for the first Sunday in Lent. Thus Powell has suggested that these manuscripts "are descended from the original *Festial* and form the earliest group of MSS."[6]

### Bodleian Library MS Gough Ecclesiastical Topography 4[7]
*Description:* Fifteenth century, 1415–1433.[8] 164 folios. Written in a single hand, it contains 69 homilies from *Festial* (ff. 1r–164r), including prayer, the homilies on St. Winifred, St. Alkemund, and the Narration on the death of Nero. It does not include the prologue. It opens with First Sunday in Advent and ends with the Lord's Prayer. This is the most well-known copy of *Festial* as it was edited by Theodore Erbe and published for the Early English Text Society in 1905 as *Mirk's Festial: A Collection of Homilies by Johannes Mirkus (John Mirk). Edited from Bodl. MS. Gough Eccl. Top. 4, with variant readings from other MSS.* A close reading of the manuscript compared with Erbe's text has revealed the printed edition to be reliable. The first ten homilies were compared and found to be the same, while the introductions and various test passages were compared throughout the remaining homilies with no discrepancies found. Yet, because Bodl. MS Gough Ecclesiastical Topography 4 is significantly different from other *Festial* manuscripts, Erbe's edition should not be used as representative of all *Festial* texts. Linguistically it stems from northern Staffordshire.[9]

---

6   St. Alkemund's tomb was (originally) at Lilleshall Abbey, and a parish church in Shrewsbury and Lilleshall Abbey were both dedicated to him. "We would assume, therefore, that the sermon for Alkemund (which is not found in the *Legenda Aureau* but presumably based on local sources) was in Mirk's original MS." Powell, "A Critical Edition of the *Temporale* Sermons," part II, appendix 8, 89–91.

7   A description can be found in Wakelin, "The Manuscripts of Mirk's *Festial*," 110; and in Horstmann, *Altenglische Legenden*, cxvii.

8   Lillian L. Steckman has provided this date. "A Late Fifteenth-Century Revision of Mirk's *Festial*," *Studies in Philology* 34 (1937), 36–48, at 37.

9   Powell, "A Critical Edition of the *Temporale* Sermons," part II, appendix 8, 90. A description can be found in Wakelin, "The Manuscripts of John Mirk's *Festial*," 104.

### Cambridge, Gonville and Caius College MS 168[10]

*Description*: Mid-fifteenth century. 168 folios (separately numbered as 336 pages). It is written in a single hand and contains 70 *Festial* homilies, including the usual prayer, prologue, and local saint days (St. Winifred and St. Alkemund). It commences with First Sunday in Advent and ends with the sermon detailing burial instructions. Linguistically it stems from northern Nottinghamshire.

### Bodleian Library MS Douce 108[11]

*Description*: Mid-fifteenth century. 354 numbered pages (although Wakelin notes "The pp. really amount to 358, since pp. 203 and 281 are triplicated"). Written in single hand that seems the same as the hands of MSS Douce 60 and 103 (contains *Instructions for Parish Priests*), it probably originates from northern Buckinghamshire.[12] It contains 44 sermons of *Festial* (1–350), opening with First Sunday in Advent and ending with Circumcision of Christ, includes usual prayer and prologue, and – again as Wakelin notes – conforms more with BL MS Cotton Claudius A II order than does Bodl. MS Douce 60 (although there are "many gaps and considerable diversions"). Like Bodl. MS Douce 60, however, the *Festial* sermons are abbreviated significantly and the manuscript is incomplete. It is one of four Group A manuscripts to lack the homily for St. Winifred (which, perhaps, is due to its incomplete form).

### Bodleian Library MS Douce 60[13]

*Description*: Mid-fifteenth century. 239 folios (although only 231 are numbered as, similar to Douce 108, 8 folios are duplicated). Manuscript written in single hand same as that of MSS Douce 103 and 108, and it seems to originate from northern Buckinghamshire.[14] A comprehensive pastoral care manual, it contains 44 *Festial* homilies (ff. 1r–146v, 189r–192v), *Instructions for Parish Priests* (ff. 147r–189r), Richard of Lavynham's Treatise on the Seven Deadly Sins (ff. 193r–213r), and a confessional (ff. 213r–228r). *Festial* lacks prayer and prologue, beginning with homily for Nativity of Our Lady and ending with All Saints, and is not arranged in a chronological nor *sanctorale/temporale* sequence (although it traditionally has been classified with Group A rather than Group B, largely because of its textual similarity to Bodl. MS Douce 108). The *Festial* sermons are abbreviated significantly, leaving out exempla and condensing sentences. It is also one of four Group A manuscripts to lack the homily for St. Winifred.

## SECOND RECENSION OF GROUP A

These manuscripts contain an alternate prayer (Prayer II). It is listed below from BL MS Lansdowne 392, f. 3r.

**Prayer II:** "The helpe and the grace of Almyȝty God þrowe þe besechyng of his

---

10 Powell, "A Critical Edition of the *Temporale* Sermons," part II, appendix 8, 90. A description can be found in Wakelin, "The Manuscripts of Mirk's *Festial*," 110; and in Horstmann, *Altenglische Legenden*, cxvii.

11 A description can be found in Horstmann, p. cxix.; and Wakelin, "The Manuscripts of Mirk's *Festial*," 105–106.

12 Powell, "A Critical Edition of the *Temporale* Sermons," part II appendix 8, 90.

13 A description can be found in Horstmann, cxix–cxx; Richard of Lavynham, *A Litil Tretys on the Seven Deadly Sins*, ed. J.P.W.M. van Zutphen (Rome: Institutum Carmelitanum, 1956), xlii–xliii; *John Mirk's Instructions for Parish Priests: Edited from MS Cotton Claudius A II and Six Other Manuscripts with Introduction, Notes, and Glossary*, ed. Gillis Kristensson, Lund Studies in English 49 (Lund, 1974), 22; and Wakelin, "The Manuscripts of Mirk's *Festial*," 104–105.

14 Powell, "A Critical Edition of the *Temporale* Sermons," part II, appendix 8, 90.

blessyd Moder/ Seynt Mary be wyth us at owre begynnyng help us and spede vs here in/ owe lyvyng, And brynge us to the blysse þat neuer shal haue endynge. Amen."

### British Library MS Lansdowne 392[15]

*Description*: Fifteenth century, Wakelin identified it as shortly before 1450. 122 folios. Linguistically it stems from northern Warwickshire. It includes 51 *Festial* homilies (ff. 3r–95v) and a different prayer that occurs in only three other major *Festial* manuscripts: BL MS Harley 2403, CUL MS Dd. X. 50, and Durham Cathedral MS Cosin V III 5. This prayer also occurs in BL MS Royal 18 B XXIII (*Middle English Sermons*), which contains three *Festial* sermons. The sermons begin with First Sunday in Advent and end with the Lord's Prayer. Post-Reformation editing seems to have occurred in this manuscript, as the majority of the homily for the Translation of St. Thomas was deliberately removed.

### British Library MS Harley 2403[16]

*Description*: Fifteenth century, 1475–1500. 194 folios. *Festial* includes the prayer found in BL MS Lansdowne 392 and the usual prologue, opens with First Sunday in Advent and ends with a fragment of the sermon providing burial instructions and a homily on the Lord's Prayer (70 homilies in all). Wakelin identified it linguistically as stemming from northwestern Warwickshire, southeastern Staffordshire.

### British Library MS Harley 2420[17]

*Description*: Mid-fifteenth century. 63 folios. Manuscript is written in a hand identical to that of BL MS Harley 2417. Fletcher has argued that the two manuscripts originally were bound together and that they stem linguistically from Southeastern Staffordshire. Like its counterpart, it is a badly damaged manuscript with numerous alterations, most of which seem to stem from the post-Reformation period since the words *pope* and *abbot* are repeatedly marked through and references to Rome erased (such as in the homily for *Quinquagesima*, f. 28v). Unlike its counterpart, it contains 27 sermons primarily from the *temporale* sermons (including the *Ascension Day* homily, 53v–56r, which Fletcher neglected on his list). It also contains the usual prayer and prologue, commences with First Sunday in Advent and ends with Corpus Christi.

### British Library MS Harley 2417[18]

*Description*: Fifteenth century. Wakelin dated it shortly before 1450. 87 folios. Manuscript is written in single hand, excluding prayer and prologue, and containing only the *sanctorale* sermons (41 homilies, including fragments). The sermons commence with a fragment on burial instructions and end with All Saints. According to Fletcher, it was originally bound with BL MS Harley 2420, which contains the *temporale* sermons along with a few sermons from the *sanctorale*. He also has argued that these two manuscripts are from Southeastern Staffordshire. It is a damaged manuscript, with the last few folios almost illegible. The manuscript also has been corrected on several occasions, with a different hand inserting words and phrases into the original text, as if comparing this version of *Festial* with another copy. For example, the homily on the nativity of the Virgin Mary read originally in BL MS Harley 2417, "… þe grete repres þat/þey hadde suffred long tyme forth þey ʒode booldely among/oþer of her lynage …" A smaller hand inked in the correction

---

15  A description can be found in Horstmann, *Altenglische Legenden*, cxviii; and Wakelin, "The Manuscripts of Mirk's *Festial*," 95–96.

16  A description can be found in Horstmann, *Altenglische Legenden*, cxvii–cxviii; and Wakelin, "The Manuscripts of Mirk's *Festial*," 96.

17  A description can be found in Fletcher, "Unnoticed Sermons from John Mirk's *Festial*," 518.

18  A description can be found in Fletcher, "Unnoticed Sermons from John Mirk's *Festial*," 519; and Wakelin, "The Manuscripts of Mirk's *Festial*," 97.

"for her bareyn þ was put awey for þat tyme," making the phrase read almost identical to that of Bodl. MS Gough Ecc. Top. 4 and BL MS Cotton Claudius A II. Also, the homily for the Translation of St. Thomas of Canterbury has been crossed out (again, possibly post-Reformation editing).

### Cambridge University Library MS Dd. X. 50[19]
*Description*: Fifteenth century. 158 folios (Wakelin suggests it was written by four different hands). *Festial* includes the prayer also found in BL MS Lansdowne 392 and the usual prologue, commences with First Sunday in Advent, ends with a 21-line fragment of the homily for Sts. Simon and Jude, and contains 59 homilies (including fragment). It is the only Group A manuscript including a prayer (either the Lansdowne or Cotton Claudius prayer) to omit the homily for St. Winifred's Day. Linguistically it stems from southern Leicestershire, northern Warwickshire.

## GROUP A MISCELLANEOUS MANUSCRIPTS

These manuscripts can be tentatively linked with the groupings above, but as they lack either prayer, I have grouped them separately.

### Southwell Minster MS 7[20]
*Description*: Sixteenth century (Wakelin notes shortly after 1500). 202 numbered folios. It contains the prologue, but omits the prayer, and includes 71 sermons. They commence with First Sunday in Advent, end with Salutations of Mary, and includes the homily for St. Winifred. The *Festial* homilies fill ff. 1r–171v, while vernacular hagiography fills the remaining ff. 172r–202v. Powell has *tentatively* suggested it should be grouped with BL MS Cotton Claudius A II and the first recension of Group A.[21] Linguistically it stems from southern Staffordshire.

### Bodleian Library MS Hatton 96[22]
*Description*: Fifteenth century, before 1461.[23] 307 folios. Written in several different hands (at least four according to Wakelin), it stems linguistically from eastern Staffordshire. It includes approximately 60 *Festial* homilies (ff. 3r–6v, 92v–305r), English homilies (ff. 8v–92r), and Latin homilies for Christmas and Advent (ff. 7r–8v). Additional Latin homilies are interspersed throughout the *Festial* homilies; some of the *Festial* homilies are duplicated; and the sermons are jumbled and disorganized. It is not surprising that Powell identified this as a "complicated" manuscript, although the sermon order adheres more closely to the BL MS Cotton Claudius A II order than any of the Group B manuscripts.[24] The manuscript also seems unfinished, as spaces remain unfilled at the beginning of each sermon for the usual large capitol letters. Wakelin tentatively linked Bodl. MS Hatton 96 with BL MSS Lansdowne 392 and Harley 2403.

---

19  A description can be found in Wakelin, "The Manuscripts of Mirk's *Festial*," 108.
20  A description can be found in Wakelin, "The Manuscripts of Mirk's *Festial*," 110.
21  Powell, "A Critical Edition of the *Temporale* Sermons," part II, appendix 8, 90.
22  For a description, see: Wakelin, "The Manuscript's of John Mirk's *Festial*," 106–107.
23  Ibid., 106–107. Wakelin referenced a note on f. 256b referring to death of Robert Whytt, B.A. He wrote that this probably referred to the Robert Whyte in A.B. Emden, *Biographical Register of the University of Oxford*, vol. III (Oxford: 1957–9), 2042–2043, who died in 1461.
24  Powell, "A Critical Edition of the *Temporale* Sermons," part II, appendix 8, 89–90.

**Dr. William's Library MS Ancient 11**[25]

*Description*: Second half of fifteenth century. 344 numbered pages. It lacks prayer and prologue, but contains 58 homilies (including fragments). It begins imperfectly with the homily for St. Andrew, ends imperfectly with Dedication of a Church, and is one of the four Group A manuscripts to lack the homily for St. Winifred. The manuscript seems to be written in a single hand, and it contains post-Reformation revisions. The inside cover contains an interesting note (probably written by a P. Dodridge whose name appears on the following page with date 1730) describing it as "part of the old popish treatise entitled *the Festivale*." A drawing of a monk with tonsure along with the penciled words "Monkish Sermons" appears under the name Dodridge. Lots of interesting comments pepper the margins, but stem primarily from the early modern period. One particularly interesting comment on p. 17 (the sermon for St. Thomas the Apostle) reads, "They who can in earnest believe [such things] are past all confutation by reason, having their minds naturally framed to believe Legends." Wakelin placed it linguistically in northern Warwickshire.

## LATER RECENSION GROUP B MANUSCRIPTS, FIRST GROUPING

These manuscripts textually correlate closely with the Group A manuscripts.[26]

**British Library MS Harley 2391**[27]

*Description*: Mid- to late fifteenth century. 238 folios. *Festial* sermons written in single hand identical with BL MS Harley 2371 (ff. 2r–133r), along with exemplum fragments (ff. 133r–134r), an English form for confession (ff. 134r–138v), and additional English homilies (ff. 138v–156r). The remainder (according to Wakelin) is written in two hands: an English *legenda* (ff. 156v–230v), Latin exempla (ff. 231r–235v), an English treatise on the Seven Deadly Sins (ff. 235v–238r), and an English fragment (f. 238v). Thus the manuscript fits the genre for comprehensive care manuals, as it contains sermons, exempla, a form for confession, and treatise on the Seven Deadly Sins. Altogether it includes 58 *Festial* homilies, commencing with First Sunday in Advent and ending with the homily for St. Katherine. Wakelin identified it linguistically as stemming from southeastern Yorkshire, northwestern Nottinghamshire. The handwriting throughout the *Festial* section is rather messy, with frequent mistakes crossed through and words reinserted. Some of the homilies are fragmentary, such as the sermon for St. Matthew, and the homily for the Translation of St. Thomas is missing.

**Bodleian Library MS Rawlinson A 381**[28]

*Description*: Mid-fifteenth century. 115 folios. It is written in three hands (according to Wakelin), double column format, and Wakelin notes that, "The manuscript is one of the most lavishly decorated of all the manuscripts of the *Festial*, which, generally speaking, are fairly plain." It lacks both prayer and prologue, but contains 63 *Festial* homilies commencing with First Sunday in Advent and ending with Dedication of a Church (ff. 7r–106v). Also containing the vernacular Great Sentence (ff. 1v–2v) and an exposition of

---

25 A description can be found in Wakelin, "The Manuscripts of Mirk's *Festial*," 111. It was originally described as New College London Z.c.19.

26 Powell, "A Critical Edition of the *Temporale* Sermons," part II, 13.

27 A description can be found in Horstmann, *Altenglische Legenden*, cxx–cxxi; Wakelin, "The Manuscripts of Mirk's *Festial*," 100.

28 A description can be found in Wakelin, "The Manuscripts of Mirk's *Festial*," 107. See also: Susan Powell, "John Mirk's *Festial* and the Pastoral Programme," *Leeds Studies in English* n.s. 22 (1991), 85–102, at 90–92.

the Ten Commandments and Seven Deadly Sins (ff. 107r–115r), the manuscript clearly was created with pastoral needs in mind. Wakelin has identified it as stemming linguistically from eastern Staffordshire.

### Bodleian Library MS University College Oxford D102[29]
*Description*: Mid-fifteenth century. 271 numbered pages. Manuscript is written in a single hand, although a possibly different hand scribbled occasionally in the margins. It contains 62 *Festial* sermons commencing with First Sunday in Advent, ending with Dedication of a Church, but lacking prayer and prologue. It also contains two Latin treatises (261–267). Wakelin placed it linguistically in northeastern Nottinghamshire, northwestern Lincolnshire.

### Durham University Library MS Cosin V III 5[30]
*Description*: Late fifteenth century. 156 folios. It contains the prayer found only in three Group A manuscripts, BL MSS Lansdowne 392, Harley 2403, and CUL MS Dd. X. 50, omits prologue, commences with First Sunday in Advent, ends with Dedication of a Church, and contains 61 *Festial* homilies. Linguistically it stems from Derbyshire. This manuscript contains an intricate drawing on the first folio of a tonsured priest standing in a pulpit, decorated in red and gold. It also contains several post-Reformation comments and what Wakelin has identified as a love poem on f. 162v. Fletcher and Powell have noted that this Durham manuscript is the most similar of all Group B manuscripts to the *Festial* revision represented by BL MS Harley 2247 and BL MS Royal 18 B XXV.[31]

### LATER RECENSION GROUP B MANUSCRIPTS, SECOND GROUPING

These manuscripts textually seem very different from the Group A manuscripts, especially the latter two which are individual redactions.

### University of Leeds, Brotherton Collection MS 502[32]
*Description*: Fifteenth century, c. 1450. 138 folios. It is written in a single hand and contains 56 *Festial* homilies (ff. 1r–115r). It commences with a fragment of Quinquagesima and ends with a fragment of All Souls. Linguistically (according to Wakelin) it seems to stem from the northern Leicestershire, eastern Nottinghamshire, and western Lincolnshire areas. The manuscript lacks prayer or prologue and appears incomplete as the first letters of each sermon disappear half way through, leaving only spaces for the missing capitals. Wakelin edited this manuscript in an unpublished dissertation for Leeds University. M.F. Wakelin, "An Edition of John Mirk's Festial as it is contained in the Brotherton Collection Manuscript," M.A. thesis (Leeds, 1960).

### British Library MS Harley 2371[33]
*Description*: Fifteenth century, 1475–1500. 149 folios. Manuscript is written in a single hand identical with that of BL MS Harley 2391. It contains 61 *Festial* homilies (although some fragmentary, ff. 1r–141v), commencing with Advent Sunday (fragment) and ending with Dedication of a Church (fragment). Like several of the other manuscripts, this one shows evidence of post-Reformation tampering: the homily for the feast day of St. Thomas of Canterbury has been blacked out, the homily for the Translation of St. Thomas has been

---

29   See Wakelin, "The Manuscripts of Mirk's *Festial*," 107–108, for a description.
30   A description can be found in Wakelin, "The Manuscripts of Mirk's *Festial*," 111–112.
31   Fletcher and Powell, "The Origins of a Fifteenth-Century Sermon Collection," nn. 12, 94.
32   A description can be found in Wakelin, "The Manuscripts of Mirk's *Festial*," 110–111.
33   Ibid., for a description, 99–100.

removed after the first eleven lines, and the fragment of the homily for the Dedication of a Church has been blackened. Wakelin placed it linguistically in southern Lincolnshire.

### British Library MS Harley 2247[34]

*Description*: Fifteenth century. 215 folios. Written in a single hand, the manuscript contains numerous intriguing sketches stemming from the first letter of each title. Sometimes these are in the shape of heads and faces; sometimes they are simply embellishments. It also contains evidence of sixteenth-century editing. This is a significantly altered version of *Festial*. It lacks prayer and prologue, frequently adds extra sermons for many of the feasts and Sunday celebrations, and greatly expands existing versions of *Festial* sermons. All told, the entire compilation is a much more scholarly manuscript than most (as Powell has successfully argued). Lillian Steckmen suggested that it, along with BL MS Royal 18 B XXV, were "later revisions, written specifically for the public as distinct from the clergy, and with an independent use of Mirk's sources."[35] Powell has provided more evidence to support this claim, suggesting that this manuscript originated in the London area and was written for a more socially distinguished clientele.[36] It contains 90 vernacular sermons, 62 of which derive from *Festial*.

### British Library MS Harley Royal 18 B XXV[37]

*Description*: Fifteenth century. 141 folios. Like BL MS Harley 2247, this is a significantly altered version of *Festial*. It lacks prayer and prologue, adds several extra homilies for existing Sunday celebrations and feast days, and expands the existing text. It also contains 90 vernacular sermons, 59 of which are derived from *Festial*.[38] Yet, despite the substantial differences, Powell has argued that the reviser of BL MSS Harley 2247 and BL MS Royal 18 B XXV was working within the same tradition as Mirk. "His approach in these additions is more scholarly than that of Mirk, and his aims are in general markedly different from those of Mirk, but his use of a key text in the dissemination of Church doctrine, John Gaytryge's vernacular version of Thoresby's 1357 Latin decree, nevertheless shows the HR reviser working in the same tradition as Mirk in his production of the *Festial*."[39] Powell also has argued that neither MS Harley 2247 nor MS Royal 18 B XXV derived from one another; rather they both descended from a common ancestor. MS Harley 2247 represents "most nearly the archetype of the collection," while MS Royal 18 B XXV descended from a common ancestor with Gloucester Cathedral MS 22.[40]

## MINOR MANUSCRIPTS OF *FESTIAL*: A BRIEF INTRODUCTION

Mirk's work also appears in several minor manuscripts.[41] These are sermons from *Festial* scattered throughout pastoral care manuals and other sermon collections. Some exist as

---

34 For a description please see: Fletcher and Powell, "The Origins of a Fifteenth-Century Sermon collection"; Wakelin, "The Manuscripts of Mirk's *Festial*," 100–101.

35 Wakelin, "The Manuscripts of Mirk's *Festial*," 100–101.

36 Powell, "A Critical Edition of the *Temporale* Sermons," Part 1, 71.

37 For a description, see: Fletcher and Powell, "The Origins of a Fifteenth-Century Sermon collection"; Wakelin, "The Manuscript's of Mirk's *Festial*," 101–102; D.S. Brewer, "Observations on a Fifteenth-Century Manuscript," *Anglia* 72 (1954), 390–399.

38 *The Advent and Nativity Sermons from a Fifteenth-Century Revision of John Mirk's Festial: Edited from B.L. MSS Harley 2247, Royal 18 B XXV, and Gloucester Cathedral Library 22*, ed. Susan Powell, Middle English Text Series 13 (Heidelberg: Winter, 1981), 8.

39 Powell, "A Critical Edition of the *Temporale* Sermons," part II, 48.

40 Powell, *The Advent and Nativity Sermons*, 17.

41 Descriptions of these texts can be found in Wakelin, "The Manuscripts of John Mirk's Festial"; Fletcher, "Unnoticed Sermons from John Mirk's *Festial*"; D.S. Brewer, "Observations on a Fifteenth-Century Manuscript."

nothing more than a single sermon: such as the Borthwick Institute of York MS H.C.C.P. 1590/5 which preserves the homily from St. John's Eve in the midst of a record of a late sixteenth-century court case; BL MS Arundel 279 which preserves part of a Rogation Days homily; and BL MS Lansdowne 379 which preserves a copy of the Easter homily. Some exist only as fragmentary exempla, such as the five found in BL MS Harley 1288.

Others manuscripts contain more substantial versions of *Festial*. Gloucester Cathedral MS 22, Lincoln Cathedral MSS 50 and 51, Bodl. MS E Museo 180, and Durham Cathedral Cosin MS V IV III shed interesting light on how *Festial* was modified to suit the needs of a commercially-minded cleric. Written by a single scribe in late fifteenth-century Bedfordshire, these manuscripts seem to have been made for retail and contain a vernacular sermon compilation incorporating many *Festial* sermons.[42] Originally each of these manuscripts would have contained the same basic sermon collection (sixty to seventy Dominican sermons). Both the Durham and Lincoln manuscripts have been damaged, however, and contain merely one and two *Festial* sermons respectively. Durham Cathedral MS Cosin V IV III is still intriguing, as, alongside the sermons, it includes drawings of sirens (women with long hair, emphasized breasts, curling tails, and in this case, a comb to identify them as sexual temptresses) penciled into the margins.[43] Gloucester Cathedral MS 22 contains the most *Festial* sermons, including the four Passiontide homilies and Ascension day; while Bodl. MS E Museo 180, although superficially undamaged, contains only two *Festial* sermons, Passion Sunday and Ascension Day. Finally, although not written by the same scribe, CUL MS Gg. VI. 16 preserves homilies from this Bedfordshire sermon collection and overlaps with the *Festial* revision represented by BL MS Harley 2247 and BL MS Royal 18 B XXV.

Four other manuscripts, BL MS Royal 18 B XXIII (*Middle English Sermons*), CUL MS Ff. 2. 38, CUL Ee. 2. 15, and Lincoln Cathedral MS 133, each contain ten or fewer *Festial* homilies that have been incorporated into various religious texts. The Royal manuscript includes Dedication of a Church, the Marriage ceremony, and the Easter homily embedded within a late fifteenth-century compilation of 54 sermons (including the items from *Festial*). CUL MS Ff. 2. 38, a fifteenth-century religious miscellany, contains three Mirk sermons from the *Sanctorale*: St. Mary Magdalene, St. Margaret, and St. Thomas. Beginning its middle English poetry collection with eight *Festial* sermons, fifteenth-century CUL MS Ee. 2. 15 incorporates the homily for St. Nicholas, Conception of Mary, St. Thomas the Apostle, Nativity of Christ, St. Stephen, St. John apostle and evangelist, Feast of Innocents, and St. Thomas of Canterbury in the order of BL MS Cotton Claudius A II. Lincoln Cathedral MS 133 was compiled by a Lancashire parish priest over a period of time, one Egredius Wryght de Flixton. "The nature of the contents strongly suggest that it was owned by a parish priest, if not written by him for his own use," Fletcher commented.[44] Along with ten well preserved sermons from *Festial*, Lincoln Cathedral MS 133 also contains a collection of clerical statues in Latin (ff. 8r–46r), Latin wills and testaments (ff. 47r–50r), a copy of the Latin and English *Speculum Christiani* (ff. 51r–67v), a Latin tract on officiating mass (ff. 68r–97 v), and ten vernacular sermons (ff. 98r–120r), including nine *Festial* homilies.

Bodl. MS Greaves 54 and BL MS Harley 2250 are the last two "minor manuscripts" of great consequence to this project. Both clearly belong to the genre of comprehensive care manuals identified by Leonard Boyle. Of the first, Bodl. MS Greaves 54, Fletcher has written that it "provides an example of how the *Festial* might be edited and adapted.

---

42   The sermon collection of Gloucester Cathedral MS 22 was later bound with a section of the *Gesta Romanorum*. As such, not all of the Gloucester manuscript was composed by the Bedfordshire scribe. For more information, see D.S. Brewer, "Observations on a Fifteenth-century Manuscript," 390–399.

43   Durham Cathedral MS Cosin V IV III, f. 11v.

44   Fletcher, "Unnoticed Sermons from John Mirk's *Festial*," 518–19. The note about Egredius Wryght de Flixton can be found in the manuscript, ff. 46r–47v.

It is a parchment manuscript written by one scribe in a script of the middle to second half of the fifteenth century, and judging by its contents, was compiled with an eye to its usefulness at a parochial pastoral level."[45] It contains a Latin and English *Speculum Christiani,* a vernacular sermon sequence (not based on *Festial*), a portion of a Latin *Gesta Romanorum,* various other Latin and English narrations which might stem from *Fasciculus Morum,* and a vernacular sermon sequence based on *Festial.* The *Festial* sermons are not copies, but rather interpolations with sections from *Festial* lifted and combined with other sermon material. The second manuscript, BL MS Harley 2250, is a very late fifteenth-century pastoral manual (between 1477 and 1500). It also contains an abridged version of *Speculum Christiani,* several versified *Sanctorale* homilies in English and Latin, three sermons and five exempla from *Festial,* and a portion of Richard of Lavynham's treatise on the Seven Deadly Sins.

---

[45]  Ibid., 516.

*Appendix II*

## THE EXEMPLA OF MIRK'S *FESTIAL*

These 110 exempla appear in the full text of Mirk's 74 *Festial* sermons. I have listed them in the order they appear in Erbe's printed edition. Due to manuscript variation in sermon content, not all of these exempla appear in each manuscript. But, aside from the significantly revised editions of BL MS Harley 2247 and BL MS Royal 18 B XXVIII, the majority of *Festial* texts continue to repeat these "original" exempla within the appropriate sermons. For information about the derivation of each exemplum, please see Albert Elsasser, "The Exempla of Mirk's *Festial*," Ph.D. diss., Princeton University, 1924. His work is dated and some conclusions are no longer accurate. But his study does provide an excellent starting point for examining the origins of these exempla.

| *Narrative* | *Page* | *Primary characters* |
|---|---|---|
| 1. A husbandman-turned-monk saw the pains of hell and performed penance through the remainder of his life, standing in water to lessen the pain of others. | 5 | husbandman-turned-monk, angel |
| 2. A bishop was tempted by a devil disguised as a princess. The devil-princess sought the bishop in confession, and told him she swore chastity and wanted to take vows to avoid an arranged marriage. The priest was saved by St. Andrew disguised as a pilgrim. | 9 | bishop, devil-princess, pilgrim, messenger |
| 3. A Jew was upset with an image of St. Nicholas which did not protect his goods from thievery. St. Nicholas appeared to the thieves in person and they returned the goods. The Jew converted. | 14 | St. Nicholas, Jew, thieves |
| 4. A penny-reeve said prayers to the BVM (Blessed Virgin Mary) in woods while collecting rents. He was protected from thieves for his devotion. | 16 | penny-reeve, BVM, thieves |
| 5. Augustus Caesar refused to be worshipped as god. He asked the sage Sybyll if there was someone greater than he. Sybyll replied that a child he saw in a vision would be greater. The Emperor worshiped the Christ child. | 25 | Caesar, Sybyll, Christ-child and BVM in vision |
| 6. A woman fouled with the sin of lechery, despaired because she compared her guilt to the innocence of Christ. But then she considered Christ in his childhood, and prayed that he would have mercy on her. A voice from heaven proclaimed she was forgiven. | 26 | lecherous woman, divine voice from heaven (presumably Jesus) |
| 7. A woman cursed her ten children; two of them, Paul and Pallida, went into a church dedicated to St. Stephen. Paul trusted the saint would intercede | 29 | Paul, Pallida, mother |

135

| Narrative | Page | Primary characters |
|---|---|---|

for him and was healed. Pallida emulated his
example after seeing Paul healed. The story notes
Pallida thanked God and St. Stephen with all her
heart.

| | | |
|---|---|---|
| 8. A Roman senator and wife traveled to Jerusalem and built a chapel to St. Stephen. The senator died and was buried in the chapel next to St. Stephen. The widow wanted to return to Italy and requested her husband's bones. She unknowingly took the bones of St. Stephen and transported them instead. | 29 | widow, senator, bishop, spiritual beings (angel of god and fiends) |
| 9. Edward the Confessor gave his ring in honor of St. John. The saint kept the ring 12 years, then gave it to a knight and had him carry it to Edward, explaining that Edward would see the saint soon. Edward died shortly after. | 34 | Edward, St. John, knight |
| 10. Constantine was sick and ordered the sacrifice of 3000 children so he could bathe in their blood. The mothers of the children gathered outside his palace weeping. The emperor refused to sacrifice the children and gave the mothers gifts. Peter and Paul appeared to him in a dream and bade him send for St. Sylvester, who healed him. | 37 | Constantine, mothers, children, Peter, Paul, St. Sylvester |
| 11. A bird that could speak witnessed a pilgrimage to St. Thomas of Canterbury. When a sparrow hawk tried to kill the bird, the bird called on St. Thomas and the hawk fell down dead. | 43 | bird, sparrow-hawk |
| 12. A sick man prayed to St. Thomas for healing, but when he was healed, the man worried that the sickness might have been good for his soul. So he prayed again to St. Thomas that if it was healthier for his soul to be physically sick, then he wanted the illness to return to him. The man became sick once more and thanked God and St. Thomas. | 43 | sick man |
| 13. An evil man was a lord's officer and he went mad. The bailey of the manor realized the man was mad and had him bound to a post. Three black dogs appeared and had eaten him completely by the next morning. | 56 | mad officer, bailey, servant, dogs |
| 14. St. Dunstan's mother went to Candlemas while pregnant. All the candles went out in the church. A fair light from heaven lit the candle of St. Dunstan's mother. | 60 | mother |
| 15. A woman devout in service to the BVM gave all of her clothes away, and could not go to church on Candlemas day because she was ashamed as she could not be "honest arayde." So she went into a chapel near the church to pray, and fell asleep. | 60 | woman, heavenly host, messengers |

She dreamed she was in the company of the heavenly
host, and received a candle to present to the BVM.
When she was asked to offer the candle to the BVM,
she refused and held fast to it. She awoke with half of
the candle in her hand.

16. A woman of evil living only did one good thing
in her life: lit a candle before an image of the BVM.
Fiends dragged her soul to hell when she was dead;
but at hell's gate they were stopped by angels. The
BVM said she lit a candle for her and thus had done
a good deed and deserved to live. The soul was
returned to the woman's body and she lived a good
life thereafter.

61    woman, fiends, BVM

17. A cheerless king who never laughed rebuked his
brother who remarked the king should be more
lighthearted. The king demonstrated to his brother
why he should also be grim, ordering knights to
point seven swords at his heart. The king stated the
swords were the seven deadly sins, and the brother
understood why he should be wiser.

64    king, brother, knights of king

18. Embellished account of the Fall
in Genesis. Used to illustrate why men and
women should not be idle but "labor busily;
for if Adam and Eve had busied them in labor,
the fiend should not have overcome them so soon."

66    Adam, Eve, devil, God

19. Adam and Eve performed penance for
the Fall, standing in water up to their chins. Eve
was tempted three times by the devil to leave her
penance, but the third time Adam severely
reprimanded her and she completed her penance.

67    Adam, Eve, devil

20. A rich man in Ireland had given many alms
in his life. After he died, he appeared to his
loved ones black as pitch and smelling horribly.
He said he had given the alms for his own glory
instead of for God. Thus he was eternally punished.

71    rich Irish man, his friends

21. During his devotions, St. Dominic witnessed
Jesus ready to punish the world. The BVM
interceded and sent Dominic to preach God's word.

73    St. Dominic, BVM, Jesus

22. A dying man became contrite for his wicked
life, weeping day and night. He died forgiven.
A monk died the same day, and returned to tell
his abbot of his state. He said he was on his way
to heaven and that the wicked man was in heaven
as well. The abbot accused the monk of lying,
but the monk explained how contrite the wicked
man had been at his death.

75    wicked man, monk, abbot,
priests

23. The Bishop of Lincoln Robert Grosseteste
was tormented by fiends on his death bed. The
BVM rescued him by having him renew his
faith in holy church.

78    bishop, BVM, fiends

| *Narrative* | *Page* | *Primary characters* |
|---|---|---|
| 24. St. Brendan in his travels saw Judas resting from his travails in hell on a rock in the sea. | 80 | St. Brendan, Judas, Brendan's companions |
| 25. An unrepentant man was brought before St. Wulstan. St. Wulstan tried to help the man, but he refused, and the saint prayed to St. Matthew that an example be made of the man. Two fiends came and dragged the evil man to hell. | 81 | wicked man, St. Wulstan, friends, fiends |
| 26. A knight suffered from the sin of gluttony and died. His son suffered from the same sin. He forgot to say his devotions at his father's grave until in the middle of hosting a dinner party. He quickly went to the grave, and when he got there he felt a great desire to see his father. So he had his men undo the tomb, and found a great foul toad devouring his father's throat. The son then reformed from his gluttonous ways. | 85 | gluttonous knight, son, feast guests, knight's men, toad |
| 27. A knight owned no land. He was handsome, but poor after spending everything he had earned from war. He wanted to marry a rich woman. She told him first to rob a rich merchant and then she would consent. He did so and killed the merchant, whose spirit prophesied the knight and woman would live together thirty years and then be punished. The knight and woman were married and built a huge castle to protect themselves from the prophecy, but after thirty years the castle was consumed with fire and sank into the earth. Only a harpist was miraculously saved. | 88 | knight, woman, merchant, harpist |
| 28. A woman had done a horrible sin and, for shame, would not confess. When she came to confession, she purposed to reveal her sin, but the fiend would make her too ashamed. One night Jesus visited her and revealed his wounds to her and placed her hand in his side and told her not to be ashamed to confess. She could not wash away the blood until she finally confessed and then her hand was cleansed. | 90 | woman, Jesus |
| 29. An evil chapman refused to repent on his death bed, despite pleas from his fellow good chapman. His friend brought priests to his bed, but the man was "overly proud" and refused to confess, saying "God would not forgive him." Finally Jesus appeared to the man and asked him to repent; the man refused again; and Jesus drew blood from his side and cast it in the man's face. The friend found the man dead and his body black as pitch. | 91 | two chapmen, Jesus, religious men |
| 30. A woman had done a horrible sin. Some differences from no. 28. | 95 | woman, Jesus, priest |
| 31. An abbess had not sinned with her body, but | 96 | Abbess, sisters, fiends |

talked "ribaldry." After she died, fiends came
at night and beat her body from the navel up.
Some of her sisters heard her soul crying in the
churchyard and she explained that she was beaten
because of the dirtiness of her mouth. She
begged them to pray for her.

32. A sick man was healed by St. Winifred, but that     100     man, monks, priest
night became sick again. Monks asked him if he
had confessed before being healed, and he had
not. So he confessed immediately and was healed
in body and soul by St. Winifred.

33. A rich man named Perys refused to give alms.     104     Perys, beggars, BVM, fiends,
A poor man tricked him into throwing a loaf of bread            servant
to him. Perys died and fiends dragged him away,
but the BVM intervened to see if he had done
anything good in life. The only good deed he had
done was throw bread to the beggar, but it was
thrown against his will and did not count. The
BVM prayed that life be returned to Perys, and it was
done. Perys then sold all his goods and gave them to
the poor and became a holy man.

34. A charcoal burner sat in a great lord's park and     105     charcoal-burner, lord, knight,
made a fire to sleep by one night. After midnight            woman
he witnessed a vision of a woman chased by a
knight on a horse. The knight killed the woman
and burned her body. This happened night after
night until the charcoal burner told the lord. The
lord went to see the sight for himself, and questioned
the knight. The knight explained that he and the
woman were lovers, but she was married to another
man. This was the penance they must suffer until
certain masses and alms-deeds were performed for
them. So the lord agreed to perform the alms-deeds,
and the knight and woman were released from their
penance.

35. A Christian man and Jewish man argued about     108     Jewish man, Christian man
the virgin birth. The Jew said when he saw a lily
spring out of the pot between them then he would
believe. Then a lily sprang out of the pot and the
Jew converted.

36. A holy maiden devout to the BVM rehearsed the     110     holy woman, BVM
Five Joys of the Virgin daily. She was taken to
bliss by the BVM when she died.

37. St. Filbert had a swollen throat and could     110     St. Filbert, BVM
not breathe. The BVM came to him and fed him
from her breast, and he was healed.

38. An idol in a city could tell of all things stolen.     111     thief, idol, victims
A young thief was afraid of the idol and threatened
to break its head if it revealed his acts of theft.
The victims of the thief asked the idol to reveal
the perpetrator. The idol answered cryptically.

| *Narrative* | *Page* | *Primary characters* |
|---|---|---|
| 39. A Roman emperor sent a great man to act as justice in a foreign land. This justice introduced swearing on books and by God in court. During session, a fair woman carrying a fair child walked into court. The child was bloody and tormented. The woman condemned the justice for introducing swearing, blaming her child's wounds on the words spoken in court. The earth then opened up and swallowed the justice. | 113 | BVM, child-Jesus, people in court, justice |
| 40. When Roman knight conquered a land, he paraded himself in honor, but also had a man stand by his chair and beat him in the mouth with an olive branch, saying "know thyself." This was to remind him that though he had the victory now, he could easily lose it. The story gives a moral at the end, "be not proud of thyself." | 116 | Roman knight, servant |
| 41. A knight rescued a lion entangled by a huge snake. The lion refused to be parted from the man thereafter, and the knight tried to leave the lion by sailing away. The lion discovered he was gone and tried to swim after him, but but drowned. | 119 | knight, lion, snake, knight's men |
| 42. A noble woman was starving and slew her own child. She cut it in half and roasted part in the fire and kept the other half for the next day. Men smelled the roasting meat and came to steal it, but soon saw it was a mother roasting her own child and refused to eat. The mother said it was her child and she would rather eat it than die of hunger. | 122 | woman, dead child, men |
| 43. A great lord had a son who died brawling with another young man. The murderer was afraid and went to church on Good Friday to find sanctuary; the knight heard of the man's attendance and came with his sword drawn to kill him. The young man knew he had sinned and ran to the knight and fell down to the ground in the form of the cross and cried for mercy and forgiveness. The knight, who had already carried arms into a church (which the story points out as a terrible deed), forgave his son's murderer. The image on the cross then hugged the knight, saying he forgave the knight as the knight had forgiven the young man. | 123 | knight, murderer, dead son, parishioners, image on cross |
| 44. St. Richard decided to shave his beard one Saturday afternoon. The devil gathered up the hairs that fell, and St. Richard conjured the devil and asked him why. The devil responded he was keeping them as evidence of Richard's disregard of God's holy day. So Richard stopped shaving, remaining half shaved half unshaved until Monday. | 125 | St. Richard, fiend |
| 45. A bishop prayed God would grant the grace for him to see the penitents worthy and unworthy to | 131 | bishop, angel, penitents, two common women |

140

receive the sacrament. He saw some with red
faces with blood dripping from their mouths, some
black faces, some white faces, and some fair and
ruddy faces, and two common women with faces
shining bright. An angel revealed that the bloody faces
were the envious men and women; the black faces
lecherous men and women; the fair faces those who
had lived good lives; and the two common women
had been so contrite for their sins that their faces
shone above all others.

| | | |
|---|---|---|
| 46. St. George (as a young knight) appeared first to a priest and then to the Christian army besieging Jerusalem and helped them conquer the Saracens. | 135 | St. George (as a young knight), priest, Christians, Saracens |
| 47. The plague fell on the people of Rome, but many were saved when Pope Pelgaius ordered them to make a cross on their mouths, to cry for Christ to help, to fast, and to go in procession. Later popes imitated his methods to "put away God's wrath," hallowing holy days and instituting fasts and processions. | 137 | Pelgaius, Roman people popes |
| 48. Destruction of Jerusalem by Vespasian and Titus as punishment for the Jews slaying Jesus. A man from Pilate's household helped Vespasian to believe in Jesus, and thus to be healed from his illness. Vespasian in turn decided to destroy the city that had killed Jesus. Vespasian became emperor soon thereafter and sent his son Titus to destroy Jerusalem. Titus did so and the siege and destruction were terrible. | 141 | man, Vespasian, Titus, people of Jerusalem, Roman soldiers |
| 49. The story of a woman slaying and eating her own child occurs again (no. 42), this time embedded within the tale of Titus conquering Jerusalem. | 141 | woman, dead child, men |
| 50. A Christian man rented a house and set up a Jewish crucifix. When he moved, he forgot the crucifix, and a Jewish man moved into the house. Friends came to dinner with the Jew, saw the crucifix, accused him of being Christian, and severely beat him. Then they attacked the image, beating it and stabbing its side until blood and water poured out. Amazed by the miracle, they told the town bishop and collected the blood in vials to use for healing sick people. | 145 | Christian man, Jewish man, friends, bishop, sick men |
| 51. Jews tried to rebuild Jerusalem, but each morning they discovered crosses in the ground, and the third morning the a fire rose from the earth and consumed the Jews. | 146 | Jews |
| 52. Edward the Confessor always gave alms to those who asked for St. John's love. One day he had nothing on him except a ring, which he gave to St. John disguised as a pilgrim. Two of his knights went on pilgrimage to Jerusalem and met St. John | 148 | Edward, St. John (pilgrim), knights pilgrims (old man and two (children) |

disguised along the way. St. John returned the ring
to the knights, instructing them to take the ring to
Edward and tell him that six months later he would
die. (Story repeated from no. 9; this is a fuller
account than the abbreviated story in no. 9.)

into the goblet, and called the clerics to witness the
blood on his finger and on the host.

| | | |
|---|---|---|
| 61. A Christian man from England went to a heathen land and hired a Saracen for a guide. He noticed that no birds sang in the woods, and the Saracen explained that they remained as if dead from Palm Sunday to Easter. The man looked into the trees and saw the birds lying as if dead with their wings spread in the form of the cross. | 171 | Christian man, Saracen guide, birds |
| 62. The earl of Venice was a very pious man, but when he was dying he became so ill that he could not swallow the host without vomiting. He laid the sacrament on his side and prayed that God would miraculously allow him to receive it. His side opened and consumed the host. | 172 | earl of Venice, men |
| 63. A woman named Lasma baked the holy bread for St. Gregory. One day St. Gregory noticed her smiling when he offered her God's body during mass. She explained her behavior by stating that she had made the bread "with her own hands," so how could it be God's body? St. Gregory bade the congregation to pray on account of her unbelief, and the host turned into raw bleeding flesh. The woman repented and received the Eucharist. | 173 | Lasma, St. Gregory, congregation |
| 64. A vicar in Devonshire beside Axe bridge discovered a female parishioner was dying. She lived half-a-mile away, and sent for him at midnight to receive extreme unction. He hastily left, placing the pix in his pocket. While riding through a meadow, the pix fell from his pocket to the ground. He did not realize the loss until the woman was ready to receive Eucharist. Distressed, he beat himself as punishment, and then began searching for the host. He found it in the meadow with a pillar of fire soaring from it to the heavens. All of the beasts bowed to it on both knees, except for a black horse that knelt on one knee. The vicar questioned this behavior, and the horse responded that he was a fiend of hell and did reverence against his will, and thus knelt on only one knee. The vicar then condemned the fiend, picked up the host, and returned with it to the woman's house. | 173 | vicar, woman, fiend, beasts |
| 65. Adam of Erkaleton suffered severe abnormalities in his arms and legs. He dragged himself to the shrine of St. Winifred and prayed all night. He awakened the next morning healed and devoted himself as a servant to St. Winifred's church. | 180 | Adam of Erkaleton |
| 66. Three men sitting together in the town of Shrewsbury were bitten by a spider. Two died; | 181 | three men, mother |

143

| *Narrative* | *Page* | *Primary characters* |
|---|---|---|

the third thought on St. Winifred and her miracles and bade his mother go offer a candle and bring water that St. Winifred's bones had been washed in to him. He was then healed and created an image of silver and offered it to St. Winifred and became her servant for the remainder of his life.

| | | |
|---|---|---|
| 67. The day St. Winifred was translated to Shrewsbury Abbey, many came from Wales to witness the event. A great man who was mute came also, and when he entered the church he suddenly fainted. St. Winifred visited him in a vision and bade him drink the water which her bones were washed in to be healed. When he awoke and audibly asked for holy water, the astounded people around him brought him the water and he was completely healed, and devoted his life to St. Winifred's service. | 181 | mute man from Wales, crowd, St. Winifred |
| 68. Two lepers, one who loved St. John the Baptist and the other who loved St. John the Evangelist, discussed which was greater. A voice from heaven settled their dispute, telling them to be at peace on earth as in heaven. The lepers were immediately healed and celebrated and thanked God and the two saints. | 186 | two lepers |
| 69. An Irish priest had a dirty mouth that often turned people to lechery. One night fiends dragged him from his bed and tortured him for three nights. When they returned him to his bed on the third night, his body was full of stinking wounds that never would heal. Whenever he heard others speaking ribaldry, he warned them to beware of what happened to him. | 192 | Irish priest, fiends |
| 70. A holy hermit prayed for ability to see a holy soul depart to heaven. An angel took him to watch the death of a holy man. Many others came to watch his death, but the hermit was aghast to see two fiends sit on his head and rake his soul from his body. The angel explained the holy man's deeds had been done for his glory, not God's. The angel then directed the hermit to the death of a pilgrim. A heavenly host wooed the soul from the body of the pilgrim and guided it to heaven. The angel explained this man was a good man who had only sought to please God. | 195 | holy man, holy hermit, angel, fiends, heavenly host, pilgrim |
| 71. A man named Bernard was imprisoned in a dungeon and cried to St. James for help. St. James came to him, comforted him, broke his chains, and helped him leap safely from the tower. | 211 | Bernard, St. James |
| 72. Three knights rode on pilgrimage to the shrine of St. James. One took the script of a poor woman | 212 | charitable knight, damned lord, two knights, poor woman, sick |

who was weary and the staff of a sick man. The
charitable knight became sick upon reaching the
shrine. On the third day of his sickness, he stated
that St. James had delivered him from fiends
with the script and staff he had carried. He also
predicted that the lord of one of the knights would die
and be damned. The charitable knight then died,
followed by the lord.

man, fiends

73. Thirty pilgrims made an agreement to stay
together in health and sickness; one refused to
pledge. But when a member of the thirty became
ill, the pilgrims left him behind except for the
one that refused to pledge. He stayed behind
and helped the sick man travel. The sick man
soon died, but St. James appeared and helped the
faithful pilgrim travel to his shrine and bury the
dead pilgrim.

212    29 pilgrims, one sick pilgrims, charitable pilgrim, St. James

74. A priest named Scatalus was helped by St.
Lawrence to rebuild a church destroyed by the
Lombards. The saint provided a quantity bread that
miraculously filled the workers for ten days.

220    priest Scatalus, workmen

75. An evil emperor died and fiends came running
to take his soul. A hermit heard the noise and called
out to the fiends. One told of his task and the hermit
asked him to return later and tell him what had
happened. The fiend returned and said that they
had lost the soul because the devotion the emperor
had done to St. Lawrence balanced the scales of
his wicked deeds.

220    hermit, fiend, fiends, emperor

76. St. Elizabeth of Spain witnessed a vision of
a tomb with a great light shining about and a fair
woman in the tomb and an angel standing above.
A glorious man bearing the sign of the cross with
a great multitude of angels took this woman into
heaven. The angel explained that Elizabeth had
witnessed the translation of the BVM into heaven.

226    St. Elizabeth, BVM, heavenly host, angel

77. A cleric was devoted to the BVM and rehearsed
the Five Joys of the Virgin daily. He feared death,
however, and the BVM came and comforted him
and took him into bliss.

226    cleric, BVM

78. A woman was tempted by a fiend that appeared
to her in the form of a man. She could not be rid
of him until a hermit taught her to say, "Saint
Mary, help me," and the fiend left in fear.

226    woman, fiend in form of a man, hermit

79. A Jewish boy went to school with Christian
children and went to church with them one day
and received the host. His father was furious and
stuffed him into a hot oven. The mother wept
so loudly that Christian men came to the
scene and opened up the oven and found the little
boy safe inside. He claimed he had been rescued

227    Jewish boy, mother, father, Christian children, BVM, Christian men

| Narrative | Page | Primary characters |
|---|---|---|
| by the fair woman he had seen at church when receiving the sacrament. | | |
| 80. A cleric was devoted to the BVM and wanted to see her. An angel came to him and said if he saw her he would lose his sight, but he still wanted to see her. So he devised a plan to hide one eye and look at her through the other. It worked, but he was so overjoyed by the sight of her that he wanted to see her again. This time when he saw her, the BVM took pity on his blindness (this time in both eyes) and his devotion and restored his sight in both eyes. | 234 | cleric, angel, BVM |
| 81. The emperor Frederick destroyed a great city that contained a chief church dedicated to St. Bartholemew. A holy man walked past the ruins and saw a great council of men in white, including St. Bartholemew. They said they had decided to punish the Emperor for his misdeeds, and he was damned to hell. | 239 | holy man, council of saints, St. Bartholemew, emperor |
| 82. St. Guthlac ventured into a wild land called "Crowland" in the fens. It was inhabited by fearsome fiends that attacked Guthlac and almost overcame him, condemning him to the pains of hell, but then he remembered St. Bartholemew and called on him for help. Bartholemew came shining bright as the sun and rebuked the fiends and Guthlac was saved; the fiends returned to hell. | 239 | St. Guthlac, St. Bartholemew, fiends |
| 83. King Athelstan engaged in a battle (the Battle of Brunanburh against the Scottish king Constantine in 937) when his sword broke. St. Ode prayed for the king and the king found a new sword at his side and was victorious in the battle. | 243 | Athelstan, St. Ode, enemy soldiers |
| 84. A holy man was praying during his devotions one night when he heard the angels in heaven singing. He prayed that he might understand the occasion for the melody, and an angel came from heaven and revealed that this was the birthday of the BVM. Thus the date was hallowed as a feast. | 247 | holy man, angel |
| 85. The son of a widow was taken prisoner by enemies. The woman prayed to the BVM that her son be freed. But the prayers went unanswered. The woman went to the church and stole the image of the Christ child from the arms of his carved mother and prayed that as the Virgin mother had not seen fit to return the widow's son, the widow had taken the Virgin's son as hostage. The BVM appeared to the widow's son in prison and opened all the doors for him and set him free. | 247 | widow, BVM, imprisoned son |

The woman then returned the carved Christ child
and devoted herself to the Virgin's service.

86. A Jew from France traveled through England    248    Jewish man, BVM, bishop
when he was attacked by thieves and bound.
The BVM appeared to him, freed him and told
him who she was and showed him the pains of hell
and the bliss of heaven. He rode through the night
to Bath and went to a bishop and converted.

87. A Jew rode into an empty church and cut the    252    Jewish man, Christian man
throat of an image of Christ. The blood spurted
out all over his clothes and the Jew became afraid
and fled. On his way home he ran into a Christian
man who guessed the blood was from Christ and the
Jewish man broke down and confessed his deeds
and was converted.

88. St. Brendan sailed to an island filled with birds.    260    St. Brendan, birds
He prayed for illumination and one of the birds
revealed that they were former angels driven out by St.
Michael during the war between Lucifer and God. They
worshipped God on the island and their only
punishment was to be cast out from God's presence.

89. The keeper of St. Peter's church in Rome was    267    keeper of St. Peter's church,
doing his devotions at midnight when he fell              heavenly host
asleep at the altar. He had a vision of the heavenly
court, which was identified to him by an angel.

90. A man lived next to a churchyard.    269    devout man, enemies, ghosts
When he rode through the churchyard, he would
pray for the Christian souls buried there. One
day he was chased by enemies on his way home.
But when he came into the churchyard, he still
remembered to pray for the dead, and ghosts rose
from the graves and drove off his enemies.

91. Before going into battle, a knight asked his    270    knight, cousin
cousin that, if he died, to sell his horse and give alms
to the poor for his soul. The knight died, but the
cousin took the horse for his own. The knight
appeared to his cousin in a vision and told him
because of his faithless actions, the cousin would
go to hell while the knight would soon be freed
from purgatory. Wild animals appeared and carried
the cousin away, "that nevermore after heard man of
him."

92. A bishop suspended an illiterate priest who    271    bishop, priest, ghosts
could only sing requiem mass. As the bishop rode
through a churchyard, dead bodies rose from the
graves and said that they had no one to sing mass
for them since the bishop had suspended the priest.
They warned the bishop would die unless
he amended his actions. So the bishop reinstalled
the priest.

| *Narrative* | *Page* | *Primary characters* |
|---|---|---|
| 93. A fisherman brought St. Theobald a block of ice in which was trapped a soul doing penance. The soul claimed he could be released from his penance at the price of thirty masses. St. Theobald began reciting masses, but was interrupted by a fiend who said the town was in an uproar. Another fiend came when he was halfway through and said enemies had besieged the town. Finally, when he reached his last mass, a fiend came again and said the town was on fire. But Theobald finished the last mass and the soul was freed. | 271 | St. Theobald, soul, fiends |
| 94. A woman who had left the service of St. Katherine witnessed a procession of fair maidens. She asked one of the maidens who the fair maiden was that refused to look on her. The maiden answered that it was St. Katherine and that she refused to look because the woman had left her. The woman returned to her devotions. | 277 | woman, fair maiden, St. Katherine, fair maidens |
| 95. When a church was hallowed and relics of saints carried within, a swine ran among the people's feet; it was the fiend that had occupied the church. The fiend was so upset about losing his home that he returned three times to the church at night and made great noise. But then he left for good. | 278 | swine-fiend, people in church |
| 96. A bishop was performing mass and his deacon bid the people to bow, but saw two women in conversation together. A fiend sat on their shoulders with a long roll writing quickly. After mass the deacon told the bishop of the sight and the bishop confronted the women. They said they had been reciting their prayers dutifully, but then the bishop commanded the fiend to read the woman's words, and the women fell down and cried for mercy. | 279 | bishop, deacon, two women, fiend |
| 97. An angel visited the wardens of a church and bade them warn the bishop that if he did not remove an unworthy corpse buried there, then the bishop would be dead within 30 days. The bishop refused and died. | 280 | bishop, angel, wardens |
| 98. An angel told a bishop that Charles king of France had been damned for withholding rights from holy church. The bishop had the king's tomb opened and a great dragon flew out and left the tomb burnt within. | 281 | angel, bishop, dragon |
| 99. Three men in Lilleshall stole the ox of the abbot. Two confessed and were shriven. The third did not and died damned. His spirit wandered the streets of the parish at night, scaring all the residents. One night the parish priest, Sir Thomas Woodward, was carrying the | 281 | three thieves, priest, abbot |

host to a sick woman when he was met by the
spirit which requested help, which the priest granted.

| | | |
|---|---|---|
| 100. King Darius asked which was the strongest: a king, wine, or a woman. Three bodyguards gave different answers, but the third argued that a woman was the strongest and thus the moral of the story was that the "foul sin of lechery" could destroy a man. | 287 | King Darius, three bodyguards |
| 101. A woman and a man were involved in an illicit love affair. The woman went to church one day and was convicted of her sin and repented. But her lover enticed her back. They both died suddenly, and a holy man prayed to see how the two had fared. Their spirits appeared in a mist and showed the two blaming one another for their eternal damnation. | 287 | woman, man, holy man |
| 102. Repetition of the story of a charcoal-burner (no. 34). | 291 | charcoal burner, lord, knight, woman |
| 103. A local priest blessed a stein of ale and it burst revealing a great toad. | 293 | priest, town people, toad |
| 104. A sick child in Northhamptonshire fell into a coma. When he awoke, he predicted many things. He told of a married man who kept a mistress. This man went to meet with the boy, but was intercepted by the fiend disguised as his mistress and he kissed her. The boy predicted that this kiss had set a canker in the man's mouth. And so the man died from the devil's kiss. | 293 | child, man, fiend-mistress |
| 105. Three brothers died at the same time and were buried together. One had not been shriven. A fiend entered his body and committed many crimes within the town. Finally an anchorite in the town saw the fiend raise the corpse. The anchorite confronted the fiend and the fiend explained he was adding guilt to the dead man. The anchorite ordered the fiend to stop, which he did. | 295 | three brothers, fiend, anchor |
| 106. A cursed man was buried in the churchyard, but the yard cast his body out naked during the night. So he was removed. | 298 | cursed man |
| 107. Repetition of the bishop who refused to remove a corpse (no. 97). | 298 | bishop, angel, holy man |
| 108. A nun from Shaftsbury named Eulalia said her prayers too quickly. The BVM appeared to her and requested she say half as many with sincere devotion, rather than as many as usual too quickly. The nun acquiesced. | 299 | nun, BVM |
| 109. One man lent money to another man, who did not pay on time. The debtor swore he had paid the man, and swore falsely. The lender fell sick on his way home from this meeting, and was shown a | 300 | two men, Christ |

| *Narrative* | *Page* | *Primary characters* |
|---|---|---|
| vision of Christ, and then scourged for allowing the man to swear falsely. | | |
| 110. A monk had a great devotion for the BVM. The emperor of Rome sent his cousin to be taught to write by this monk. This young man envied the monk and conspired against him by writing a false letter. For punishment, the emperor smote off the monk's writing arm below the elbow and then sent him to be imprisoned by an abbot. The BVM visited him in prison and healed his arm, and the monks heralded it as a miracle. The emperor heard of the event and discovered the plot of his cousin, and so returned the monk to his station and punished his cousin in the same manner he had punished the monk. Then the monk went on pilgrimage and converted a Jew by showing him an image of the BVM that miraculously suckled the baby Jesus. | 301 | monk, emperor, cousin, abbot, monks, Jew, BVM image and Christ-child |

# BIBLIOGRAPHY

## MANUSCRIPT SOURCES

Cambridge University Library
    Dd. X. 50: Mirk's *Festial*, see Appendix I.
    Ee. II. 15: Religious miscellany containing 8 Mirk's *Festial* sermons.
    Ff. II. 38: Religious miscellany containing 3 Mirk's *Festial* sermons.
    Ff. V. 48: Mirk's *Instructions for Parish Priests*.
    Gg. VI. 16: Sermon compilation, overlaps with Sidney Sussex 74, Mirk's *Festial*, and the Bedfordshire cycle sermon compilation.
    Nn. III. 10: Copy of a printed edition of Mirk's *Festial*.
Cambridge, Gonville and Caius College
    168 (89): Mirk's *Festial*, see Appendix I.
Cambridge, St. John's College
    G. 19 (187): Copy of a printed edition of Mirk's *Festial*.
    S. 35: Pastoral handbook.
Cambridge, Sidney Sussex College
    74: Lollard sermon compilation.
Dublin, Trinity College
    201: [m] Mirk's *Festial*, see Appendix I.
    428: [m] Mirk's *Festial*, see Appendix I.
Durham University Library
    Cosin V. III. 5: Mirk's *Festial*, see Appendix I.
    Cosin V IV. 2: Pastoral handbook.
    Cosin V IV. 3: Bedfordshire cycle sermon compilation, containing sermons from Mirk's *Festial*.
Gloucester Cathedral Library
    22: Bedfordshire cycle sermon compilation, containing sermons from Mirk's *Festial*.
Leeds, Brotherton Library
    501: Mirk's *Festial*, see Appendix I.
Lincoln Cathedral Library
    50 and 51: Bedfordshire cycle sermon compilation, containing sermons from Mirk's *Festial* (originally this was a single manuscript artificially separated when bound).
    133: Pastoral handbook containing 10 sermons from Mirk's *Festial*.
London, British Library
    Additional 32320: Pastoral handbook.
    Additional 37691: *Speculum Sacerdotal*.
    Additional 37677: Sermon compilation, contains Alkerton's sermon from 1406.
    Arundel 279: Sermon compilation preserving fragment of *Festial* Rogation Days homily.
    Cotton Claudius A. II: Mirk's *Festial* and *Instructions for Parish Priests*, see Appendix I.
    Harley 211: Richard of Lavynham's treatise on the seven deadly sins.
    Harley 1288: Pastoral handbook preserving 5 *exempla* from *Festial*.
    Harley 2247: Revision of Mirk's *Festial*, see Appendix I.
    Harley 2371: Mirk's *Festial*, see Appendix I.
    Harley 2391: Mirk's *Festial*, see Appendix I.

Harley 2403: Mirk's *Festial*, see Appendix I.
Harley 2417: Mirk's *Festial*, see Appendix I.
Harley 2420: Mirk's *Festial*, see Appendix I.
Harley 2250: Pastoral handbook with 3 sermons and 5 *exempla* from *Festial*.
Lansdowne 379: Sermon compilation preserving *Festial* Easter Day homily.
Lansdowne 392: Mirk's *Festial*, see Appendix I.
Royal 18 B. XXIII: Sermon compilation, overlaps Mirk's *Festial* and Sidney Sussex 74.
Royal 18 B. XXV: Revision of Mirk's *Festial*, see Appendix I.
Royal 17 C. XVII: Mirk's *Instructions for Parish Priests*.
Sloane 3160: Pastoral handbook.
Sloane 1584: Pastoral handbook.
London, Dr. William's Library
Anc. 11 (New College Z. C. 19): Mirk's *Festial*, see Appendix I.
Oxford, Bodleian Library
Bodley 95: Sermon compilation, overlaps with Sidney Sussex cycle.
Bodley 110: Pastoral manual overlapping Harley 4172.
Bodley 806: Sermon compilation, overlaps with Sidney Sussex cycle.
Douce 60: Mirk's *Festial* and *Instructions for Parish Priests*, see Appendix I.
Douce 103: Mirk's *Instructions for Parish Priests*.
Douce 108: Mirk's *Festial*, see Appendix I.
E Museo 180: Bedfordshire cycle sermon compilation, overlaps with Mirk's *Festial*.
Gough Ecc. Top. 4: Mirk's *Festial*, see Appendix I.
Greaves 54: Sermon compilation with interpolations of *Festial* sermons.
Greaves 57: Mirk's *Instructions for Parish Priests*.
Hatton 96: Mirk's *Festial*, see Appendix I.
Rawlinson A. 381: Mirk's *Festial*, see Appendix I.
Tanner 196: [m] Mirk's *Instructions for Parish Priests*.
Shrewsbury School
III: Sermon compilation, overlaps Sidney Sussex 74 and Bodley 806
Southwell Minister.
7: Mirk's *Festial*, see Appendix I.
Worcester Cathedral Library
142: [m examined in Birmingham University Library] Pastoral handbook.
F. 10: [m examined in Birmingham University Library] Sermon compilation.
York, Borthwick Institute
H.C.C.P. 1590/5: Court case preserving a *Festial* homily from St. John's Eve.

## PRINTED PRIMARY SOURCES

Amt, Emilie. *Women's Lives in Medieval Europe: A Sourcebook*. New York and London: Routledge, 1993.

Banks, Mary Macleod, ed. *An Alphabet of Tales: An English 15th Century Translation of the Alphabetum narrationum of Étienne de Besançon. From Additional MS. 25, 719 of the British Museum*, EETS original series 126 and 127. London: Kegan Paul, Trench, Trubner & Co. for the EETS, 1904 and 1905.

Blake, N.F., ed. *Quattuor Sermones: Printed by William Caxton*, Middle English Texts 2. Heidelberg: Winter, 1975.

Brandeis, Arthur, ed. *Jacob's Well: An English Treatise on the Cleansing of Man's Conscience. Edited from the Unique MS about 1440 A.D. in Salisbury Cathedral, Part 1* (all published), EETS original series 115. London: Kegan Paul, Trench, Trubner & Co. for the EETS, 1900.

Bryant, Geoffrey F. and Vivien M. Hunter. *'How Thow Schalt Thy Paresche Preche': John Myrc's Instructions for Parish Priests. Part One: Introduction and Text*. Barton-on-Humber: Worker's Educational Association Barton-on-Humber Branch, 1999.

Cigman, Gloria. ed. *Lollard Sermons*, EETS original series 294. Oxford: Oxford University Press, 1989.

Cromarty, D., and R. Cromarty. *The Wealth of Shrewsbury in the Early Fourteenth Century: Six Local Subsidy Rolls 1297–1322: Text and Commentary*. Shrewsbury, Shropshire: Shropshire Archaeological and Historical Society, 1993.

Fletcher, Alan J. "A Critical Edition of Selected Sermons from an Unpublished Fifteenth Century de Tempore Sermon Cycle," B. Litt. thesis. Oxford University, 1978.

Francis, W. Nelson, ed. *The Book of Vices and Virtues: A Fourteenth Century English Translation of the Somme le Roi of Lorens d'Orléans*, EETS original series 217. London: Oxford University Press, 1942.

Grisdale, D.M., ed. *Three Middle English Sermons from Worcester Chapter Manuscript F. 10*, Leeds School of English Language Texts and Monographs 5. Kendal: Printed by T. Wilson for Members of the School of English Language in the University of Leeds, 1939.

Gurney, Norah K.M. and Sir Charles Clay, eds. *Fasti Parochiales Vol. IV: Being Notes on the Advowsons and Pre-Reformation Incumbents of the Parishes in the Deanery of Craven*, Yorkshire Archaeological Society Record Series 133. Leeds: Yorkshire Archaeological Society, 1971.

Harper-Bill, Christopher, ed. *The Register of John Morton II*, The Canterbury & York Society, vol. 78. Woodbridge, Suffolk: Boydell Press, 1991.

Heath, Peter, ed. *Medieval Clerical Accounts*, Borthwick Papers 26. York: St. Anthony's, 1964.

Herrtage, Sidney J.H., ed. *The Gesta Romanorum*, EETS extra series 33. London: Oxford University Press, 1932.

Jacobus de Voragine. *The Golden Legend: Readings on the Saints*, trans. William Granger Ryan. Princeton: Princeton University Press, 1993.

Julian of Norwich. *Showings*, trans. and ed. Edmund Colledge and James Welch. New York: Paulist, 1978.

Kempe, Margery. *The Book of Margery Kempe: The Text from the Unique MS Owned by Colonel W. Butler-Bowdon*, ed. Sanford Brown Meech with prefatory note by Hope Emily Allen and notes and appendices by Sanford Brown Meech and Hope Emily Allen, EETS original series 212. London: Oxford University Press, 1940.

Lavynham, Richard. *A Litil Tretys on the Seven Deadly Sins*, ed. J.P.W.M. van Zutphen. Rome: Institutum Carmelitanum, 1956.

Mannyng, Robert. *Robert of Brunne's Handlyng Synne, A.D. 1303 with Those Parts of the Anglo-French Treaties on which it was Founded, William of Wadington's 'Manuel des pechiez'*, ed. Frederick J. Furnivall, EETS original series 119 and 123. London: Kegan Paul, Trench, Trubner & Co. for the EETS, 1901 and 1903.

McNeill, John T., and Helena M. Gamer, trans. and eds. *Medieval Handbooks of Penance: A Translation of the Principal Libri Poenitentiales and Selections from Related Documents*. New York: Columbia University Press, 1990.

Mirk, John. *Instructions for Parish Priests: Edited from MS Cotton Claudius A II and Six Other Manuscripts with Introduction, Notes and Glossary*, ed. Gillis Kristensson, Lund Studies in English 49. Lund: Gleerup, 1974.

Mirk, John. *Mirk's Festial: A Collection of Homilies by Johannes Mirkus*, ed. Theodore Erbe, EETS extra series 96. London: Kegan Paul, Trench, Trubner & Co. for the EETS, 1905.

Nelson, Venetia, ed. *A Myrour to Lewde Men and Wymmen: A Prose Version of the Speculum vitae, ed. from B.L. MS Harley 45*, Middle English Texts 14. Heidelberg: Winter, 1981.

Offer, Clifford J., trans. and ed. *The Bishop's Register: A Translation of Documents from Medieval Episcopal Registers Designed to Illustrate their Contents as well as Various Phases of Medieval Episcopal Activity*. London: Society for Promoting Christian Knowledge, 1929.

Powell, Susan, ed. *The Advent and Nativity Sermons from a Fifteenth-Century Revision of John Mirk's Festial: Edited from B.L. MSS Harley 2247, Royal 18 B XXV, and Gloucester Cathedral Library 22*, Middle English Texts 13. Heidelberg: Winter, 1981.

————. "A Critical Edition of the *Temporale* Sermons of MSS. Harley 2247 and Royal 18 B. xxv," Ph.D. diss., University of London King's College, 1986.

Powicke, F.M., C.M. Chenye, Arthur West Hadden, M. Brett, Dorothy Whitelock and Christopher N.L. Brooke, eds. *Councils & Synods, with Other Documents Relating to the English Church, 1205–1313*, 2 vols. Oxford: Clarendon, 1964–1981.

Ross, Woodburn O., ed. *Middle English Sermons edited from BM MS Royal 18 B xxiii*, EETS original series 209. London: Oxford University Press, 1940.

Rothwell, Harry, ed. *English Historical Documents III, 1189–1327*. New York and Oxford: Oxford University Press, 1975.

Simmons, Thomas Frederick and Henry Edward Nolloth, eds. *The Lay Folk's Catechism*, EETS original series 118. London: Kegan Paul, Trench, Trubner, & Co., 1901.

Swanson, R.N., trans. and annotator. *Catholic England: Faith, Religion and Observance before the Reformation*. New York: Manchester University Press, 1993.

Thoresby, John, and John Wycliffe. *The Lay Folks' Catechism, or, the English and Latin Versions of Archbishop Thoresby's Instruction for the People; Together with a Wycliffite Adaptation of the Same and the Corresponding Canons of the Council of Lambeth*, eds. John Peckham, Thomas Frederick Simmons, Henry Edward Nolloth and John De Taystek, EETS original series 118. London: Kegan Paul, Trench, Trubner & Co. for the EETS, 1901.

Timmins, T.C.B., ed. *The Register of John Chandler, Dean of Salisbury, 1404–17*, Wiltshire Record Society series 39. Devizes: Wiltshire Record Society, 1984.

Wakelin, M.F. "An Edition of John Mirk's *Festial* as it is contained in the Brotherton Collection Manuscript." M.A. thesis, University of Leeds, 1960.

Weatherly, Edward H. ed., *Speculum Sacerdotal: Edited from British Museum MS. Additional 36791*, EETS original series 200. London: Oxford University Press, 1936.

## SECONDARY SOURCES

Aldredge-Clanton, Jann. *In Whose Image? God and Gender*. New York: Crossroad, 1992.

Alldridge, Nick. "Loyalty and Identity in Chester Parishes," in *Parish, Church, and People: Local Studies in Lay Religion 1350–1750*, ed. S. J. Wright. London: Hutchinson, 1988, pp. 85–124.

Aston, Margaret. "Segregation in Church," in *Women in the Church: Papers Read at the 1989 Summer Meeting and the 1990 Winter Meeting of the Ecclesiastical History Society*, eds. W.J. Sheils and Diana Wood, Studies in Church History 27. Oxford: Basil Blackwell, 1990, pp. 237–94

Atkinson, Clarissa. *Mystic and Pilgrim: The Book and World of Margery Kempe*. Ithaca and London: Cornell University Press, 1983.

Aylmer, G.E. "Unbelief in Seventeenth Century England," in *Puritans and Revolutionaries: Essays in Seventeenth-Century History Presented to Christopher Hill.*, eds. Donald Pennington and Keith Thomas. Oxford: Oxford University Press, 1978, pp. 22–46.

Ayscough, Samuel. *A Catalogue of the Manuscripts Preserved in the British Museum hitherto Undescribed: Consisting of Five Thousand Volumes; Including the Collections of Sir Hans Sloane Bart. The Rev. Thomas Birth, D.D., by Samuel Ayscough, Clerk*. London: John Rivington, 1782.

Baldwin, Marshall W., ed. *Christianity through the Thirteenth Century*. New York: Harper and Row, 1970.

Barr, Beth Allison. "Gendering Pastoral Care: John Mirk and his *Instructions for Parish Priests*," in *Fourteenth Century England*, vol. IV, ed. J.S. Hamilton. Woodbridge, Suffolk: Boydell Press, 2006, pp. 93–108.

Barron, Caroline. "The 'Golden Age' of Women in Medieval London," in *Medieval Women in Southern England*, Reading Medieval Studies 15. Reading, England: Graduate Centre for Medieval Studies, University of Reading, 1989, pp. 35–58.

Baugh, A.C., and T. Cable. *A History of the English Language*, 3rd ed. Englewood Cliffs, N.J.: Prentice-Hall, 1978.

Beattie, Cordelia. "The Problem of Women's Work Identities in Post Black Death England," in *The Problem of Labour in Fourteenth-Century England*, eds. James Bothwell, P.J.P. Goldberg, and W.M. Ormnrod. York: York Medieval Press, 2000, pp. 1–19.

Bell, Susan Groag. "Medieval Women Book Owners: Arbiters of Lay Piety and Ambassadors of Culture," in *Sisters and Workers in the Middle Ages*, ed. Judith M. Bennett, et al. Chicago: University of Chicago Press, 1989, pp. 135–161.

Bem, Sandra, and Daryl Bem. "Does Sex-Biased Job Advertising 'Aid and Abet' Sex Discrimination?" *Journal of Applied Social Psychology* 3:1 (1973), pp. 6–18.

Bennett, Judith M. *Ale, Beer, and Brewsters in England: Women's Work in a Changing World, 1300–1600*. New York and Oxford: Oxford University Press, 1996.

———. "England: Women and Gender," in *A Companion to Britain in the Later Middle Ages*, ed. S.H. Rigby. Malden, Mass.: Blackwell Publishers, 2003, pp. 87–106.

———. "Medieval Women, Modern Women: Across the Great Divide," in *Culture and History 1350–1600: Essays on English Communities, Identities, and Writings*, ed. David Aers. Detroit: Wayne State University Press, 1992, pp. 147–75.

———. "Misogyny, Popular Culture, and Women's Work." *History Workshop* 31 (Spring 1991), pp. 166–88.

———. *Women in the Medieval English Countryside: Gender and Household in Brigstock Before the Plague*. New York and Oxford: Oxford University Press, 1987.

Bennett, Judith M., and Amy M. Froide. "A Singular Past," in *Singlewomen in the European Past, 1250–1800*, eds. Judith M. Bennett and Amy M. Froide. Philadelphia: University of Pennsylvania Press, 1999, pp. 1–37.

Berlioz, Jacques and Marie Anne Polo de Beaulieu. "*Exempla*: A Discussion and a Case Study," in *Medieval Women and the Sources of Medieval History*, ed. Joel T. Rosenthal. Athens: University of Georgia Press, 1990, pp. 37–65.

Biller, Peter. A. "Childbirth in the Middle Ages." *History Today* 36 (1986), pp. 42–49.

———. "The Common Woman in the Western Church in the Thirteenth and Early Fourteenth Centuries," in *Women in the Church: Papers Read at the 1989 Summer Meeting and the 1990 Winter Meeting of the Ecclesiastical History Society*, eds. W.J. Sheils and Diana Wood, Studies in Church History 27. Oxford: Basil Blackwell, 1990, pp. 127–157.

———. "Confession in the Middle Ages: Introduction," in *Handling Sin: Confession in the Middle Ages*, eds. Peter Biller and A.J. Minnis. York: York Medieval Press, 1998, pp. 1–33.

———. "Marriage Patterns and Women's Lives: A Sketch of a Pastoral Geography," in *Women in Medieval English Society 1200–1500*, ed. P.J.P. Goldberg. Stroud, Gloucestershire: Sutton, 1997, pp. 60–107.

———. *The Warwickshire Parish Clergy in the Late Middle Ages*, Dugdale Society Occasional Papers 17. Stratford-upon-Avon: Dugdale Society, 1967.

Blake, Norman. *The English Language in Medieval Literature*. London: J.M. Dent, 1977.

Blamires, Alcuin. *The Case for Women in Medieval Culture*. Oxford: Clarendon, 1997.

———, and Karen Pratt, eds. *Woman Defamed and Woman Defended: An Anthology of Medieval Texts*. Oxford: Clarendon, 1992.

Blench, J.W. *Preaching in England in the Late Fifteenth and Sixteenth Centuries*. Oxford: Basil Blackwell, 1964.

Bock, Darrell L. "Do Gender Sensitive Translations Distort Scripture? Not Necessarily," *Journal of the Evangelical Theological Society* 45:4 (December 2002), pp. 651–69.

Boyle, Leonard E. "The Fourth Lateran Council and Manuals of Popular Theology," in *The Popular Literature of Medieval England*, ed. Thomas J. Heffernan, Tennessee Studies in Literature 28. Knoxville: University of Tennessee Press, 1985, pp. 30–43.

———. "The *Oculus Sacerdotis* and Some Other Works of William of Pagula," in *Pastoral Care, Clerical Education, and Canon Law, 1200–1400*, ed. Leonard E. Boyle. London: Variorum Reprints, 1981, pp. 81–110.

Braswell, Mary Flowers. *The Medieval Sinner: Characterization and Confession in the Litera-*

*ture of the English Middle Ages.* Rutherford, Madison and Teaneck: Fairleigh Dickinson University Press, 1983.

———. "Sin, the Lady, and the Law: The English Noblewoman in The Late Middle Ages." *Medievalia et Humanistica* 14 n.s. (1986), pp. 81–101.

Brewer, D.S. "Observations on a Fifteenth-Century Manuscript," *Anglia* 72 (1954), pp. 390–99.

Brooke, C.N.L. "Gregorian Reform in Action: Clerical Marriage in England, 1050–1200." *Cambridge Historical Journal* 12:1 (1956), pp. 1–20.

Brown, Andrew. *Popular Piety in Late Medieval England: The Diocese of Salisbury, 1250–1550.* Oxford: Clarendon, 1995.

Brundage, James A. "Sexual Equality in Medieval Canon Law," in *Medieval Women and the Sources of Medieval History*, ed. Joel T. Rosenthal. Athens: University of Georgia Press, 1990.

Bunn, Margaret J. "John Mirk's *Festial*: A Study of the Medieval English Sermon," M.A. thesis, University of Leeds, 1954.

Burnley, J.D. *The Language of Chaucer.* London: Macmillan Education, 1989.

Burrow, J.A. and Thorlac Turville-Petre. *A Book of Middle English: Second Edition.* Oxford: Blackwell Publishers, 1996.

Bynum, Caroline Walker. *Fragmentation and Redemption: Essays on Gender and the Human Body in Medieval Religion.* New York: Zone Books, 1992.

Cameron, Deborah. "Extracts from *Man Made Language*," in *The Feminist Critique of Language: A reader*, ed. Deborah Cameron. (New York: Routledge, 1990), pp. 102–110.

Carruthers, Leo. "'No Woman of No Clerk is Preysed': Attitudes to Women in Medieval English Religious Literature," in *A Wyf There Was*, eds. Paule Mertens-Fonck and Juliette Dor. Liège, Belgium: Dép. d'anglais, Université de Liège, 1992, pp. 49–60.

Challis, M.G. *Life in Medieval England as Portrayed on Church Misericords & Bench Ends.* Nettlebed: Teamband, 1998.

Cobban, Alan. *English University Life in the Middle Ages.* Columbus: Ohio State University Press, 1999.

Courtenay, William J. "The Effect of the Black Death on English Higher Education." *Speculum* 55:4 (1980), pp. 696–714.

Crawford, Patricia. *Women and Religion in England, 1500–1720.* New York: Routledge, 1993.

Cressy, David. "The Churching of Women." *Past and Present* 141 (1993), pp. 106–146.

———. *Education in Tudor and Stuart England.* New York: St. Martin's, 1975.

———. *Travesties and Transgressions in Tudor and Stuart England: Tales of Discord and Dissension.* New York and Oxford: Oxford University Press, 2000.

Cullum, P.H. "'And Hir Name was Charite': Charitable Giving by and for Women in Late Medieval Yorkshire," in *Women in English Society 1200–1500*, ed. P.J.P. Goldberg. Stroud, Gloucestershire: Sutton, 1992, pp. 182–211.

Dalarun, Jacques. "The Clerical Gaze," in *A History of Women: Silences of the Middle Ages*, eds. Georges Duby, Michelle Perrot and Christine Klapisch-Zuber. Cambridge: Belknap Press of Harvard University Press, 1992, pp. 15–42.

Davis, Natalie Zemon. "From 'Popular Religion' to Religious Cultures," in *Reformation Europe: A Guide to Research*, ed. Steven Ozment. St. Louis: Center for Reformation Research, 1982, pp. 399–426.

Dohar, William J. *The Black Death and Pastoral Leadership: The Diocese of Hereford in the Fourteenth Century.* Philadelphia: University of Pennsylvania Press, 1995.

Duffy, Eamon. *The Stripping of the Altars: Traditional Religion in England, c.1400–c.1580.* New Haven and London: Yale University Press, 1992.

Edwards, William Alpheus. "John Myrc's Conception of the Function of Medieval Parish Priests," B.D. thesis, Duke University, 1943.

Elliott, Dyan. "Bernardino of Siena versus the Marriage Debt," in *Desire and Discipline: Sex and Sexuality in the Premodern West*, eds. Jacqueline Murray and Konrad Eisenbichler. Toronto: University of Toronto Press, 1996, pp. 168–200.

————. *Fallen Bodies: Pollution, Sexuality, and Demonology in the Middle Ages.* Philadelphia: University of Pennsylvania Press, 1999.

————. "Sex in Holy Places: An Exploration of a Medieval Anxiety." *Journal of Women's History* 6:3 (1994), pp. 6–34.

Elliott, Ralph W.V. *Chaucer's English.* London: A. Deutsch, 1974.

Elsasser, Albert R. "The *Exempla* of Mirk's *Festial*," Ph.D. diss., Princeton University, 1924.

Farmer, Sharon. "'It Is Not Good That [Wo]man Should Be Alone': Elite Responses to Singlewomen in High Medieval Paris," in *Singlewomen in the European Past, 1250–1800*, eds. Judith M. Bennett and Amy M. Froide. Philadelphia: University of Pennsylvania Press, 1999, pp. 82–105.

————. "Persuasive Voices: Clerical Images of Medieval Wives." *Speculum* 61:3 (1986), pp. 517–543.

Ferrante, Joan. *Woman as Image in Medieval Literature.* New York: Columbia University Press, 1975.

Fletcher, Alan. "John Mirk and the Lollards." *Medium Aevum* 56:2 (1987), pp. 217–24.

————. "Unnoticed Sermons from John Mirk's *Festial*." *Speculum* 55:3 (1980), pp. 514–22.

————, and Susan Powell. "The Origins of a Fifteenth-Century Sermon Collection: MSS Harley 2247 and Royal 18 B XXV." *Leeds Studies in English* 10 (1978), pp. 74–96.

Ford, Judy Ann. *John Mirk's Festial: Orthodoxy, Lollardy, and the Common People in Fourteenth-Century England.* Cambridge: D.S. Brewer, 2006.

Foss, D.B. "John Mirk's *Instructions for Parish Priests*," in *The Ministry: Clerical and Lay: Papers Read at the 1989 Summer Meeting and the 1989 Winter Meeting of the Ecclesiastical History Society*, ed. W.J. Sheils, Studies in Church History 26. Oxford: Basil Blackwell, 1989, pp. 131–40.

French, Katherine. "Maidens' Lights and Wives' Stores: Women's Parish Guilds in Late Medieval England." *Sixteenth Century Journal* 29:2 (1998), pp. 399–425.

————. "Parochial Fund-Raising in Late Medieval Somerset," in *The Parish in English Life 1400–1600*, eds. Katherine French, Gary G. Gibbs and Beat A. Kümin. New York: St. Martins Press, 1997, pp. 115–32.

————. *The People of the Parish: Community Life in a Late Medieval English Diocese.* Philadelphia: University of Pennsylvania, 2001.

————. "'To Free Them From Binding': Women in the Late Medieval English Parish." *Journal of Interdisciplinary History* 27:3 (1997), pp. 387–412.

Froide, Amy M. "Marital Status as a Category of Difference," in *Singlewomen in the European Past, 1250–1800*, eds. Judith M. Bennett and Amy M. Froide. Philadelphia: University of Pennsylvania Press, 1999, pp. 236–69.

Gillespie, Vincent. "Vernacular Books of Religion," in *Book Production and Publishing in Britain 1375–1475*, eds. Jeremy Griffiths and Derek Pearsall. Cambridge: Cambridge University Press, 1989, pp. 317–41.

Girsch, James M. "An Elizabethan Manuscript of Mirk's *Festial* Sermon on St. Winifred and Observations on the 'Shrewsbury Manuscript.'" *Neuphilologische Mitteilungen* 96:3 (1995), pp. 265–69.

Gold, Penny Schine. *The Lady and the Virgin: Image, Attitude, and Experience in Twelfth-Century France.* Chicago: University of Chicago Press, 1985.

Goldberg, P.J.P. "'For Better, For Worse': Marriage and Economic Opportunity for Women in Town and Country," in *Women in English Society 1200–1500*, ed. P.J.P. Goldberg. Stroud, Gloucestershire: Sutton, 1997, pp. 108–125

————. "Pigs and Prostitutes: Streetwalking in Comparative Perspective," in *Young Medieval Women*, eds. Katherine J. Lewis, Noel James Menuge, and Kim M. Phillips. New York: St. Martin's Press, 1999, pp. 172–194

————. "Women's Work, Women's Role, in the Late-Medieval North," in *Profit, Piety, and the Professions in Later Medieval England*, ed. M.A. Hicks, Gloucester: A. Sutton, 1990, pp. 34–50.

————. *Women, Work, and Life Cycle in a Medieval Economy: Women in York and Yorkshire c. 1300–1520.* Oxford: Clarendon, 1992.

Graham, Helen. "'Woman's Work …': Labour and Gender in the Late Medieval Country-side," in *Women in English Society 1200–1500,* ed. P.J.P. Goldberg. Stroud, Gloucester-shire: Sutton, 1997, 126–48.

Gregg, Joan Young. *Devils, Women, and Jews: Reflections of the Other in Medieval Sermon Stories.* Albany: State University of New York Press, 1997.

Hadley, D.M, ed. *Masculinity in Medieval Europe.* New York: Longman, 1999.

Hanawalt, Barbara. "Peasants' Contribution to the Home Economy in Late Medieval England," in *Women and Work in Preindustrial Europe,* ed. Barbara Hanawalt. Bloom-ington: Indiana University Press, 1986, pp. 3–19.

Haren, Michael. *Sin and Society in Fourteenth-Century England: A Study of the Memoriale Presbiterorum.* Oxford: Clarendon, 2000.

Harper-Bill, Christopher. *The Pre-Reformation Church in England 1400–1530.* New York: Longman, 1996.

Hayman, Richard. *Church Misericords and Bench Ends,* Shire Album 230. Risborough, Buckinghamshire, UK: Shire, 2000.

Heal, Felicity. "The Economic Problems of the Clergy," in *Church and Society in England: Henry VIII to James I,* eds. Felicity Heal and Rosemary O'Day. Hamden, Conn.: Archon Books, 1977, pp. 99–118.

Heath, Peter. *The English Parish Clergy on the Eve of the Reformation.* Toronto: University of Toronto Press, 1969.

Herbert, J.A. *Catalogue of Romances in the Department of Manuscripts in the British Museum,* vol. III. London: Trustees of the British Museum, 1910.

Horstmann, Carl. *Altenglische Legenden Neue Folge.* Heilbronn, Germany: Gebr. Henniger, 1881.

Hudson, Anne. "'*Laicus Litteratus*': The Paradox of Lollardy," in *Heresy and Literacy, 1000–1530,* eds. Peter Biller and Anne Hudson. Cambridge: Cambridge University Press, 1994, pp. 222–36.

Hufton, Olwen. *The Prospect before Her: A History of Women in Western Europe,* vol. 1, *1500–1800.* New York: Alfred Knopf, 1996.

Hutton, Diane. "Women in Fourteenth Century Shrewsbury," in *Women and Work in Pre-Industrial England,* eds. Lindsay Charles and Lorna Duffin. London: Croom Helm, 1985, pp. 83–99.

Huxley, Aldous. *Words and Their Meanings.* Los Angeles: Ward Ritchie, 1940.

Jewell, Helen. *Education in Early Modern England.* New York: St. Martins, 1998.

————. "Women at the Courts of the Manor of Wakefield, 1348–1350." *Northern History* 26 (1990), pp. 59–81.

————. *Women in Medieval England.* New York: University of Manchester Press, 1996.

Joliffe, P.S. *Check-List of Middle English Prose Writings of Spiritual Guidance,* Subsidia Mediaevalia 2. Toronto: Pontifical Institute of Mediaeval Studies, 1974.

Karras, Ruth Mazo. *Common Women: Prostitution and Sexuality in Medieval England.* New York and Oxford: Oxford University Press, 1996.

————. "Gendered Sin and Misogyny in John of Bromyard's *Summa Predicantium*." *Traditio: Studies in Ancient and Medieval History, Thought, and Religion* 47 (1992), pp. 233–57.

————. "Sex and the Singlewoman," in *Singlewomen in the European Past,* eds. Judith M. Bennett and Amy M. Froide. Philadelphia: University Pennsylvania Press, 1999, pp. 127–45.

Keene, Derek. "Tanners' Widows, 1300–1350," in *Medieval London Widows,* ed. Caroline Barron. London: Hambledon, 1994, pp. 1–27.

Kettle, Alice J. "Ruined Maids: Prostitutes and Servant Girls in Later Medieval England," in *Matrons and Marginal Women in Medieval Society,* eds. Robert R. Edwards and Vickie Ziegler. Woodbridge, Suffolk: Boydell Press, 1995, pp. 19–32.

Klein, Peter. *The Misericords & Choir Stalls of Ludlow Parish Church*. Birmingham: Ludlow Parochial Church Council, 1986.

Kowaleski, Maryanne. "Singlewomen in Medieval and Early Modern Europe: The Demographic Perspective," in *Singlewomen in the European Past*, eds. Judith M. Bennett and Amy M. Froide. Philadelphia: University of Pennsylvania Press, 1999, pp. 38–81.

———. "Women's Work in a Market Town: Exeter in the Late Fourteenth Century," in *Women and Work in Preindustrial Europe*, ed. Barbara Hanawalt. Bloomington: Indiana University Press, 1986, pp. 149–159.

Kuhn, Sherman M., and John Reidy, eds. *Middle English Dictionary*, vol. M, part 1. Ann Arbor: University of Michigan Press, 1975.

Lawson, John, and Harold Silver. *A Social History of Education in England*. London: Methuen, 1973.

Lee, Charles. "'Tales Olde': The *Festial* of John Mirk and Its Historical Context," Ph.D. diss., University of Missouri-Columbia, 1992.

Leyser, Henrietta. *Medieval Women: A Social History of Women in England 400—1500*. New York: St. Martins, 1995.

Little, A.G. *Studies in English Franciscan History*. Manchester, UK: The University Press, 1917.

Lupton, J.H. *A Life of John Colet, D.D., Dean of St. Paul's, and Founder of St. Paul's School. With an Appendix of Some of his English Writings*. London: G. Bell and Sons, 1887, 2nd edition 1909.

Lytle, G.F. "Patronage Patterns and Oxford Colleges, c. 1300–1500," in *The University in Society*, vol. 1, ed. Lawrence Stone. Princeton: Princeton University Press, 1974, pp. 111–149.

Makowski, Elizabeth. "The Conjugal Debt and Medieval Canon Law." *Journal of Medieval History* 3 (1977), pp. 99–114.

Martyna, Wendy. "The Psychology of the Generic Masculine," in *Women and Language in Literature and Society*, eds. Sally McConnell-Ginet, Ruth Borker, and Nelly Furman. New York: Praeger, 1980, pp. 69–78.

McHardy, A.K. "Careers and Disappointments in the Late-Medieval Church: Some English Evidence," in *The Ministry: Clerical and Lay: Papers Read at the 1989 Summer Meeting and the 1989 Winter Meeting of the Ecclesiastical History Society*, ed. W.J. Sheils, Studies in Church History 26. Oxford: Basil Blackwell, 1989, pp. 111–130.

McIntosh, Angus, M.L. Samuels and Michael Benskin. *A Linguistic Atlas of Late Mediaeval English*, 4 vols., with the assistance of Margaret Laing and Keith Williamson. Aberdeen: Aberdeen University Press, 1986.

McIntosh, Marjorie K. *Controlling Misbehavior in England, 1370–1600*. Cambridge: Cambridge University Press, 1998.

McLaughlin, Eleanor. "Equality of Souls, Inequality of Sexes: Women in Medieval Theology," in *Religion and Sexism: Images of Women in the Jewish and Christian Traditions*, ed. Rosemary Radford Ruether. New York: Simon and Schuster, 1974, pp. 213–66.

McNeill, John T., and Helena M. Gamer, trans. and eds. *Medieval Handbooks of Penance: A Translation of the Principal Libri Poenitentiales and Selections from Related Documents*. New York: Columbia University Press, 1990.

McSheffrey, Shannon. *Gender and Heresy: Women and Men in Lollard Communities, 1420–1530*. Philadelphia: University of Pennsylvania Press, 1995.

———. *Marriage, Sex, and Civic Culture in Late Medieval London*. Philadelphia: University of Pennsylvania Press, 2006.

Milton, G.A. "Sex Differences in Problem Solving as a Function of Role Appropriateness of Problem Context." *Psychological Reports* 5 (1959), pp. 705–8.

Moorman, John R.H. *Church Life in England in the Thirteenth-Century*. Cambridge: Cambridge University Press, 1946.

Moran, Jo Ann Hoeppner. "Clerical Recruitment in the Diocese of York, 1340–1530: Data and Commentary." *Journal of Ecclesiastical History* 34:1 (1983), pp. 19–54.

———. *The Growth of English Schooling, 1340–1548: Learning, Literacy, and Laicization in Pre-Reformation York Diocese.* Princeton: Princeton University Press, 1985.

Moran Cruz, Jo Ann Hoeppner and Richard Gerbeding, eds. *Medieval Worlds: An Introduction to European History 300–1492.* Boston: Houghton-Mifflin, 2004.

Morey, James H. *Book and Verse: A Guide to Middle English Biblical Literature.* Urbana: University of Illinois Press, 2000.

Murray, Alexander. "Counseling in Medieval Confession," in *Handling Sin: Confession in the Middle Ages*, eds. Peter Biller and A.J. Minnis. York: York Medieval Press, 1998, pp. 63–77.

Murray, Jacqueline. "The Absent Penitent: The Cure of Women's Souls and Confessors' Manuals in Thirteenth-Century England," in *Women, the Book, and the Godly: Selected Proceedings from the St. Hilda's Conference 1993*, vol. 1, eds. Lesley Smith and Jane H.M. Taylor. Cambridge: D.S. Brewer, 1995, pp. 13–26.

———. "Gendered Souls in Sexed Bodies: The Male Construction of Female Sexuality in Some Medieval Confessor's Manuals," in *Handling Sin: Confession in the Middle Ages*, eds. Peter Biller and A.J. Minnis. York: York Medieval Press, 1998, pp. 79–94.

Myers, W. David. *"Poor, Sinning Folk": Confession and Conscience in Counter-Reformation Germany.* New York: Cornell University Press, 1996, pp. 27–60

Nevanlinna, Saara. "The Sermon on the Day of St. Katherine in John Mirk's *Festial* in Southwell Minister MS 7," in *English Far and Wide: A Festschrift for Inna Koskenniemi*, ed. Risto Hiltunen. Turku: Turun Yliopisto, 1993, pp. 183–94.

Nichols, Ann Eljenholm. "The Etiquette of Pre-Reformation Confession in East Anglia." *Sixteenth Century Journal* 17:2 (Summer 1986), pp. 145–163.

———. *Seeable Signs: The Iconography of the Seven Sacraments, 1350–1544.* Woodbridge, Suffolk: Boydell Press, 1994.

O'Mara, Veronica M. "A Middle English Sermon Preached by a Sixteenth Century 'Atheist': A Preliminary Account." *Notes and Queries* n.s. 34:2 (1987), pp. 183–85.

———. "Middle English Sermons: A Brief Overview." *Medieval Sermon Studies*, 41 (1998), pp. 37–40.

Owen, Dorothy Mary. *Church and Society in Medieval Lincolnshire*, History of Lincolnshire 5. Lincoln: History of Lincolnshire Committee, Lincolnshire Local History Committee, 1971.

———. *The Medieval Canon Law: Teaching and Transmission.* Cambridge: Cambridge University Press, 1990.

Owst, G.R. *Literature and Pulpit in Medieval England: A Neglected Chapter in the History of English Letters and of the English People*, 2nd rev. ed. Cambridge: Cambridge University Press, 1961.

———. *Preaching in Medieval England: An Introduction to Sermon Manuscripts of the Period, c. 1350–1450.* Cambridge: Cambridge University Press, 1926.

Pantin, W.A. *The English Church in the Fourteenth Century*, Medieval Academy of America Reprints for Teaching 5. Toronto: University of Toronto Press in association with the Mediaeval Academy of America, 1980.

Petalas, Urania Contos. "The Sermons of John Mirk," Ph.D. diss., University of California at Los Angeles, 1970.

Peters, Christine. *Patterns of Piety: Women, Gender and Religion in Late Medieval and Reformation England.* New York and Cambridge: Cambridge University Press, 2003.

Petroff, Elizabeth A. "Male Confessors and Female Penitents: Possibilities for Dialogue," in *Body and Soul: Essays on Medieval Women and Mysticism*, ed. Elizabeth A. Petroff. New York and Oxford: Oxford University Press, 1994, pp. 139–60.

Phillips, Kim M. "Written on the Body: Reading Rape from the Twelfth to Fifteenth Centuries," in *Medieval Women and the Law*, ed. Noel James Menuge. Woodbridge, Suffolk: Boydell Press, 2000, pp. 125–144.

Platt, Colin. *The Parish Churches of Medieval England.* London: Secker and Warburg, 1981.

Pollock, Frederick, and Frederick William Maitland. *A History of English Law Before the Time of Edward I*, 2 vols., 2nd ed. London: Cambridge University Press, 1968.

Powell, Susan. "John Mirk's *Festial* and the Pastoral Programme." *Leeds Studies in English* n.s. 22 (1991), pp. 85–102.

———. *The Medieval Church in the Sixteenth Century: The Post-Reformation History of a Fourteenth-Century Sermon Collection*. Salford: European Studies Research Institute, University of Salford, 1998.

———. "A New Dating of John Mirk's *Festial*." *Notes and Queries* n.s. 29 (1982), pp. 487–89.

Power, Eileen. *Medieval Women*, ed. M.M. Postan. Cambridge: Cambridge University Press, 1995.

Ranft, Patricia. *Women and Spiritual Equality in Christian Tradition*. New York: St. Martin's Press, 1998.

Rawcliffe, Carole. "Women, Childbirth, and Religion in Later Medieval England," in *Women and Religion in Medieval England*, ed. Diana Wood. Oxford: Oxbow, 2003.

Remnant, G.L. and M.D. Anderson. *A Catalogue of Misericords in Great Britain*. Oxford: Clarendon Press, 1998.

Rosser, Gervase. "Communities of Parish and Guild in the Late Middle Ages," in *Parish, Church, and People: Local Studies in Lay Religion 1350–1750*, ed. S.J. Wright. London: Hutchinson, 1988, pp. 29–55.

Rubin, Miri. *Corpus Christi: The Eucharist in Late Medieval Culture*. Cambridge and New York: Cambridge University Press, 1991.

Russell, G.H. "Vernacular Instruction of the Laity in the Later Middle Ages in England: Some Texts and Notes." *The Journal of Religious History* 2:2 (1962–1963), pp. 98–119.

Saunders, Corinne. *Rape and Ravishment in the Literature of Medieval England*. Cambridge: D.S. Brewer, 2001.

Schulenberg, Jane Tibbetts. "Gender, Celibacy, and Proscriptions of Space: Symbol and Practice," in *Medieval Purity and Piety: Essays on Medieval Clerical Celibacy and Religious Reform*, ed. Michael Frasseto. New York: Garland, 1998, pp. 353–76.

Sheard, J.A. *The Words We Use*. London: A. Deutsch, 1954.

Shinners, John, and William J. Dohar. *Pastors and the Care of Souls in Medieval England*. Notre Dame: University of Notre Dame Press, 1998.

Silveria, Jeanette. "Generic Masculine Words and Thinking," in *The Voices and Words of Women and Men*, ed. Cheris Kramarae. Oxford: Pergamon, 1980, pp. 165–78.

Spencer, H. Leith. *English Preaching in the Late Middle Ages*. Oxford: Clarendon, 1993.

Spender, Dale. "Extracts from *Man Made Language*," in *The Feminist Critique of Language: A Reader*, 2nd rev. ed., ed. Deborah Cameron. New York: Routledge, 1998, pp. 93–99.

Steckman, Lillian L. "A Late Fifteenth-Century Revision of Mirk's *Festial*." *Studies in Philology* 34 (1937), pp. 36–48.

Storey, R.L. "Ordination of Secular Priests in Early Tudor London, Part One." *Nottingham Medieval Studies* 33:1 (1989), pp. 122–31.

Strang, Barbara M.H. *A History of English*. London: Methuen, 1974.

Stroup, Herbert W. "John Mirk: Tutor to England's Medieval Preachers." *Lutheran Theological Seminary Bulletin* 47:3 (Summer 1967), pp. 26–38.

Swanson, R.N. "Angels Incarnate: Clergy and Masculinity from Gregorian Reform to Reformation," in *Masculinity in Medieval Europe*, ed. D.M. Hadley. New York: Longman, 1999, pp. 160–177.

———, trans. and annotator. *Catholic England: Faith, Religion and Observance before the Reformation*. Manchester and New York: Manchester University Press, 1993.

———. *Church and Society in Late Medieval England*. Oxford and New York: Basil Blackwell, 1989.

———. *Religion and Devotion in Europe, c.1215–c.1515*. Cambridge: Cambridge University Press, 1995.

———. "Universities, Graduates, and Benefices in Later Medieval England." *Past and Present* 106 (1985), pp. 28–61.

Taylor, Larissa. *Soldiers of Christ: Preaching in Late Medieval and Reformation France*. New York and Oxford: Oxford University Press, 1992.

Tentler, Thomas N. *Sin and Confession on the Eve of the Reformation*. Princeton: Princeton University Press, 1977.

Thorne, Barrie, Cheris Kramarae, and Nancy Henley. "Language, Gender, and Society: Opening a Second Decade of Research," in *Language, Gender, and Society*, eds. Barrie Thorne, Cheris Kramarae, and Nancy Henley. Rowley, Mass.: Newbury House, 1983, pp. 7–24.

Tubach, Frederic C. *Index Exemplorum: A Handbook of Medieval Religious Tales*. Helsinki: Suomalainen Tiedeakatemia, 1969.

Wakelin, Martyn F. "An Edition of John Mirk's *Festial* as it is contained in the Brotherton Collection Manuscript," M.A. Thesis, University of Leeds, 1960.

———. "The Manuscripts of John Mirk's *Festial*." *Leeds Studies in English* n.s. 1 (1967), pp. 93–118.

Watkins, Keith. *Faithful and Fair: Transcending Sexist Language in Worship*. Nashville: Abingdon Press, 1981.

Wells, John E. *A Manual of the Writings in Middle English 1050–1400*. New Haven: Yale University Press, 1916.

White, Mary Frances. *Fifteenth Century Misericords in the Collegiate Church of Holy Trinity, Stratford-upon-Avon*. Stratford-upon-Avon, UK: Phillip Bennet, 1974.

Wiesner, Merry E. *Gender, Church, and State in Early Modern Germany*. New York: Longman, 1998.

Witherup, Ronald D. *A Liturgist's Guide to Inclusive Language*. Collegeville, Minnesota: Liturgical, 1996.

Wood, Juanita. *Wooden Images: Misericords and Medieval England*. Madison: Fairleigh Dickinson University Press, 1999.

Young, Karl. "Instructions for Parish Priests." *Speculum* 11:2 (1936), pp. 224–31.

# INDEX

# GENDER IN THE MIDDLE AGES

Printed in the United States
by Baker & Taylor Publisher Services